# DOING SOCIAL RESEARCH

# DOING SOCIAL RESEARCH
## A Source Book for Preparing Dissertation

DR. D.K. LAL DAS

PUBLICATIONS
KALPAZ PUBLICATIONS
DELHI-110052

Doing Social Research : A Source Book for Preparing Dissertation

Rs. 720



ISBN: 81-7835-667-8



Published in 2008 in India by
Kalpaz Publications
C-30, Satyawati Nagar,
Delhi-110052
E-mail: kalpaz@hotmail.com
Phone : 9212729499

*Lasser Type Setting by*: Rudra Computer Graphics, Delhi
*Printed at* : Singal Print Media, Delhi

*To my wife-Pushpa-whose patience, understanding, and encouragement has helped me to complete this assignment*

# Contents

# Preface

As a supervisor of Post Graduate and Ph.D. dissertations for over three decades, I have spent a great deal of time searching for a suitable text on preparation of dissertations for my students and research scholars. It became increasingly evident that most research books describe research as any other theory papers. Consequently, most of the books skip a very important aspect of research, that is : How to do research? As a result, even though a student who has cleared the theory paper on research may be with distinction, come to supervisor and ask the very basic questions like:

How to select a research problem?
How to identify objectives of the study?
How to formulate a hypothesis?
How to select a sample?
How to construct a research instrument?
How to process data?
How to analyse data?
How to write a research report?

I am of the view that since research is a skill oriented course we need to include the "How to do research?" aspect too while we teach research. I trust if we include this aspect in our research curriculum it would certainly help researchers to execute the research project.

In preparing this text on 'doing social research' my intent, therefore, is to help students, research scholars and research educators to execute the research project.

This book includes the details about various stages of research, such as, selection of problem, the objectives, research questions, formulation of hypothesis, selection of sample, construction of research instrument, processing and analysis of data and writing of report. In other words, this book aims at helping the researcher to prepare a scientific report-the dissertation.

Keeping in view the above objective, the book-doing social research-has unique role to play in enabling the students, research scholars as well as educators to conduct research study and present research report.

Against this background, the book deals with the subject in a very specific way. That is, while the book describes the basics of social research, the focus of the book is on 'how to do research'.

**Salient Features**

1. Each chapter includes illustrations from practice, which discuss how research can be conducted.
2. In Chapter I basics of social research have been presented in very concise form. The purpose was to reduce the material that has minimal or no relevance in doing research.
3. The remaining seven chapters written exclusively for 'doing social research'.
4. Data processing and analysis have been explained with SPSS commands in Chapter VI and Chapter VII respectively.

Finally, I trust, the book will help the reader to do social research.

**D.K. Lal Das**

# Acknowledgments

For me there is nothing more satisfying than helping my colleagues and students understand research. In the last three decades my colleagues and students have contributed to my understanding of research. I am therefore grateful to both my colleagues and students.

First of all I would like to thank Dr B.T. Lawani, Director, Social Science Centre, Bharati Vidyapeeth, Pune, for his "kind" as well as "forceful" suggestion that helped me to write this book.

I would like to express my gratitude to the students whom I had taught research and statistics over the years. They may not be aware of the fact that their queries have helped me a lot to organise my thoughts, which are now presented through this text.

My colleagues at R.M. College of Social Work have generously shared their views on preparing dissertation. I especially want to express my gratitude and appreciation to my colleague Mrs. Vanila Bhaskaran who in spite of her busy schedule not only did proof reading meticulously but also read the whole type script and offered valuable suggestions on some of the chapters of this text. I express my gratitude to Mr. A. Ravindra Chary and Mr. Hari Babu, my colleagues who readily and promptly made available the books and journals whenever I needed.

Finally, I acknowledge the support of Pushpa, my wife, who understood, with great patience, my working on computer for long hours and even on holidays which, was unavoidable. I thank my family members – Hemendra, Rathindra, Sneha and Kalpana, who created an atmosphere that helped me to complete the project more speedily than it would have been without their support. Finally, I would like to thank my grand children -Harsh, Yash, Eshant, Swati and Shree – who missed my company – for constantly reminding me to complete the work at the earliest.

**D.K. Lal Das**

# List of Tables

# List of Figures

# List of Boxes

# 1

# Introduction to Social Research

## Introduction

Research is a process by which one acquires authentic and reliable information about a phenomenon. Therefore, the term research may be broadly defined "as a systematic inquiry towards understanding a social phenomenon". It follows the scientific approach to gain knowledge. The most important characteristic of this approach is its thrust on objectivity. To what extent is the research using scientific approach is useful in studying the problems of society? How can we acquire reliable knowledge about the various aspects of human experience? To be more specific how can the scientific approach be of value in understanding social phenomena? In this chapter we will discuss these questions. Our approach would be first, to understand the meaning of the terms 'research' and 'scientific research' then to examine the scientific method, its application in social sciences, its assumptions and finally to take a close look at the approach to find out how it can help researchers to understand social phenomena.

## Meaning of Research and Scientific Research

### Research

When we observe certain objects or phenomena, we are often unaware of our biases, we do not question them and so we attribute our observations entirely to the objects or phenomena being observed. In this process, it is possible to arrive at right decision on the basis of wrong reasons or vice versa. This questions the process of observation. Was the observation error free? While observing are we aware of our limitations? Every method of knowing has certain limitations. Any study to create new knowledge or aims to increase existing fund of knowledge may it be through observation or by some other methods, is called research if it takes into account the biases, the errors and limitations. As such, research may be described as systematic and critical investigation of phenomena toward increasing the stream of knowledge (Lal Das, 2000).

## Scientific Research

Science aims at description, explanation and understanding of various objects or phenomena in nature. Research is a special endeavour, which involves systematic and critical investigation towards increasing the stream of knowledge. Now it is easier to define scientific research. We may define scientific research as a "systematic and critical investigation about the natural phenomena to describe, explain and finally to understand the relations among them".

## Conceptual Foundations of Scientific Research

The scientific research is based on two conceptual foundations, namely, facts and theory. In the context of scientific research fact simply means some phenomenon that has been observed. Scientific research aims at systematic description of observed facts and of their relations. It also aims at understanding the nature and interpreting the observed facts and relations. This involves the reduction of observed facts and their relations into a limited number of general statements that account for the observed facts and their relations. These general statements embody a theory (Mohsin. 1984, p. 4).

There is little agreement among social scientist on what theory is. For example, according to Goode and Hatt (1952): A theory refers to the relationship between facts or the ordering of them in some meaningful ways, whereas to Kerlinger (1973) a theory is a set of interrelated constructs (concepts), definitions and propositions that present a systematic view of phenomena by specifying relations among variables, with the purpose of explaining and predicting the phenomena.

There are many more explanations of what a theory is. Despite the disagreement there are certain common points in almost all the explanations. Keeping this in view we can understand a theory as a systematic explanation for the observed facts and their interrelations.

## Scientific Method

It is obvious that it would be impossible to comprehend the nature and content of research without an appreciation of a method. The method used in scientific research is usually designated as scientific method. According to George Lundberg (1946), scientific method consists of three basic steps; systematic observation, classification and interpretation of data. Through these steps, scientific method brings about not only verifiability of the facts, but also it lays the confidence in the validity of conclusions.

The definition requires some more explanations. First when Lundberg (1946) says that scientific method is systematic observation, he means, the scientific investigation is ordered. It aims at discovering facts as they actually are and not as they are desired to be and as such the investigators can have critical confidence in their conclusions. Second, the scientific method is concerned with 'classes of objects' not 'individual objects' especially universality and predictability. The method makes it possible to predict about a phenomenon with sufficient accuracy.

The major characteristics of scientific method are:

1. Objectivity,
2. Verifiability.
3. Replication and
4. Prediction.

Let us look at these characteristics more closely:

## Objectivity

The most important characteristic of scientific method is objectivity. Research is beyond the subjective bias of the researcher. The researcher makes deliberate efforts to eliminate personal bias and prejudices and resist the temptation to seek only such data that supports his/her hypothesis. The emphasis is on testing, rather than proving the hypothesis. The researcher is prohibited to make personal judgment and make the data and logic to lead a sound conclusion. Objectivity is achieved through standardisation of research instruments and analytical tools (Lal Das, 2005).

### Verifiability

This is another characteristic of scientific method. Research findings presented for other researchers must be verifiable. Research is a scientific endeavour and hence its findings are open for scrutiny. This characteristic of scientific method, i.e. verifiability, is related to the criteria of objectivity. That is, a study which is based on objective facts can be verified. Verifiability is achieved through two different approaches: first, analysing the same data on the same sample through alternative analytical tools (statistical methods), second, replicating the study on a different sample.

### Replication

The third characteristic of scientific method is 'replication'. Only through replication of a research study the conclusions/results can be confirmed. As such, Through the use of scientific method it is possible to replicate the study and verify the results. Only if the research has been carried out by using a scientific method, it can be replicated for verification.

### Prediction

Prediction is achieved through the uses of statistical methods and techniques. For example, regression analysis is the most common statistical procedure in quantitative research which predicts about the phenomena under study.

### Use of Scientific Method in Social Science

Social sciences primarily deal with human behaviour, which is, by and large, complex and dynamic in nature. One cannot, therefore investigate the human behaviour under guided conditions as in natural and physical sciences. This creates many problems to the researcher such as the problems of subjectivity and individualistic generalisations etc.

The problem arising out of the nature and content of social sciences do not seriously diminish the importance of scientific method for social scientists. Notwithstanding the inherent defects of social sciences, scientific method can be acceptable with its own limitations for the study of social phenomena so far as it helps to arrive at valid generalisations.

## Possibilities and Limitations of Use of Scientific Method in Social Sciences

As described above, the social sciences deal with human beings. Hence, the subject of scientific research poses much greater complexity than that in natural sciences. Although problems of discovering principles of human behaviour are difficult, they are not impossible. Social scientists will need to carry out observations as carefully as are done in natural sciences. Subjective, qualitative judgments need to be supplemented by more exact, quantitative measurements which are not easy to achieve in the case of human beings.

Social sciences have not been able to establish generalisations equivalent to theories of the natural sciences or, to predict events accurately. Perhaps, social sciences will never realise the objective of science as completely as natural sciences do. In fact, there are several limitations involved in the application of the scientific method in social sciences.

## Meaning of Social Research

In a very broad sense, social research is scientific inquiry of issues pertaining to society'. To be specific, social research is the study of causal relationships in human behaviour. It is generally acknowledged that in human behaviour a large degree of measurable and predictable sets of associations occur. Social research, then seeks to establish, measure and analyse these associations in all their variety and intensity (Thomas, 1968, p. 294).

## Nature of Social Research

The object of social research is clearly the discovery of causal relationships in human behaviour. It is generally acknowledged that in human behaviour, as much as in natural phenomena, a large degree of measurable and predictable sets of associations occur. Social research, then, like research in physical and natural sciences, seeks to establish, measure, analyse these associations in all their variety and intensity (Thomas, 1968, p. 294). Social research, however assumes a distinct character of its own in a significant measure when it comes to the application of scientific process, characteristics of research in natural and physical sciences, to social phenomena. Unlike, physical and natural sciences, in social research the objects are conscious and active human beings. The individual behaviour of the objects whether it is free or determined makes the social research really a difficult job. Further, the researcher and object being similar the scope of an objective approach in social research is limited to a considerable extent.

Social research concerns with social data, which are much more complex than that of the physical data. The basis of all social interactions, whether it is a large complex group or a small cohesive group, is expectations of behaviour, which in turn is result of many factors. The complex nature of social data reduces the power of exact prediction in social research. Most of the subject matter of social research is qualitative and does not admit quantitative measurement. It is more so, because social phenomena are known only symbolically through concepts or terms representing such phenomena.

## Basic Presumptions of Social Research

The problems posed by the nature of social data are not in any way insurmountable. The limitations, which appear to preclude the application of scientific process in social research, derive from our unfamiliarity with social data rather than from the nature of the social data themselves.

Social research presumes that the applicability of scientific process in the study of social phenomena is possible because of the following situations (Galtung, 1970).

(1) It is presumed that all social interaction follows some kind of natural law. Social phenomena are social actions. Therefore, it is possible to make studies of social phenomena.

(2) It is presumed that the social phenomena follow certain definite trends at least in the short period. Thus, it is possible to predict with quite a high degree of accuracy the social behaviour.

(3) Social data are complex to us, because our knowledge of them is inadequate and we have not been able to develop tools of study, which can explain them in more simple way.

(4) In social research we presume that it is possible by stratification or classification of social data on the basis of certain traits or properties, to ensure fairly high degree of internal homogeneity within each stratum. Thus, valid

generalisation based on conclusions of a social inquiry is possible.

(5) It is presumed that the various characteristics in nature are uniformly distributed and hence, social interaction follows certain definite order. Therefore, it is presumed that similar cause produce similar result under similar circumstances. As such it is possible to find out the effects from the cause(s) or cause from the effect.

## Approaches to Social Research

A problem can be studied with different approaches. A researcher may take into consideration the phenomenon as a whole and describe it as it exists or may wish to analyse it by its components in measurable or quantifiable terms. The former approach is termed as qualitative. approach and the later are known as quantitative approach. Thus, there are two prominent approaches to study a problem in social research. They are:

1. Qualitative approach
2. Quantitative approach

## Qualitative Approach

In some situations it is difficult to analyse a phenomenon into various components or variables which can be measured in quantified terms. In such cases the researcher takes into consideration the phenomenon as a whole and assumes that there is some quality in the phenomenon in its entirety. When the researcher attempts to retain the totality of a phenomenon while verifying propositions regarding it, he / she adopt a qualitative approach. This approach describes the experiences of people in depth and permits the researcher to record and understand people in depth in their own perceptions. Qualitative approach helps us to examine the nature of human behaviour and experience and social conditions. It also permits the researcher to study selected issues, cases or events in depth. While using this approach the researcher seeks to capture what people have to say in their own words.

Qualitative approach takes into consideration 'detailed descriptions' of situations, events, people, interactions and observed behaviours. These data are also available in the form of 'direct quotations' from people about their experiences, attitudes, beliefs, and thoughts. Data in qualitative approach are collected through direct observation, participant observation, in-depth interviewing, case studies, recorded documents, open-ended questionnaires and journals.

The validity and reliability of qualitative data depend to a great extent on the methodological skills, sensitivity, and integrity of the researcher. Systematic and rigorous observation involves far more than just being present and looking around. Skillful interviewing involves much more than just asking questions. Content analysis requires considerably more insights into the data than reading to see what's there. Thus, generating useful, credible qualitative findings through observation, interviewing and content analysis requires discipline, knowledge, training, practice, creativity and hard work (Lal Das, 2005).

## Quantitative Approach

Quantitative approach focuses on objective and standardized means of inquiry and application of statistical analysis for attainment of objectivity and generalisations. Quantitative researchers use interview, questionnaire and structured observation as major methods to collect data. Quantitative approach use standardized measures that fit diverse opinions and experiences into predetermined response categories. This approach measures the reactions of a large number of individuals to a limited set or questions, thus facilitating comparison and analysis of data with the help of close-ended questionnaires, attitude scales, rating scales and postal surveys.

## Social Research Process

The research process is the paradigm of research project. In a research project, there are various scientific activities in which researcher engage him in order to produce knowledge. Although each research project is unique in some ways, all projects, regardless of the phenomenon being studied, involve, by and large, some common activities. Each of these activities is interdependent. The research process is thus the system of these interrelated activities. The various activities are conveniently grouped into following stages:

Stage I : Selection and Formulation of a Problem
Stage II : Formulation of Hypothesis
Stage III : Collection of Data
Stage IV : Analysis and Interpretation of Data
Stage V : Drawing Conclusions

The stages of research are interdependent. The researcher usually enters the research process at stage I. However, when he/she enters second stage, he/she has to draw on past studies to formulate his/her hypothesis. Similarly, to collect data the researcher has to keep in mind the problem and the hypothesis. A researcher, who has no knowledge of how to collect and analyse data, may find himself / herself unable to formulate a testable hypothesis. The final stage of a research process, that is drawing of conclusions-totally depends on data analysis and interpretations. This brief discussion on the cyclic nature of research process makes it very clear that each of these five stages of research process is dependent upon others.

The research process is also cyclic in nature (as shown in Figure 1). In fact, the research process is not complete at the stage V. The process leads to two situations: The first situation may be that the data did not support or partially support the hypothesis. In this situation the researcher must return to the stage I. He/she, then, may decide to reformulate the problem and hypothesis and then list it exactly as before. In the second situation, that is, even if the research is successful and the findings of stage V confirm the hypothesis of stage II, it is advisable to repeat the study preferably with a different sample as to reconfirm the findings. This will also support the contention that the hypothesis cannot be rejected. The exact repetition of a study is called replication.

Another characteristic feature of the research process is 'self correction'. In a situation, when the data did not support or only partially support the hypothesis and the researcher has sufficient reasons to decide that the hypothesis is adequate then he/she may decide that the failure to confirm the hypothesis is due to error in selecting a sampling design or in measurement of the key concepts or in analysis of data. In these situations the researcher may decide to repeat the study beginning with the faulty stage after rectifying the faults. Finally, the five stages of the research process make the study potentially replicable. The researcher designs his/her study

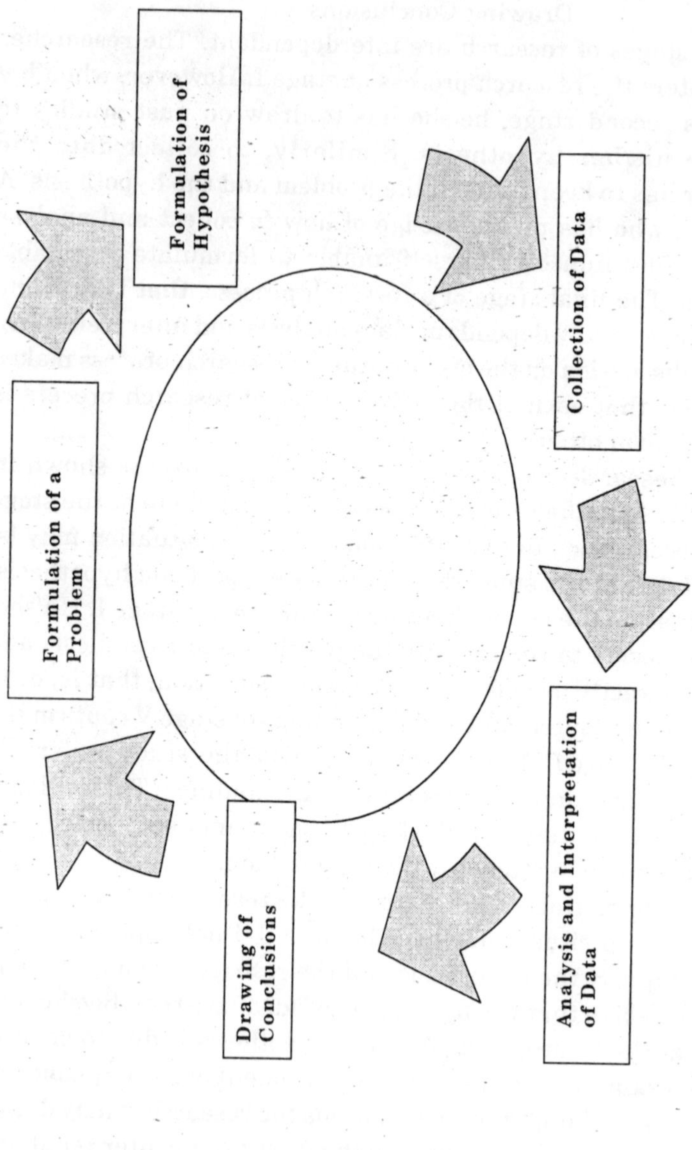


**Figure 1. Research Process**

in such a way that either the researcher or others can replicate it. The replication of study substantiates the fact further that the findings are not due to mere coincidence.

## Doing Social Research

The meaning of social research, as presented above, appears simple and straightforward (and is often understood that way), but in practice social research is multistage scientific process. Then the very fundamental question is : 'How to handle the research process?'. The basic premise of this resource book is that just knowing what social research is not enough to do research. The knowledge of social research is certainly necessary but not enough to 'do' research. In other words the knowledge is not in itself sufficient for 'doing' research that is to begin designing and carrying out a research study.

If you want to learn about research methods in general and quantitative methods in particular, then you will need to see how research studies actually get done, rather than simply reading about how they are supposed to be done. We will discuss the various stages of an actual research study-from planning the research and developing the hypotheses to collecting the data and analyzing the findings. The research study we are going to discuss is 'a study of sex discrimination against women at work'. This research study runs as a continuous theme throughout this book. At every step from research design through data collection to the final analysis, I have written the book in such a way that you can actively use and contribute to the research study.

## Steps of a Research Study

In a research study there are various scientific activities in which researcher engage him in order to produce knowledge. Although each research study is unique in some ways, all research studies, regardless of the phenomenon being studied, involve, by and large, some common activities. Each of these activities is interdependent. The research process is thus the system of these interrelated activities. The various activities of a research study conveniently grouped into following steps:

**Step 1 : Identification of a Research Problem**

The first step in planning a research project is the identification of a suitable problem. In each area/field of social sciences innumerable problems exists. The choice of a suitable problem is one of the most difficult tasks for a researcher, especially if he/she is a beginner.

There are many sources to which a researcher may go to identify his / her research problem. Once you decide to take up a problem for a research study immediately you need to evaluate the proposed problem in the light of your competence, possible difficulties, in terms of availability of data, the financial and field constraints , and limitations of time.

After evaluating the problem you have to make it a specific problem. Let us assume that you have chosen the 'problem of street children' . To undertake a research study on this problem you have to narrow it down to specific research problem. You may make it specific by saying that you would like to study the "Psychosocial Problems of Street Children with specific reference to a slum".

It is very commonly experienced in social sciences in general and social work in particular, that students respond to this assignment by drawing a total blank. Other students grasp eagerly onto a topic, such as "the causes of delinquency," and rush off with total confidence that they are about to solve this enduring problem. It is very obvious that in each case, the student will be having difficulty in formulating a research problem. In the first case, the difficulty is in locating a problem to investigate whereas, in the second, it is in formulating a problem sufficiently specific that it is amenable to scientific research. This problem is not unique to students. Every student researcher must grapple with the issue of problem formulation. Because it is the initial step and provides the basis for the complete research project, problem formulation is of crucial importance. Many potentially serious research problems can be avoided – or at least minimized-by careful process of problem formulation. In this section of this unit, we will present the major issues to be considered in problem formulation, beginning with how to select a problem on which to conduct research.

## Selecting a Research Problem

The first hurdle confronting a researcher is to select a topic that is appropriate for scientific inquiry. Actually, this is not as difficult as it may fist appear because the social world around us is literally full of unanswered questions. Selecting a problem calls for some creativity and imagination, but there are also a number of sources you can look for inspiration. Some of the more common sources of research problems are discussed here.

## Personal Interest

A researcher often selects a research topic simply because he / she has an interest in some aspect of human behaviour, possibly owing to some personal experience. A researcher might, for example, be interested in the problem of alcoholics because he or she has been experiencing the ill effects of it in his/her family. Truancy or delinquency might be the focus of research attention because of contact with some youngsters in trouble in the neighborhood. A research study generally focuses on behaviour that is unique and thus compelling to some.

If a researcher who selects a topic out of his / her personal interest must be careful to demonstrate the scientific worth of his / her projects. The goals of scientific research are to describe, explain, predict, and evaluate. The aim of a research study to advance our knowledge, not just satisfy personal curiosity. A researcher who chooses a topic based on his/her personal interest- especially if it deals with some unusual aspect of human behavior – should be prepared for the possibility that others will fail to see the worth of that research.

## Social Problems

To identify a topic for a research study, you need to look through the daily newspaper, where you can read about the many social problems that our society faces. Problems such as crime, delinquency, poverty, pollution, overpopulation, drug abuse, alcoholism, mental illness, sexual deviance, discrimination, exploitation and oppression have all been popular sources of topics for social research. A number of journals such as "The Indian Journal of Social work", "Social Welfare", "Social Change" etc. communicate the results of scientific investigations into current social problems.

Within each of these broad categories of social problems, there is a range of issues that can be studied. Many studies, for example, focus on the origin of a problem. Others are concerned with the effects and consequences these problems have for individuals, groups and society. Still others deal with the impact of social programs and other intervention efforts intended to ameliorate these problems. People associated with non-governmental organisations , who are routinely involved with many of these problems, can find opportunities for research that are directly related to their professional activities.

**Step 2: Define the Research Topic**

Once a research problem has been identified, the research topic needs to be defined In this stage of research the overall plan for the research project must be set out in logical order to see if it makes sense.

Your research topic should be defined in such a way that it is clearly understood. If you are studying, say for example, alcoholism; you need to put your research question into a framework which suggests that you are very clear and specific about the problem of alcohol consumption and abuse. In short, topics of research must be grounded in some already-known factual information which is used to introduce the topic and from which the research question will emerge.

**Step 3: Review of Existing Literature**

The beginning of this section has suggested you to get literature relevant to the topic before you want to study it. Social research topics are usually embedded in so many different kinds of literature that the researcher must be careful in to selecting the best literature to examine. While many researchers collect every material which has some linkages with the topic, you need to keep the central theme of your topic in mind to guide you through your search of the literature in the field. It is also important to examine different types of literature where relevant inferences are drawn from scientific data interpretations. It would be very useful if research findings from studies using various methods are critically examined.

For your research study, you should refer to the significant findings you have gathered. This will help you to raise questions or which will guide you to decide your area and unit of study. You must be able to draw out these findings from the studies and summarize them in such a way that someone unfamiliar with study can easily grasp their meaning and importance. To help you to do this, you should look at the background literature review sections which generally come at the beginning of published research articles. Most of these reviews are very condensed; they extract a few salient points from numerous studies, summarizing them in a way that is relevant to the study in question.

**Step 4: Clarification of Concepts and Their Measurement**

In a study, a set of concepts is used to explain the phenomenon. These concepts need clarifications with reference to the particular topic. Through the clarifications and discussion of the concepts a research model is developed at this stage. Precision in conceptualization is critical in the social sciences, and it is not easy to achieve. Concepts like alcoholism, autonomy and juvenile delinquency may all seem to be familiar terms. However, the precise meanings you attach to these concepts must be defined and clarified, and then an appropriate way to measure concepts must be found or devised.

In the research plan, a clear definition of the main concept or concepts is most essential. It is also essential to discuss the process of measurement of the concepts. In the research plan you should also touch upon the potential problems in measuring the concepts. These include two critical issues: *validity*, that is, whether the measurement of a concept in fact produces a result that truly represents what the concept is supposed to mean, and *reliability*, that is, whether the measurement would lead to same results, whenever it is repeated, that one could have some confidence in the results.

**Step 5: Identifications of Objectives of the Study**

Once the problem, the theoretical background, the clarification of concepts, and the major methods of data collection have been explained, it is time to address the aim and objectives of the study.

At this stage you are required to present the aim and the objectives of the study in brief justify your study in terms of both its rationale and the implications that it might raise. But in a proposal the study design must be presented before the rationale Here it is important to note that rationale for doing the project will be accomplished only if the study is done well. Preparing a plan of your study will show that you have devised a plan to study your problem that seems feasible; you reinforce the sense that the aims and objectives of the study will be achieved. The value of the study lies not only in what it alone will produce, but also in how it may add to or challenge other research in the area.

**Step 6 : Formulation of Hypotheses**

A common strategy in scientific study is to move from a general theory to a specific researchable problem. A part of this exercise is to develop hypotheses, which are testable statements of presumed relationships between two or more constructs or Hypotheses state what we expect to find rather than what has already been determined to exist. For example, we might hypothesise that the acceptance of the use of alcohol among adolescent's peers will lead to increased likelihood that the adolescents will consume alcohol.

**Step 7: Operationalization of Concepts and development of Research Instruments**

Once you are settled with the concepts for your study, you need to operationalise the concepts so that you can develop your measuring instruments such as your questionnaire. In a survey, the questionnaire is nothing but concepts in operational form. In an experiment, the operationalization of the independent variable (concept) is the actual stimulus. In field studies, this process of operationalization occurs in a very different manner. It is often carried out after the field notes have been collected. After that the researcher may find evidence that suggests certain meanings, at which time the process of conceptualizations are carried out. To test whether you are correct, you may go back to the field to see if another instance of this operationalized concept occurs.

It is always advisable to use more than one indicator for better measurement of the concept. This will strengthen your study.

**Step 8: Selection of Method of Data Collection**

There are three primary means of data collection, namely, observation, interview and questionnaire. You will learn about these methods in subsequent Chapters of this book. In these Chapters the methods are explained in details so that you can use them to design and carry out a study based on questionnaires or interviews, and in field studies using different types of observation techniques It also describes different forms of what might be called data collection procedures for using secondary data.

While preparing the research plan you must describe how you will collect primary data. In case you are planning to use secondary data you must mention which sources of available data you will actually use. You may also very briefly discuss about issues of access to the data. It is important for a researcher to see that, he/she must be able to get the data he/she proposes. If you anticipate problems in securing the proposed data, these problems should be discussed and possible alternate sources of data might be suggested. Most researchers propose to use one source of data yet you may propose few more sources through which you may also collect data from other sources to widen their scope.

**Step 9: Selection of Sample**

The selection of sample whom you will study depends on many factors and it is not possible to take into account all. However, there are some factors which affect the selection of the sample to a great extent. We will discuss a few of them. The homogeneity or heterogeneity of the universe is one such factor which affects the sample selection procedure to a great extent. For example, if you are interested in studying medical students, which is a very homogeneous group, even a very small ample will be representative of the universe where as if you plan to study a college having arts, science and commerce faculties you may have to chose a very large sample and even then you may not have confidence to say that your sample is representative.

You may be interested in generalizing your findings to others beyond those studied. When probability samples are used, it is possible to determine how representative your sample is of the population who might have gotten into your study. Sampling plans may be very simple or complex. When the rules of probability are not followed and you merely select a sample of subjects who seem to fulfill the needs of your study, you have a non-probability sample. For many studies, such a sample is sufficient; and for some, it is the best that can be achieved. Whatever the design of your sample, it needs to be explained in detail in your research plan. It should be so precise that someone else could generate a similar sample by following your procedures. Remember that even if you select a representative sample you have to be very careful in making generalisations.

### Step 10: Collection of Data

There are different methods of data collection. Each method of data collection has its special concerns which need to be considered fully before doing the study. This is why pretesting is so valuable, because it helps you to find and address potential problems before they enter your study and cause bigger problems.

The plans for collecting data should be described carefully. In a field study, it is always more difficult to be precise, and you may need to make changes once you enter the field. Nevertheless, it is better to have a clear plan that can be changed as you move forward For an experiment; data collection procedures can usually be described very precisely. This is also true of a survey. Surveys using mailed questionnaire tend to have multiple stages in the data collection procedure to increase the *response rate*. If you are using secondary data, you need to describe at this stage how you will collect the data.

### Step 11: Processing of the Data

Once the data are collected, they must be processed. If the responses are in qualitative terms you have to prepare a codebook where you have to give numbers for the qualitative responses. This is very much essential if you wish to process your data through computer. If they are field notes, they must be organized and categorized.

In the research plan, a concise statement may be included to address this subject. It may describe what type of computer facilities is available, what possible sources of assistance are available, and what efforts are being made to increase accuracy in the handling of the data. There are now some technological advances in data gathering which speed the process from data gathering to data entry. An example is the SPSS (Statistical Package for Social Sciences) now becoming quite common for social research.

**Step 12: Analysis of the Data**

We need to plan how we will analyze the data. It is advisable to prepare a plan of analysis of data spelling out the various applications of statistical tests carefully while the study is being designed. It is better to have a planned strategy that can be adapted than to end up with piles of data for which you have no organized plan.

You are also required to explain how you are planning to compare or contrast different variables, for example, men with women, one rehabilitation program with another, length of time spent in an organisation by the attitude of employees towards the new incentive introduced recently?

In addition, you need to consider which statistical tests you plan to apply to evaluate the association / differences between the variables. For example, if you propose to measure correlation between the variables to test whether there are significant correlations between them you have to select an appropriate test of correlation that could get the result you need.

**Step 13: Present the Results**

At the end of the study, you have to present the results of the study in the form of a report. While preparing a research report you have to follow a number of writing conventions. These conventions are commonly known as research formats.

The steps discussed above are presented below in a flow chart form to help the learners to comprehend the complete research process quickly :

The steps of a research study have been sown here in a flow chart. This must not lead to the impression that the process is linear in nature. In fact, the research process is not complete at the stage 13. There are two possibilities : The first possibility may be that the data did not support or partially support the hypothesis. In this situation the researcher must return to the step I. He/she, then, may decide to reformulate the problem and hypothesis and then test it exactly as before. In the second possibility, that is,

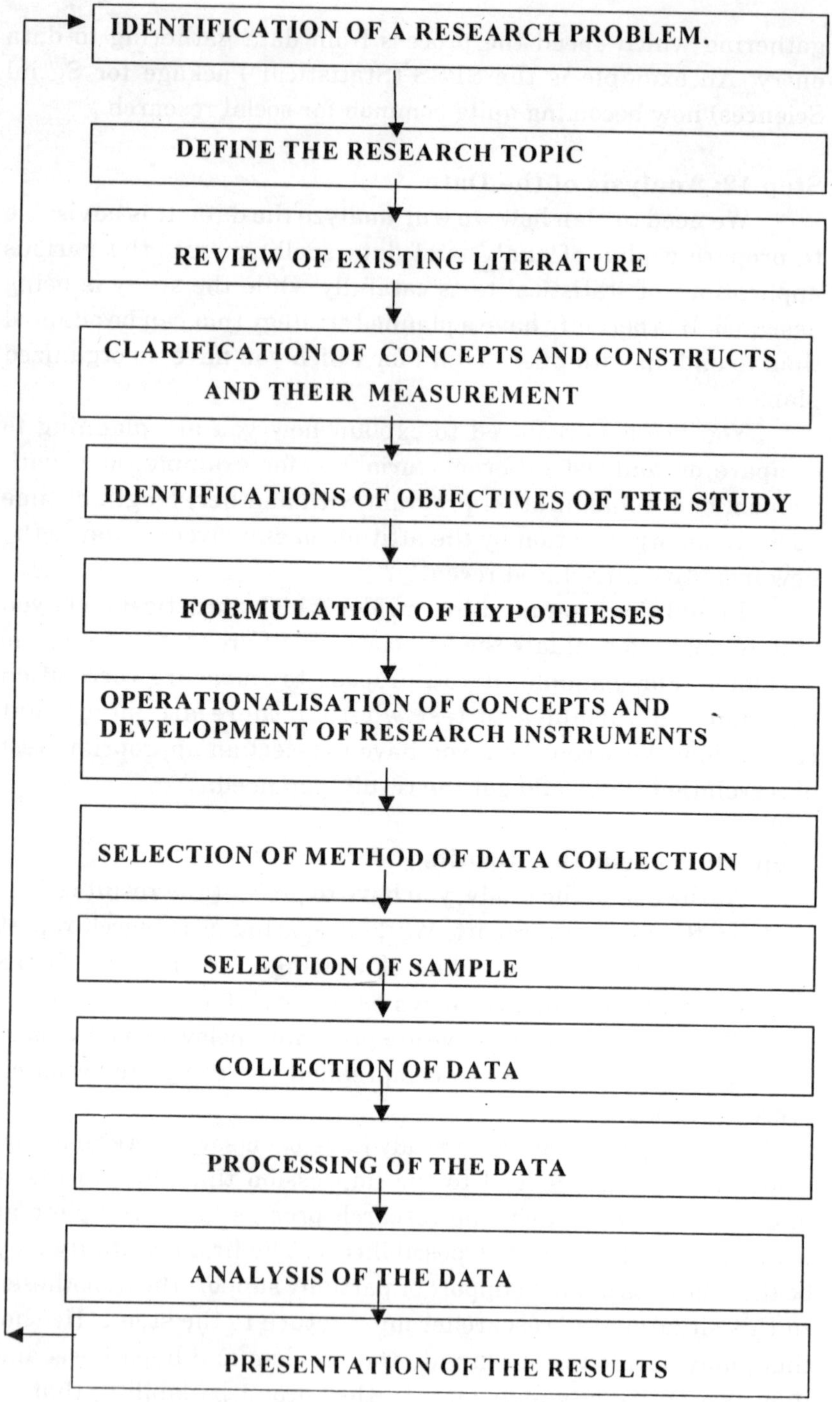
IDENTIFICATION OF A RESEARCH PROBLEM.
DEFINE THE RESEARCH TOPIC
REVIEW OF EXISTING LITERATURE
CLARIFICATION OF CONCEPTS AND CONSTRUCTS AND THEIR MEASUREMENT
IDENTIFICATIONS OF OBJECTIVES OF THE STUDY
FORMULATION OF HYPOTHESES
OPERATIONALISATION OF CONCEPTS AND DEVELOPMENT OF RESEARCH INSTRUMENTS
SELECTION OF METHOD OF DATA COLLECTION
SELECTION OF SAMPLE
COLLECTION OF DATA
PROCESSING OF THE DATA
ANALYSIS OF THE DATA
PRESENTATION OF THE RESULTS

even if the research is successful and the findings of step 13 confirm the hypothesis formulated at step 6, it is advisable to repeat the study preferably with a different sample as to reconfirm the findings. This will also support the contention that the hypothesis cannot be rejected. The exact repetition of a study is called replication.

Another characteristic feature of the research process is 'self-correction'. In the situation, when the data did not support or only partially support the hypothesis and the researcher has sufficient reasons to decide that the hypothesis is adequate then he may decide that the failure to confirm the hypothesis is due to error in selecting a sample or in measurement of the key variables/concepts or in analysis of data. In these circumstances the researcher may decide to repeat the study beginning with the faulty step after rectifying the faults. Finally, the steps of the research process make the study potentially replicable. The researcher designs his/her study in such a way that either the researcher or anybody other than him/her can replicate it. The replication of study substantiates the fact further that the findings are not due to mere coincidence.

## Plan of the Book

This book is about "doing social research". Then the very fundamental question is : 'How to handle the research project?'. With this view in mind, this book is organized in nine chapters.

Chapter I provides a brief overview of the fundamentals of social research and plan of a research project. The chapter starts with the meaning of research, followed by brief explanations of the terms like 'scientific research', scientific method' and 'social research'. Two important issues, namely, basic presumptions of social research and possibilities and limitations of social research, have also been briefly discussed in this chapter. Then 'How to do research ?'. the basic premise of this resource book is explained. The chapter ends with details of planning a research project.

In chapter II the first step in the research process - formulation of research problem has been dealt with. This step starts with the selection of a research problem and is followed by identification of objectives, construct, concepts and variables. Finally, formulation and testing of hypotheses have been explained in this chapter.

The various social research designs have been covered in chapter III. How to decide the most appropriate research design in order to execute the study to find the answers of research questions raised - is the major subject matter of this chapter.

Chapter V deals with the sampling procedures which includes topic like representativeness and adequacy of sample, types of sampling, choice of sampling method, technique of drawing sample and determination of size of sample.

Selection of tools of data collection has been discussed in chapter VI. This chapter includes topics like sources of data, measurement in social research and tools of data collection. Under the section on "Tools of Data Collection" various tools of data collection such as questionnaire, interview, interview schedule, observation etc. have been explained in detail.

Chapter VII describe in detail the steps of data processing and analysis. The subject has been explained with an example of a hypothetical data. The steps like editing, coding, categorizing, preparation of master chart etc. have been discussed in this chapter. The discussion on processing is followed by steps of data analysis. It includes, univariate, bivariate, trivariate and multivariate analysis of data. While explaining the steps of data analysis examples are cited from a real research study.

In chapter VIII selection and application of statistical measures have described. Each statistical test has been introduced with brief description before the description of its selection and application. When and how to use the tests have been explained with an example of a table that might be analysed using the tests, to give readers a concrete example.

The final chapter discusses about the writing of a research report. The chapter starts with the purposes of writing a research report, followed by the components of the report itself (the beginning, the main body, and the end). Standard patterns, conventions, styles and formats of research report are some of the topics discussed in this chapter.

## References

Buckingham, A and Saunders, (2004). P. *The Survey Methods Workbook.* Cambridge : Polity Press.

Goode. W.J. and Hatt. P.K. (1952). *Methods of Social Research*, New York, McGraw Hill.

Lal Das, D. K. (2000) . *Practice of Social Research : Social Work Perspectives*: Jaipur : Rawat Publications,

Lal Das, D. K. (2005). *Designs of Social Research* : Jaipur : Rawat Publications.

Monette, Duane R. et. al. (1986).Applied Social Research: Tool for the Human Services, Chicago: Holt.

O'Leary Z. (2004). *The Essential Guide to Doing Research*. New Delhi : Vistaar Publications.

Rubin, Allen & Babbie E. (1989). *Research Methods for Social Work*, Belmont, California, Wadsworth,

Thomas , P.T. (1968). "*Social Research*" in M.S. Gore (ed.) *Encyclopaedia of Social Work in India*, New Delhi : Government of India, p. 204.

# 2

# Formulation of Research Problem

## Introduction

The first step in the research process is formulation of research problem. It is considered as the most important phase of a research process. This step starts with the selection of a suitable problem from the field chosen by the researcher. In the area of social sciences, several problems exists which may have reference to pure, applied, or action research. The choice and formulation of a suitable problem is one of the most difficult tasks for a researcher, especially if he/she is a beginner. There are many sources to which a researcher may go for a suitable research problem, or from which he/she may develop a sense of problem awareness.

## Formulation of Research Problem

### Step 1 : Identification of a Research Problem

The first hurdle confronting a researcher is to select a topic that is appropriate for scientific inquiry. Actually, this is not as difficult as it may first appear because the social world around us is literally full of unanswered questions. Selecting a problem calls for some creativity and imagination, but there are also a number of sources you can look for inspiration.

A researcher often selects a research topic simply because he / she has an interest in some aspect of human behavior, possibly owing to some personal experience. A researcher might, for example, be interested in the problems of working women because he or she has been experiencing the ill effects of it in his/her family. Truancy or delinquency might be the focus of research attention because of contact with some youngsters in trouble in the neighborhood. A research study generally focuses on behaviour that is unique and thus compelling to some.

Essentially, two issues are involved in selection of research problem viz., understanding the problem thoroughly, and rephrasing the same into meaningful terms from an analytical point of view.

The best way of understanding the problem is to discuss it with dissertation supervisor. It would also be helpful to discuss with other teachers having some expertise in the subject.

Often the dissertation supervisor put forth the problem in general terms and the researcher narrows it down and phrases the problem in operational terms.

Say, for example, a researcher, is interested in following broad areas of research:

1. Problems of Working Women
2. Domestic Violence
3. Marital Conflicts
4. Sex Discrimination.

After discussions with supervisors and other teachers the researcher develops interest in undertaking research in the specific areas of research, say for example; Sex Discrimination.

**Definition of the Problem**

Once a research problem has been identified, it needs to be defined. The definition of a problem amounts to specifying it in detail and narrowing it down to workable size. Your research topic should be defined in such a way that it is clearly understood. In short, topics of research must be grounded in some already-known factual information which is used to introduce the topic and from which the research questions will emerge.

Let us assume that researcher has briefly considered a number of possible aspects of his/her specific area of research. After this the researcher rephrases the problem into analytical or operational terms i.e., to define the problem in as specific as possible. The specific area of research, namely, "sex discrimination" can be defined as: **"Sex Discrimination against Women at Work".**

### Evaluation of the Research Problem

As a researcher, you are required to evaluate a proposed research problem in the light of your competence and professional experience, possible difficulties in the availability of data, the financial and field constraints, and limitations of time.

It is worthwhile for you to ask yourself a series of questions before you undertake the research. The questions should be helpful in the evaluation of the problem on various criteria. All such questions must be answered affirmatively before the study is undertaken. What are the questions that we should ask?

### Is the Problem Researchable?

There are certain problems that cannot be effectively studied through the process of research. A researchable problem is always concerned with the associations between two or more variables that can be defined and measured. The problem should be capable of being stated in the form of workable research question that can be answered empirically.

### Is the Problem New?

There is no use in studying a problem which has already been frequently investigated by other researchers. To avoid such duplication, it is essential to examine very carefully the literature available in the field of study. The problem should be selected only when you are convinced that it is really a new problem which has not before been investigated successfully. However, it must be noted that a researcher may repeat a study when he/she wants to verify its conclusions or to extend the validity of its findings in a situation entirely different from the previous one.

### Is the Problem Significant?

The problem should be such that it is likely to fill in the gaps in the existing knowledge, to help to explain some of the inconsistencies in the previous research studies, or to help in the interpretation of the known facts. The results or findings of a study should either become a basis for a theory, generalisations or principles. Besides, they should lead to new topic for further research or have some useful practical applications.

**Is the problem feasible for the particular researcher?**

(a) **Research Competencies**

The problem should be in an area in which the researcher is qualified and competent. He/she must possess the necessary skills and competencies that may be needed to develop and execute the research study. The researcher should also have the necessary knowledge of research design, qualitative and quantitative techniques of data analysis etc. that may be required to carry out the research to its completion.

(b) **Interest and Enthusiasm**

The researcher should be genuinely interested in and enthusiastic about the problem he/she wants to undertake for research.

(c) **Time**

Research projects are a time bound exercise. It is important to assess the time required to complete a study, besides the assessment of total period, it is necessary to identify the period of the year in relation to the nature of the study.

After evaluating a broad research problem you have to narrow it down to a highly specific research problem. In fact, formulation of the problem often follows a sequential pattern where a number of formulations are set up, each formulation more specific than the preceding one, each one phrased in more analytical terms, and each more realistic in terms of the available data and resources. Following are some examples of specific research problems :

1. Research problem to be undertaken in specific sector of industries ;
   **"Sex Discrimination against Women at Work in Unorganised Sector".**
2. Research problem to be undertaken in specific sector of industries of a state;
   **"Sex Discrimination against Women at Work in Unorganised Sector in Andhra Pradesh".**
3. Research problem to be undertaken in specific sector of industries in a particular region ;
   **"Sex Discrimination against Women at Work in Unorganised Sector in Telangana Region of Andhra Pradesh".**

4. Research problem to be undertaken in specific sector of industries in cities ;
**"Sex Discrimination against Women at Work in Unorganised Sector in Twin Cities of Hyderabad and Secunderabad".**

**Statement of the Problem**

The statement of the problem determines the data which are to be collected, the characteristics of the data which are relevant, relations between variables which are to be examined, and the choice of the method and techniques to be used in these investigations. So, you are required to describe the background of the study, its theoretical basis and underlying assumptions, and specify the issues in concrete terms.

For example, the research problem : **"Sex Discrimination against Women at Work"** could be stated as shown below:

**Box 2.1. Statement of the Problem**

**The principle of "Equal Pay for Equal Work" has been accepted all over the world. The Indian Constitution categorically asserts equal pay for equal work, and the Indian Government reinforces this commitment with a legislative measure that provides for the payment of equal remuneration to men and women workers. Nonetheless, sex discrimination against women at work exists in various forms. The various dimensions of work place where women face discrimination are nature of work, wages, preference for jobs, duration of work, benefits and facilities available for women, employees attitude, job security, satisfaction with job etc. What causes these discriminations? What is the relationship between discrimination and other variables? The study intends to investigate the extent of discrimination and its correlates.**

**Research Questions**

A research question is a question that you seek to answer through the research study. Statement of a problem must clarify exactly what is to be determined or solved or what is the research question. It must restrict the scope of the study to specific and workable research questions. So, you are required to specify the issues in concrete, specific, and workable questions. All questions raised must be related to the problem. Each major issue or element should be separated into subsidiary or secondary elements, and these should be arranged in a logical order under the major divisions.

For example, following research questions emerges from the statement of the research problem stated above :

**Box 2.2. Research Questions**

**What causes sex discriminations?**
**What are the dimensions of sex discrimination?**
**What is the nature and extent of sex discrimination?**
**Why there is wage disparity between men and women workers doing same jobs?**
**What is the relationship between sex discrimination and other variables?**

It is important to examine whether the researcher has raised very clearly the questions to which he/she is looking for answers. These questions should be explicit – the researcher should categorically put down the questions on paper.

**Review of Literature**

A researcher needs to examine all available literature to get himself/herself acquainted with the selected problem. He/she may review the conceptual literature concerning the concepts and theories, and the empirical literature consisting of studies made earlier which are similar to the one proposed. The basic outcome of this review will be the knowledge as to what research questions have been explored and what were the findings. This will enable the researcher to specify his/her own research problem in a meaningful context.

The beginning of this section has suggested you to get literature relevant to the topic before you want to study it. Social research topics are usually embedded in so many different kinds of literature that the researcher must be careful in to selecting the best literature to examine. While many researchers collect every material which has some linkages with the topic, you need to keep the central theme of your topic in mind to guide you through your search of literature in the field. It is also important to examine different types of literature where relevant inferences are drawn from scientific data interpretations. It would be very useful if research findings from studies using various methods are critically examined.

While presenting review of research literature, a researcher should touch upon the introduction justifying the research, methodological details and findings and their implications. But most researchers present only findings. Very few researchers look into findings as well as research methodology in their reviews. From the perspectives of findings, major objectives of a review are to: (a) find gaps in research, (b) identify the areas of overlap, and (c) identify contradictions.

For preparing a research proposal, you should refer to the gaps in research, the areas of overlap, contradictions and significant findings you have noted through review of literature. This will help you to raise questions or which will guide you to decide the subsequent steps of the research process such as identification of objectives, formulation of hypothesis (if any), determination of research design and sample for your study. You must be able to draw out findings from the studies and summarize them in such a way that someone unfamiliar with study can easily grasp their meaning and importance. To help you to do this, you should look at the background literature review sections which generally come at the beginning of published research articles. Most of these reviews are very condensed; they extract a few salient points from numerous studies, summarizing them in a way that is relevant to the study in question.

The following paragraphs illustrate a brief review of literature for the research problem : **"Sex Discrimination against Women at Work in Unorganised Sector".**

**Box 2.3. Review of Literature**

There have been quite a few micro-studies (Gambhir, 1979; Khanna and Mathew, 1979; Patel, 1982), that show that the disparities in wages/salary of male and female employees for work of similar nature, is part of the general discrimination against women at the work place. Particularly, in unorganised sector, women are invariably paid much less than the males.

According to the studies conducted by Pais (1980), Labour Bureau (1979), Occupational Wages Surveys (1963), with respect of select industries as well as employment, the adoption of the principle of "equal pay for equal work" has discouraged employers from employing women workers profitably. Most probably, one of the reasons for employing women workers was that it was cheaper.

What is the relationship between wage differential and regional development? This aspect was studied by the Prgoramme Evaluation Organisation of the Planning Commission (1961). The results show that inter-state variations are quite significant.

### Identification of Objectives of the Study

Once the research problem is defined it is time to address the aim and objectives of the study. At this stage you are required to present the aim and the objectives of the study in brief to justify your study in terms of both its rationale and the implications that it might raise.

### Formulation of Objectives

This set of research questions mentioned above can be converted into objectives. Objectives are the foundations of a research project. Eventually the objectives guide the entire process of research. The major attributes of well-written objectives are:

### Clarity of Expression and Direction

The objectives must have been stated clearly enough to indicate what the researcher is trying to investigate. It is equally important to avoid overlaps in stating objectives.

### Measurability

The objectives must be stated in a manner that they are measurable; in case of qualitative research it should be possible to at least codify the data and information so that assessment can be made whether the objectives have been achieved or not.

### Comprehensiveness

The objectives provide the guiding framework for a research study. Hence, the statement of objectives should be comprehensive enough to cover each and every aspect of the research study. Stating differently, nothing should be outside the purview of the stated objectives.

### Judiciousness

Another important attribute is the judiciousness in choosing and stating objectives. For example, many young scholars, in their postgraduate dissertations and doctoral theses mention "recommending future research" or "recommending suggestions" as one of the objectives. In all fairness, this is not feasible. Similarly, in a short time-bound project, a research objective that actually calls for sustained and long-term study becomes less feasible.

Here it is important to note that rationale for doing the study will be accomplished only if the study is done well. Preparing a proposal of your study will show that you have devised a plan to study your problem that seems feasible; you reinforce the sense that the aims and objectives of the study will be achieved. The value of the study lies not only in what it alone will produce, but also in how it may add to or challenge other research in the area.

To illustrate, consider the following aim and objectives of a study entitled : **"Sex Discrimination against Women at Work in Unorganised Sector".**

**Box 2.4. Aim and Objectives of the Study**

**Aim of the Study**

The aim of the present study is to investigate in to the sex discrimination at the work place on the ground of sex against women at work

**Objectives of the Study**

The specific objectives of the study are :

1. To assess the nature and extent of discrimination on the basis of sex against women at work
2. To explore the factors responsible for sex discrimination against women at work.
3. To determine the extent of disparities in wages/salary (wage differential) of male and female employees for work of similar nature, and
4. To identify the important correlates of wage differential.

## Identification of Concepts , Constructs and Variables

### Concepts

A concept is an abstraction representing objects, such as, 'water', "glass", "gold" etc. Concept may be a property of an object, or a phenomenon. For example, 'mass', 'weight', 'density' are properties of objects. These concepts are frequently used by physical scientists. Concepts such as 'village', 'rural', and 'urban', 'family' 'house' are common among social scientists. Concepts are terms or words which we can point to an object the term or word represents. For example, when we say "house", we can point to an object, the word represents. We can also measure the area on which it exists, the height, width and thickness of walls and such other dimensions of the house. There are many similar terms such as "tree", "temple", "book", "chalk", and so on for which we can point out numerous objects and measure theirs dimensions (Black and Champion, 1976).

To illustrate further , let us examine the research problem we have formulated above. The research problem includes terms like "Women", "Work" and "Unorganised Sectors". These are terms or words which we can point to objects the terms or words represent. In research terminology we call these terms or words concepts.

**Constructs**

A construct is a deliberately adopted concept having an added meaning for a specific purpose (Black and Champion, 1976). Let us take an example, - 'achievement' as a concept. It is an abstraction formed from the observation of certain characteristics of achievers and non-achievers. Achievement as a construct is defined in such a way that it serves two distinct purposes. One, a construct can be related to other constructs in various ways which will serve as the theoretical frame work of the research. For example, we can say that achievement is in part a function of motivation. Two, achievement as a construct is so consciously and deliberately defined and specified that it can be observed and measured (Goode and Hat, 1952).

A construct of more interest to social researchers is 'social status'. It is an abstraction formed from the observation of certain traits of individuals. These traits are associated with the position of individuals in the society, which are ascertained by certain indicators such as level of education, social group, and recognition by the society, etc. The assessment of various indicators put together and expressed in a word – 'social status'.

The most important step in this direction is to specify the constructs involved in the research problem and define them in operational terms. To illustrate, suppose you state that you want to study the **"Sex Discrimination against Women at Work in Unorganised Sector"**. The constructs involved in the problem are **"Sex Discrimination"** and **"Wage Disparities"** . Please note that the expressions are to be understood beyond their dictionary meanings. For example, the dictionary meaning of **"Sex Discrimination"** is "to treat someone unfairly because of their sex". This meaning is not sufficient for research purposes. It is important for you to specify exactly what indicators of **'Sex Discrimination'** you will use or what you will do to measure the presence or absence of the phenomenon denoted by the term **"Sex Discrimination"**. Similarly, you have to define the other construct **"Wage Disparities"** also in terms of the operations or processes that will be used to measure them. In this study, you might choose to define **"Sex Discrimination"** and **"Wage Disparities"** as follows :

**Box 2.5. Definitions of Constructs**

**Sex Discrimination**
Discrimination may be defined as withholding of certain rewards or facilities with regard to employment and matters connected therewith on the basis of sex. In other words, it refers to providing women workers with fewer rewards or facilities than legitimately deserved.

**Wage Disparities (Wage Differential)**
The term 'wage disparity' would refer to the difference in time rate wages of men and women workers when work done by men and women workers is demonstrably identical (same work or work of similar nature)

### Variable

A variable is an empirical property that takes two or more values. In other words, if a property can change in value or kind it can be regarded as variable. For example, 'income' is a variable because it can be assigned two or more values.

### Dependent and Independent Variables

In most of the cases researchers focus on cause –effect relationships and start with an effect, then search for its causes. The variable which represents the cause is termed as independent variable. The variable that is the effect or is the result or outcome of another variable is the dependent variable. In other words the variable expected to explain change in the dependent variable is referred to as the independent variable. The independent variable is also known as explanatory variable. Independent variable is considered as the presumed cause of changes in the values of dependent variable. Process wise the dependent variable is the expected outcome of the independent variable. Independent variable and dependent variable are also termed as predictor and criterion variables.

### Operationalisation of Variables

In stating a problem, the researcher should make sure that it is neither stated in terms so general as to make it vague nor specified so narrowly as to make it insignificant and trivial. The most important step in this direction is to specify the variables involved in the problem and define them in operational terms. To illustrate, suppose you state that you want to study the **"Sex Discrimination against Women at Work in Unorganised Sector"**. This statement is broad and it communicates in a general way what you want to do. But it is necessary to specify the problem with much greater precision. For this the first step is to specify the variables involved in the problem and define them in operational terms.

Say for example, for the study referred above the variables identified could be :

**Box 2.6. Independent and Dependent Variables**

**Independent Variables :**
**Age, Marital Status, Type of Family, Level of Education, Castes, Nativity, Income, Religion, Designation.**

**Dependent Variables :**
**Sex Discrimination and Wage Disparitis**

## Hypothesis

After the selection and formulation of research problem, the formulation of hypothesis(es) is the next important step in the research process. A hypothesis is defined as "a tentative proposition" suggested as a solution to a problem or as an explanation of some phenomenon (Goode and Hatt, 1952). This step establishes the problem and the logic underlying the research study. Research questions which the researcher has designed to answer (tentatively) are usually framed as hypothesis to be tested on the basis of evidence. The formulation of the hypothesis(es) is typically determined with the help of the implications of the related literature and the deductive logic of the problem under investigation.

## Importance of Hypothesis

It may be mentioned here that hypotheses are not essential to all researches, particularly, in the early stages of exploration of a problem. And it should not be assumed that failure to develop a hypothesis is necessarily a sign of lack of scientific orientation. However, a hypothesis may be conceived as an assumption which merits consideration and needs to be tested against the available empirical evidence. That is why it is suggested that a hypothesis is to be used as a pivot around which the investigation revolves, limiting thereby the field of investigation to a definite target and also determining the observations to be made and the ones to ignore.

A good hypothesis has several basic characteristics. We discuss some of them as follows:

(i) **Providing direction:** Hypotheses provide direction to research and prevent collection of irrelevant data. This is necessary because, a given fact may be relevant with respect to one hypothesis and irrelevant with respect to another. Thus, hypotheses ensure the collection of relevant data necessary to answer research questions arising from the statement of the problem. For example, in a research problem, **"Sex Discrimination against Women at Work in Unorganised Sector"**, the researcher may frame the hypothesis – higher the development, higher will be the level of discrimination on the basis of sex. The researcher will collect data about the indicators of development and discrimination against women .

(ii) **Hypothesis should be testable:** Hypotheses should be stated in such a way as to indicate an expected difference or an expected association/relationship between the variables used in the research. The researcher should not state any hypothesis that she/he does not have reason to believe that it can be tested or evaluated by some objective means. Hypotheses are the propositions about the association / relationships between variables. These can be tested empirically.

(iii) **Hypothesis should be brief and clear:** Hypothesis should be stated clearly and briefly. It makes problems easier for the reader to understand and also for the researcher to test. The statement should be a concise statement of the association / relationship / difference expected.

## Formulation and Testing of Hypothesis

Hypotheses are formulated to explain observed facts, conditions, or behaviour and to serve as a guide in the research process. The statements or tentative generalisations which constitute hypotheses are partly based on facts and explanations, and partly conceptual formulation of hypothesis. Some examples of hypotheses are :

> **Box 2.7. Hypotheses :**
>
> - **It is likely that women belonging to lower socio-economic status would experience higher discrimination.**
> - **Personal characteristics and sex discrimination against women at work are likely to be associated.**
> - **There may be a direct association between regional development and wage disparities and level of sex discrimination.**

**Testing of Hypothesis**

Testing hypothesis is an important activity in the research process. As a researcher you should know the important steps in testing hypothesis. The steps are:

(1) State the research hypothesis ($H_1$).
(2) Formulate the null hypothesis ($H_0$).
(3) Choose a statistical test.
(4) Specify a significance level.
(5) Compute the statistical test.
(6) Reject/accept the $H_0$.
(7) Draw the inference i.e. accept/reject $H_0$.

**Step 1: State the Research Hypothesis**

$H_1$: It is likely that women belonging to lower socio- economic status would experience higher discrimination.

**Step 2: Formulate the Null Hypothesis ($II_0$)**

Ho: There is no significant association between socio-economic status of women and sex discrimination.

**Step 3: Choose a Statistical Test**

Let us suppose that we have decided to use Chi-Square statistic ($\chi^2$ ) to test the association between the variables considered in the research hypothesis (To choose statistics please refer Chapter VIII).

**Step 4: Specify a Significance Level**

Further we suppose that we would like to test our hypothesis at 0.05 level of significance. ( For further details please refer Chapter VIII )

**Step 5: Compute the Statistical Test**

In this step the researcher has to cross tabulate his/her data and compute Chi-square test ( $\chi^2$ ) . On computation of the test, let us say that the test yielded a value of 6.78 , df = 1. (For computation of $\chi^2$ using SPSS refer Chapter VIII. For manual calculation of $\chi^2$ refer Appendix A)

**Step 6: Reject/accept the $H_0$**

Since the calculated value of Chi-square is more than the critical value we reject the null hypothesis ( For further details please refer Chapter VIII).

**Step 7: Draw the inference i.e. Accept/reject $H_1$**

We accept the research hypothesis because the null hypothesis has been rejected. Hence, we can infer that there is significant association between socio-economic status of women and sex discrimination.

## References

Black, James A. and Champion, Dean J. (1976). *Methods and Issues in Social Research,* New York: John Wiley.

Buckingham, A and Saunders, (2004). P. *The Survey Methods Workbook.* Cambridge : Polity Press.

Goode. W.J. and Hatt. P.K. (1952). *Methods of Social Research,* New York, McGraw Hill.

Lal Das, D. K. (2000) .*Practice of Social Research : Social Work Perspectives*: Jaipur : Rawat Publications.

Lal Das, D. K. (2005). *Designs of Social Research* : Jaipur : Rawat Publications.

Monette, Duane R. et. al. (1986). Applied Social Research: Tool For the Human Services, Chicago: Holt.

O'Leary Z. (2004). *The Essential Guide to Doing Research.* New Delhi : Vistar Publications.

Ramachandran, P. (2000). *Research and Statistics for Social Work.* Secnderabad : Andhra Pradesh Social Service Society.

Rubin, Allen and Babbie E. (1989). *Research Methods for Social Work*, Belmont, California, Wadsworth.

# 3

# Selection of Research Design

### Introduction

In the previous chapter we discussed about the first step of the research process that is formulation of research problem. The step starts with the selection of a research topic followed by identification of objectives, concepts, constructs and variables. At the end we had clear statement of objectives as well as hypotheses and detailed listing of the variables. The next stage is to plan how we are going to conduct the study. That is to say, we have to decide what would be the most appropriate research design you should adopt in order to execute the research study.

A research design is the 'blue print' of the research study. It describes the plan of research study. The research design results from translating the plan of action with regard to the execution of the study. As such, research design- a detailed plan outlining how the research will be carried out–has to addresses it to certain key questions like:

How to find out the answers to the research question?
How to achieve the objectives of the study?
What type of sample will be appropriate for the study?
What methods and techniques will be used to collect data from them?
What methods and techniques will be used to analyse data?
What statistical methods and techniques will be used to draw inferences?

The answers and the details about these questions constitute a research design. To be more specific, a research design includes the details about the problem, the objectives, research questions , area of study (population), sampling plan, and method and techniques of data collection and analysis. In fact the research design spells out in considerable detail what occur in the following steps of the research process. It also reflects the dimensions of research designs. Keeping in view the various dimensions, research designs can be organized into four groups : (1) research designs indicating the purpose of doing research, (2) research designs indicating its intended use, (3) research designs indicating the effects of time and (4) research designs to ascertain cause effect relationships. Before we select a suitable research design, we will have a quick review of some important research designs.

## Research Designs by Purpose of a Study

Research designs are closely linked with the purpose/ objectives of a research study/ problem (Seltiz et. al (1959, p.50). The purposes of social research may be clubbed into three groups based on what the researcher is trying to accomplish-explore a new topic, describe a social phenomenon, or explain why something occurs. Studies may have a combination of purposes, e.g. a study may aim at exploring a new topic as well as describing a social phenomenon. However, one purpose is usually dominant . Most probably this is the reason that many a researchers label his/her research design as "exploratory research design" or "descriptive research design".

## Exploratory Research Designs

The purpose of exploratory studies is to formulate a problem for a more precise investigation or to develop hypotheses. However, an exploratory study can also be conducted to enhance the familiarity of researcher with the phenomena; he/she wishes to study some time later in a more scientific way.

For instance, if a researcher wanted to study social interaction patterns of AIDS/HIV patients but knew little or nothing about the phenomenon; an exploratory research would be appropriate. A preliminary interview with the relatives of AIDS/HIV patients would enable the researcher to develop a specific study design.

Exploratory studies, therefore, helps researchers to acquaint themselves with the characteristics of their research problem.

**Descriptive Research Designs**

Descriptive studies, as name suggests, describe as accurately as possible the characteristics of a group of people or a community. A researcher who is interested in studying people of a community, their age and sex composition, castewise distribution, affiliation to religion, level of education, occupational status, designs his study as descriptive study. Another researcher may formulate a descriptive design of study to know the proportion of people in a particular population who favours dowry or who feels that child labour should be banned. Still others may be concerned with specific prediction. For example, what percentage of population would enter voter's list in the next census operations? What will be the size of the handicapped population who will need financial assistance in the next five-year plan? And so on.

**Explanatory Research Designs**

When we have a problem that is already known and have a description of it, we may like to know why things are the way they are. The purpose of explanatory research designs is to explain "why". In explanatory research designs, the researcher goes beyond focusing on a topic or portraying it. He or she looks for causes and reasons. For example, a descriptive researcher may discover that 30 per cent of the elders are abused by their children, whereas the explanatory researcher is more interested in knowing why children abuse their elders.

**Research Designs by its Intended Use**

Research designs differ with its intended use. Some researchers focus on using research to assess the effectiveness of interventions, whereas, others use it to solve problems. Yet, another group of researcher may be interested in evaluating a programme to know if it was organized effectively. Impact analysis is yet another area of research which needs a different research designs. These researches may be grouped into three categories : (1) Intervention Research Designs, (2) Action Research Designs, and (3) Evaluation Research Designs.

### Intervention Research Designs

The process of improving social functioning of individuals, groups and communities involves study, assessment, intervention and evaluation. It requires use of a research design called intervention research design commonly known as single-subject designs trough which social work practitioners attempt to improve social functioning of individuals, groups, families and communities.

Intervention research designs or single subject designs are basically quasi-experimental research designs, which use time series analysis technique of social researches to the evaluation of the impact of interventions on individual cases, groups, family and community. Such designs involve repeated measure of the dependent variable before and after a particular intervention, to see if a sustained pattern of change in the dependent variable commences shortly after the onset of intervention (Rubin and Babbie, 1989).

### Action Research Designs

Action research establishes a link between knowledge generated by the research study and social action to be undertaken based on the knowledge. The goal of action research is to improve conditions of research participants. It attracts researchers who hold specific expertise of issues related with practice. For example, most feminist research has dual objectives: to contribute to the advancement of knowledge and to create social change by transforming gender relations. An action researcher may undertake a research study effects of lay offs and work together with union officials and management to redesign work schedule to prevent lay offs. There are several other examples where action research designs are employed , such as , working among illiterates to teach functional literacy and make them aware of their socio-economic conditions, and to attempt to improve them.

### Research Designs Indicating the Effects of Time

Another dimension of research which has to be considered while designing the research is the effect of time. Knowledge of time dimension helps researchers to design his /her research to assess the effect of time on the variables under consideration. Some studies are conducted at single fixed time which gives a snapshot view of the problem. Other studies provide a moving description that helps researchers to follow events , people or social relations over periods of time. Research designs incorporating time dimension of research can be categorized into two groups: a single point in time (cross-sectional research) and multiple time points ( longitudinal research).

**Cross-Sectional Research Designs**

Studies using cross-sectional research design a researcher collects data for his/her research at one point of time. This research design is most frequently used by social researchers because it is the simplest and least costly alternative. The most striking disadvantage of this research design is that it cannot cover social processes or change.

**Longitudinal Research Designs**

To describe the social changes or social processes longitudinal research designs are used. In this research designs the phenomenon is studied at more than one time. It is usually more complex and costly than cross-sectional research designs. It is also more powerful, especially when researchers seek answers to questions about social change or social processes.

**Research Designs to Ascertain Cause-Effect Relationships**

Some researchers focus on using research to ascertain cause-effect relationships. Yet, another group of researchers may be interested in evaluating a programme to know if it was organised effectively. Impact analysis is yet another area of research which needs a different research designs. A causal relationships refers to relationships between two variables where one variable (characteristic or occurrence) X determines another variable (characteristic or occurrence) Y. Research designs focusing on causal relationships can be categorized into two groups: (a) Experimental Research Designs and (b) Non-Experimental or Survey Research Designs.

**Experimental Research Designs**

Experimental researches are designed for testing causal relationships. For example, if a researcher wishes to test a causal relationships that punishments (X) cause low self-esteem (Y) by comparing a group of students who have been exposed to punishments (X) with one that has not been exposed , he has to measure the two groups with respect of Y, either during or after exposure to X.

**Non-Experimental Research Designs or Survey Research Designs.**

Survey research designs are used to collect detailed descriptions of existing phenomena and with the aim of examining the data to ascertain cause-effect relationships. The objective may not only be to ascertain cause-effect relationships , but also to determine the nature and extent of relationships by comparing it with selected set of variables. Survey research is probably the most widely used method for obtaining descriptive and evaluative information.

Survey researches are appropriate for research questions about self- reported beliefs or behaviours. Survey research is considered as most appropriate method in case of measuring variables through answers of questions.

**Selection of Research Designs**

In the previous chapter we have selected a research problem and defined the research topic. We have also clearly stated the problem, objectives, hypotheses and a set of variables. In brief, you now have clear idea of what you want to study through a research project.

Now you need to prepare a detailed plan outlining how the research will be carried out. That is, we have to answer the questions in the beginning of this chapter with reference to the topic of research selected. We have to decide what would be the most appropriate research design in order to execute the study to find the answers of research questions raised earlier and achieve the objectives.

First we will look at the aim and objectives of the research study entitled : **"Sex Discrimination against Women at Work in Unorganised Sector in Andhra Pradesh".**

The purposes of the research study are to describe a social phenomenon, namely, sex discrimination, and to probe why there is sex discrimination. That means the research study has twin purposes. As such, you may adopt descriptive research design as well as explanatory research design. However, when we examine the objectives and hypotheses little seriously , it becomes very clear that the purpose "why discrimination' is dominant . Therefore, it would be appropriate to adopt explanatory research design for the study.

Considering time dimension of research study objectives and hypotheses suggest that study is to be conducted at single fixed time which will give a snapshot view of the problem. When you collect data for your research study at one point of time you have to use cross-sectional research design.

The objectives and hypotheses of the study also suggest that it intends to collect detailed descriptions of sex discrimination with the aim of examining the data to ascertain cause-effect relationships analysing the data about self- reported beliefs or perceptions of selected respondents. Therefore, survey research design is appropriate for the study. In sum, you can explain the research designs of your research project as shown in the box:

**Box 3.1 : Research Designs of the Study**

**This study would adopt a combination of research designs ; survey research design, explanatory research design and cross-sectional research design.**

## References

Abram, M. (1950), *Social Surveys and Social Action,* London : Heinemann.

Ackoff, R.L. (1953) *The Design of Social Research,* Chicago: University of Chicago Press.

Bailey, Kenneth D. (1978). *Methods of Social Research*, London: The Free Press.

Baker, L. Therese. ( 1988).*Doing Social Research,* New York: McGraw Hill.

Black, James A. and Champion, (1976) .Dean J. *Methods and Issues in Social Research* New York: John Wiley.

Buckingham, A and Saunders, (2004). P. *The Survey Methods Workbook.* Cambridge :Polity Press.

Festinger. L. and Katz. D. (eds.). (1953). *Research Methods in the Behavioral Sciences,*New York: The Dryden Press.

Goode. W.J. and Hat. P.K. (1952). *Methods in Social Research,* New York : McGraw Hill.

Kerlinger. Fred R. (1964). *Foundations of Behavioral Research,* Delhi : Surjeet Publications.

Kidder, Louise H. (1981). *Research Methods in Social Relations,* New York: Holt.

Lal Das, D.K. (2000), *Practice of Social Research : A Social Work Perspective,* Rawat Publications, Jaipur.

Lal Das, D.K. (2005), *Designs of Social Research,* Jaipur: Rawat Publications.

Miller. D.C. .(1964). *Handbook of Research Design and Social Measurement* New York : David Mckey Co.

Monette, Duane R. et. al. (1986). *Applied Social Research: Tool for the Human Services* Chicago: Holt.

Moser. C.A. and Kalton. *Survey Methods in Social Investigation* London : Heinemann Educational Books, 1975.

Nachmias D and Nachmias C. (1981). *Research Methods in the Social Sciences*, New York: St. Martins press.

Rubin, Allen & Babbie E. (1989). *Research Methodology for Social Work*, Belmof, California, Wadsworth.

Sellitz. G. et. al. (1973). *Research Methods in Social Relations.* New York: Holt. Rinehart and Winston (3rd edition.

Stouffer. S.A. *Social Research to Test ideas* New York: Free Press of Glencoe, 1962.

Suchman, E.A. (1953). *The Principles of Research Design.* In John T Dobyet. al., An Introduction to Social Research, New York: The Stackpole.

Wilkinson, T.S. and Bhandarkar, P.L. *Methodology and Techniques of Social Research*: Bombay: Himalayan, 1977.

Young. P.V. (1953) *Scientific Social Surveys and Research* Englewood Cliff. N.J. Prentice Hall.

# 4

# Selection of Sample

## Introduction

Once, we decide our research design, our next step would be to select the respondents. In the previous chapter we have decided that we would adopt survey research design for our study : **"Sex Discrimination against Women at Work in Unorganised Sector in Andhra Pradesh".** We have also decided that it would be a **cross sectional study** and **explanatory in nature**. Therefore, it is almost clear that we would study a section of respondents (women workers in this case) at one point of time considering a set of variables.

From the topic of research it is very clear that the area of study would the state of Andhra Pradesh. Thus, all the women workers in the unorganized sector in the state would be the population of the study. A single unit of study (a woman worker in this case) is referred to as an element of population. When we select a group of elements (women workers) for the purpose of the study we refer to that group of elements as a sample.

The basic logic of survey research design is that the results obtained from the sample are true of the population as a whole. That is, we collect data from a sample in order to make generalization to the population. How closely the sample statistics corresponds to the population depends largely on the way the sample is selected. (Kidder, 1981)

For instance, suppose we want to know what percentage of a population agrees with a statement : "Women workers should not be engaged in hazardous jobs" . We might put the statement to a sample, compute the percentage that agrees, and take this result as an estimate of the percentage of the population who agrees. We can devise a sampling plan that will carry the assurance that our sample estimates will not differ from the corresponding true population parameters by, say, more than five per cent ; the estimates will be correct within the limit of five per cent (commonly known as "margin of error" or "limit of accuracy") 95 percent of the time (commonly termed as the "probability" or "confidence level"). We can similarly devise another sampling procedure, which will produce results within the limits of one per cent 99 per cent of the time.

The sampling procedures, which ensure that the sample statistics will be correct within certain limits, are referred to as a "representative sampling plan." Here the usage of the word "representative" does not qualify sample, but sampling plan. A representative sampling plan ensures that the selected sample is sufficiently representative of the population to justify our running the risk of taking it as representative. (Kidder, 1981).

Based on this assumption probability sampling makes it possible to select a sample which will be representative . This helps researchers to estimate the extent to which the sample statistics are likely to differ from population parameters. This means, if probability sampling method is used, it is possible to ascertain the size of the sample that will be needed if we want to have a given degree of certainty that their sample results do not differ by more than a specified value from those of the population parameters.

There are a number of sampling methods which decrease the likelihood of misleading generalisations based on sample statistics. These techniques assure the inclusion of diverse elements of the population in the sample by controlling the proportions of the various types of elements. Alternatively, statistical procedures are used in the analysis of the data.

Another important factor, which affects the representativeness of samples, is data collection procedures used in the study. This is reason why the sample study can produce more valid and reliable results than can a census. For instance, it is always difficult to get skilled interviewers in large numbers to cover wide spread area of study. Even if we manage to get required number of skilled interviewers, it is not possible to get anything beyond the most superficial data in a census study. Moreover, the reliability of such data is also not beyond doubts. On the contrary, in a sample study, which requires lesser number of skilled interviewers, not only can we probe thoroughly by spending more time with each respondent but also we can depend on data collected there in. In addition to this, a sample study reduces the large expenses required for census study to a large extent.

**Representativeness and Adequacy**

Basically, there are two requirement of a sample: it has to be 'representative' and 'adequate'. If the nature of the population has to be interpreted from a sample, it is necessary for the sample to be truly representative of the population. Moreover, it calls for a drawing a representative 'proportion' of the population. The population may contain a finite number of members or units. Sometimes, the population may be 'infinite'. Therefore, a population has to be defined clearly so that there is no ambiguity as to whether a given unit belongs to the population or not. Otherwise, a researcher will not know what units to consider for selecting a sample.

The second issue related to the representation of a sample is to decide about the 'sampling frame', i.e., listing of all the units of the population in separate categories. In a study, there can be different sampling frames, such as male/female students, employed/ unemployed students, etc. The sampling frame should be complete, accurate and up-to-date, and must be drawn before selecting the sample.

Thirdly, a sample should be unbiased and objective. Ideally, it should provide all information about the population from which it has been drawn. Such a sample based on the logic of induction, i.e., proceeding from the particular to the general, falls within the range of random sampling errors. This leads us to the results expressed in terms of "probability".

A sample should not only provide representativeness, but should also be adequate enough to render stability to its characteristics. What, then, is the ideal size of a sample? An adequate sample is the one that contains enough cases to ensure reliable results. If the population under study is homogenous, a small sample is sufficient. However, a much larger sample is necessary, if there is greater variability in the units of population. Thus the procedure of determining the sample size varies with the nature of the characteristics under study and their distribution in the population. Moreover, the adequacy of a sample will depend on our knowledge of the population as well as on the method used in drawing the sample.

Before we decide sampling method for our research study we will briefly discuss the various sampling methods and techniques of selecting sample units.

## Methods of Sampling

Sampling methods can be broadly classified into two categories:

(i) Probability Sampling, and

(ii) Non-probability Sampling.

## Probability Sampling

Probability sampling is based on random selection of units from a population. In other words, the sampling process is not based on the discretion of the researcher but is carried out in such a way that the probability of every unit in the population of being included is the same. For example, in the case of lottery, every individual has equal chance of being selected. In probability sampling each unit of population has probability of being included in the sample,

Probability sampling can be done through different methods, each method having its own strengths and limitations. A brief account of these is given below:

## Simple Random Sampling

Simple random sampling is a method of selecting a sample from a finite population in such a way that every unit of population is given an equal chance of being selected. In practice, you can draw a simple random sample through the following steps:

(i) Define the population.

(ii) Make a list of all the units in the population and number them.

(iii) Decide the size of the sample, or the number of units to be included in the sample.

## Techniques of Selecting Sample Units

One of the following techniques can be used to select the sample units:

1. Lottery Method,
2. Tippet's Random Number Tables,
3. Sequential List Method.

## Lottery Method

You -may use the lottery method to draw sample units. In this method, first of all you have to write names or serial numbers of all the units of population using a set of chits. Then you need to put all the chits in a box. After shuffling the chits thoroughly, you can draw the sample of a required size, say x, by picking the required number of chits. The units which have the serial numbers occurring on these chits will be considered selected. The assumption underlying this method is that the chits are shuffled so that the population can be regarded as arranged randomly. Similarly, to select five wards from the total number of wards (60 wards) in the city you will write the serial numbers of all the wards on small pieces of paper. Jumble the chits as well and then choose five numbers.

## Tippet's Random Number Tables

The best method of drawing a simple random sample is to use a table of random numbers. These random number tables have been prepared by Tippet. After assigning consecutive numbers to the units of population, the researcher starts at any point on the table of random numbers and reads the consecutive numbers in any direction horizontally, vertically or diagonally. If the read out number corresponds with the one written on a unit card, then that unit is chosen for the sample.

Let us, suppose that a sample of five wards is to be selected at random from a serially numbered population of 60 wards. Using a part of a table of random numbers reproduced below: Table 4.1: Tippet's Random Number five two digit numbers (as the total population of wards, is a two-digit figure) are selected from the Table 4.1. Say for example we wish to select a sample of 5 **(N=5)**

Any point can be selected to start with the random numbers for drawing the desired sample size. Suppose, the researcher selects

**Table 4.1 : Tippet's Random Numbers**

| | | |
|---|---|---|
| 29935 | **03** | 971 63175 52579 10478 |
| 15114 | **07** | 126 51890 77787 75510 |
| 03870 | 99 | 225 10589 87629 22039 |
| 79390 | **43** | 188 40756 45259 65959 |
| 30035 | 85 | 915 79196 54428 64819 |
| 29039 | **39** | 861 28759 79802 68531 |
| 78196 | **09** | 108 24107 49777 09599 |
| 15847 | 08 | 493 91442 91391 80130 |
| 36614 | 62 | 248 49194 97209 92587 |
| 40549 | 54 | 884 91465 43862 35541 |
| 40878 | 18 | 997 14286 09982 90308 |

→

| |
|---|
| **3** |
| **7** |
| **43** |
| **39** |
| **9** |

columns sixth and seventh from row one, the number to start with 03. In this way he/she can select first five numbers from this column starting with 03.

If you start with the first row and the columns, 03 is the first two-digit number, 07 is the next number and so on. The sample, then, is 3, 7, 43, 39, 9

Now, in selecting the sample of five wards, two numbers, 99 and 85, need to be deleted as they are bigger than 60, the size of the population. The processes of selection and deletion are stopped after the required number of five units gets selected. If any number is repeated in the table, it may be substituted by the next number from the same column. The researcher will go on to the next column until a sample of the desired size is obtained.

Simple random sampling ensures the best results. However, from a practical point of view, a list of all the units of a population is not possible to obtain. Even if it is possible, it may involve a very high cost which a researcher or organisation may not be able to afford. Therefore, simple random sampling is difficult to realize.

### Sequential List Method

Sequential list method of selecting sample units provides a more even spread of the sample over the population list and leads to greater precision. The process involves the following steps:

(i) Make a list of the population units based on some order – alphabetical, seniority, street number, house number or any such factor.

(ii) Determine the desired sampling fraction, say 100 out of 1000; and also the number of the $K^{th}$ unit. [K = N/n = 1000/100 = 10].

(iii) Starting with a randomly chosen number between 1 and K, both inclusive, select every $K^{th}$ unit from the list. If in the above example the randomly chosen number is 6, the sample shall include the $16^{th}$, $26^{th}$, $36^{th}$, $46^{th}$, $56^{th}$ units in each of the series going up to the $996^{th}$ unit.

This method provides a sample as good as a simple random sample and is comparatively easier to draw. If a researcher is interested to study the average telephone bill of an area in his/her city, he/she may randomly select every fourth telephone subscriber from the telephone directory and find out their annual telephone bills. sampling.

**Stratified Sampling**

Stratified random sampling takes into account the stratification of the main population into a number of sub-populations, each of which is homogenous with respect to one or more characteristic(s). Having ensured this stratification, it provides for selecting randomly the required number of units from each sub-population or any mode of selection. The steps involved in the stratified sampling are given as follows:

(i) Deciding upon the relevant stratification criteria such as gender, nativity, courses of study, etc.

(ii) Dividing the total population into sub-population based on the stratification criteria.

(iii) Listing the units separately in each sub-population.

(iv) Selecting the requisite number of units from each sub-population by using an appropriate random selection technique.

Thus, stratification improves the representativeness of a sample by introducing a secondary element of control. However, the efficiency of the stratified random sample depends on the allocation of sample size to the strata. Rendering proportional weightage to each criterion improves it further by allowing the use of a smaller sample and by helping in achieving higher efficiency at a reduced cost.

Stratified random sample is very useful when lists of units or individuals in the population are not available. It is also useful in providing more accurate results than simple random sampling. For example, while selecting a sample of undergraduate student of a university, the researcher may decide the whole population of undergraduate students as boys and girls, science, arts and commerce. All these will be different strata. From each stratum researcher may select 30 students as a sample.

### Proportionate Stratified Random Sampling

In the sampling plan the sample will have specified characteristics in exact proportion to those same characteristics which are distributed in the population. To understand this sampling plan we will consider the following example.

Let us consider the students of College of Social Work. The researcher wishes to have proportionate stratified random sample of them taking year of study in the college as basis of stratification. Let us suppose that the students at the college are distributed as is shown in Table 4.2.

**Table 4.2**
**Distribution of Students According to Year in College**

| *Year* | *Population* | *Proportion of each class* |
|---|---|---|
| BSW I | 50 | .25 |
| BSW II | 40 | .20 |
| BSW III | 30 | .15 |
| MSW I | 40 | .20 |
| MSW II | 40 | .20 |
| **Total** | 200 | 1.00 |

Further, we suppose that the researcher decides to have a sample of 60 students. First, he determines the proportion of students in each class (as shown in the third column). Then he/she calculates the composition of the sample taking each proportion of the stratifying characteristics in the population and multiplying it by the desired size of the sample. Thus, he/she multiplies 60, the desired sample size by .25, the proportion of BSW first year students in the population or (60) (.25) = 15

As such, he/she has to include 15 students from the BSW first year in his sample. This precedence is repeated for each year as described below: (60) (.25) = 15 , (60) (.20) = 12, (60) (.15) = 9, (60) (.20) = 12, (60) (.20) = 12. Thus the sample size (N) = 15+12+9+12+12=60.

**Table 4.3**
**Distribution of Students by Proportion**

| *Year* | *Sample Break-up* | *Proportion* |
|---|---|---|
| BSW I | 15 | .25 |
| BSW II | 12 | .20 |
| BSW III | 9 | .15 |
| MSW I | 12 | .20 |
| MSW II | 12 | .20 |
| Total Sample (n) = | 60 | 1.00 |

After having determined the sample size from each subcategory, the researcher uses simple random sampling for drawing the desired number of elements from each category.

**Disproportionate Stratified Random Sampling**

This sampling plan is almost similar to proportionate stratified random sampling except that the sub samples are not necessarily distributed according to their proportionate weight in the population from which they were drawn. It is possible that some sub samples are over represented while other sub groups are under represented.

Let us suppose that the researcher stratifies the population into two sub-strata using sex as the criteria. He would get, the following break-up of the population: Table 4.4 : Distribution of Students by Sex.

**Table 4.4**
**Distribution of Students by Sex**

| *Sex* | *No. of Students* | *Percentage* |
|---|---|---|
| Male | 160 | 80 |
| Female | 40 | 20 |
| Total | 200 | 100 |

If the researcher wants to draw a disproportionate stratified random sample of 60 from this population, stratified by sex, then he has to draw 30 from each substrata, this means male students (30) will be under- represented and female students (30) will be over represented in the sample. In other words disproportionate sampling gives equal weights to each substratum.

## Cluster Sampling

In case the area of study is markedly wide spread, large expenses are involved if simple and stratified random sampling are used. For example , in the preparation of sampling frame from the population and in covering the wide spread areas by interviewers a large amount of expenditure is required. The more widely spread the area of study, the greater are the travel expenses, the greater is the time spent in traveling, and hence expensive- and the tasks of administering, monitoring and supervision of the research project and in particular supervising the field staff become more complicated. For the reasons mentioned above and few other reasons, large-scale research studies make use of the methods of cluster sampling.

In cluster sampling, first the whole research area is divided into sub area, more commonly known as "clusters". The simple random or stratified method is used to select clusters. Finally, researcher arrives at the ultimate sample size to be studied by selecting sample from within the clusters which is carried out on a simple or stratified random sampling basis.

Let us suppose, for example, that we want to do a survey of beggars in urban areas of a state. We may proceed as follows: prepare a list of districts and group them into clusters, and select a simple or stratified random sample from each cluster. For each of the districts included in the sample, list the cities/towns and take a simple or stratified random sample of them. If some or all of the towns/cities thus selected for the sample have more numbers of beggars that can be studied, we may take a sample of these towns/cities in each district. The questionnaires may then be administered to all the beggars in these towns/cities or, if it is desirable and administratively feasible to do so, to a sample of the beggars.

Characteristically, the procedure moves through a series of stages-hence the common term, "multistage" sampling is frequently used for cluster sampling.

## Non-probability Sampling

Non-probability sampling is based on the judgement of the researcher. The guiding factors in non-probability sampling include the availability of the units, the personal experience of the researcher and his/her convenience in carrying out a survey. Since these samples are not prepared through random sampling techniques, they are known as non-probability samples. Depending on the technique used, non-probability samples are classified into accidental, quota and purposive sampling. A brief description of these sampling is given below.

## Accidental Sampling

Accidental sampling refers to a method of selecting respondents who happen to meet the researcher and are willing to be interviewed. Thus, a researcher may take the first hundred people he/she meets who are willing to be interviewed.

For example, let us consider the situations where a researcher wishes to make some generalisation about the programme in progress, selects beneficiaries who have come to the agency for a service or a community organiser, trying to know how "the people" feel about health status in that community, interviews available community dwellers like shop-keepers, daily wage earners, barbers and others who are presumed to reflect public opinion. In both the situations those who are available for study are included in the samples. This is exactly what we call accidental sampling. It is very obvious that the sample so collected are biased and there is no known way (other than by doing a parallel study with a probability sample) of evaluating the biases introduced in such samples. However, in the situation illustrated above, most probably, accidental sampling is the only way out because of the reason that the population parameters of the beneficiaries or the community people are not available with the researcher.

**Quota Sampling**

Quota sampling ensures inclusion of diverse elements of the population in the sample and make sure that these diverse elements take account of the proportions in which they occur in the population. For example, we take a sample from a population with equal number of boys and girls, and that there is a difference between the two groups in the characteristic we wish to study and we fail to interview any girls, the results of the study would almost certainly be extremely misleading generalisations about the population. In practice, elements in small numbers are frequently underrepresented in accidental samples. In anticipation of such possible exclusion of small groups, quota sampling ensures inclusion of enough cases from each stratum in the sample. It should be noted here that the major goal of quota sampling is the selection of a sample that is a replica of the population to which one wants to generalise.

Hence it should be clear that the critical requirement in quota sampling is not that the various population strata be sampled in their correct proportions, but rather that there be enough cases from each stratum to make possible an estimate of the population stratum value (Kidder, 1981, p.426). Quota-sampling, however, is more or less similar to the earlier described accidental sampling procedure except that it ensures the inclusion of diverse elements of the population.

**Purposive Sampling**

Purposive sampling is based on the presumption that with good judgment one can select the sample units that are satisfactory in relation to one's requirements. A common strategy of this sampling technique is to select cases that are judged to be typical of the population, in which one is interested, assuming that errors of judgment in the selection will tend to counterbalance each other. For example, if a researcher were conducting a study of patients who are not regular in attending out patient department it might be desirable to choose patients for the sample from among those who are frequently irregular. Because, the causes of irregularity can be described by irregular patients only. If he selects a random sample he would have got patients who are regular and that might influence the findings of the study. It is also possible that in a truly random sample, the regular patients would nullify the effects of irregular patients.

**Snowball Sampling**

Snowball sampling is extremely helpful in studying some special sampling situation like getting a sample of drug abusers, or alcoholics or pickpockets. In snowball sampling we start with a few respondents of the type we wish to include in our study and who in turn are expected to guide us to get more respondents and so on. Like the rotating snowball, sample increases in its size as we continue to get more units of study. The technique is especially useful in the investigation of sensitive topics mentioned above because this sampling technique depends on sampled cases having knowledge of other similar cases. Another argument in favour of using this sampling technique is that, the victims might be hesitant to identify themselves if approached by a stranger but might be friendly to someone who they know and share their experiences or deviant status (Gelles, 1978).

**Special Applications of Non-probability Sampling**

In general, the major advantages of non-probability sampling are convenience and economy. However, in social research, most often we have no option other than non-probability sampling. For example, a social researcher who is interested in studying why cancer out patients are not regular in reporting to the doctor or what are the problems of the parents of the mentally challenged children and the like, will have to use any one of the non-probability sampling plan. It is likely, therefore, that many sampling operations in social research will be conducted according to non-probability principles. Social researchers are convinced that these sampling procedures work reasonably well, despite the fact that they do not provide any basis for estimating how far the sample results are likely to deviate from the true population figures. Social researchers, in other words, will continue to use non-probability methods and to justify their use on the grounds of practical experience, even while conceding the representativeness in principle of probability sampling. Moreover, many researchers argue that, many a times, this so-called representativeness exists only on paper. They believe that there is a difference between the sampling plan and its actual implementation; there can be many a slip in the implementation of the plan, which would nullify its theoretical merits.

For example, in situations where investigators may fail to follow the instructions in selecting respondents, or some of the selected respondents may refuse to be interviewed or not be available, investigators are allowed to substitute other respondents when those selected for the sample are not available for interview. Truly speaking, the sample thus obtained may, hence, not be the probability sample as it was planned to be.

In fact, there are situations, in which probability sampling is unnecessary or inappropriate. One such situation arises from the fact that many a times social researchers do not necessarily carry out studies of samples only for the purpose of generalisation to the populations from which samples have been drawn. If samples are used for other reasons, ability to evaluate the likelihood of deviations from the population values is irrelevant.

For example, a social researcher who wants to study the problems of parents of mentally challenged children would be interested in obtaining ideas, good insights and critical appraisals rather than assessing the status of opinion among the parents. In this situation researcher has to select a non-probability sample most probably a purposive sample. The situation is almost exactly analogous to one in which a social researcher tries to evaluate the effectiveness of a new technique of educating alcoholic patients. The alcoholics-also a purposive sample-are not called in order to get an average opinion that would correspond to the average opinion of the entire alcoholic population. They are called in precisely because of their special problems.

Another example of sampling for diagnosing the problems of a group of delinquent children rather than for the estimation of population values is provided by the single subject research known as evaluative research. The typical problem of evaluative research is to find out something about motives, attitudes, and associations that are evoked by certain social conditions, but that may not be obvious even to the respondents themselves. The results of such studies are reported to agencies, which make use of them in developing treatment plans for their inmates. Interestingly, the evaluative researchers are quite happy with accidental samples, or with purposive samples selected in such a way as to maximize the likelihood of differences among the elements in the sample. They are looking for causative factors to transmit to the agency people, not for correct estimates of population distributions.

**Combinations of Probability and Non-probability Sampling**

If sampling is carried out in a series of stages, it is, of course, possible to combine probability and nonprobability sampling in one design. That is, one or more of the stages can be carried out according to probability sampling principles and the balance by nonprobability principles.

The investigators may select clusters by probability cluster sampling techniques, but, at the final stage, select the elements as a quota sample. Thus, it is possible to select a probability sample of districts in a state, within each of these districts, a probability sample of towns: and within each of the selected towns, a quota sample controlled for, say, age and sex.

The advantage of such a design is the cost of obtaining cases for the sample. It is relatively inexpensive to select the areas within which the final stage of sampling will take place by probability sampling, and we thereby gain the advantages of probability sampling, at least for the areas. There is some evidence, for instance, that quota samples built up in selected areas are more successful in controlling such variables as socioeconomic status than quota samples in which the control of these variables depends on the judgments of the interviewers.

The second example of combining probability and nonprobability sampling involves the opposite strategy. The investigator takes a probability sample of elements within a nonprobability sample of areas. The areas are selected as a purposive sample. For example, a number of districts may be selected on the grounds that they have lower rate of literacy, within each of the "typical" districts, the investigator selects a probability sample of respondents.

Social researchers do not, generally, engage in sampling process like those used for conventional research process. Yet, the process of sampling in social sciences is based on principles of sampling discussed in this chapter.

### Choice of the Sampling Method

The choice of sampling method depends on several considerations unique to each individual project. These include issues related to the definition of population, availability of information about the structure of the population, the parameters to be estimated, the objectives of the analysis including the degree of precision required, and the availability of financial and other resources. This calls for appropriate selection of a sample for the conduct of any research study.

### Drawing of A Sample

Now we will discuss the process of drawing a sample. The process of drawing a sample includes selection of a method of sampling, determination of size of sample and selection of a technique of drawing elements of sample.

### Selection of a Method of Sampling

The topic of research, objectives and hypotheses point out very clearly who would be the respondents of the study. Briefly, they can be categorized as follows :

(a) Women workers in unorganized sector of industry in Andhra Pradesh.

(b) Men workers working on similar jobs in unorganized sector of industry in Andhra Pradesh.

Another point to be considered in selection of sample is the area of study. It is very clear from the topic of research that the study is to cover the whole state of Andhra Pradesh which is markedly wide spread. For the reasons mentioned above and few other reasons, for proposed research study we have to use a combination of methods of sampling.

Since the area of study is quite wide spread we have to use a combination of stratified and cluster/multistage sampling method. First of all the whole research area has to be divided into sub areas. The three administrative zones of Andhra Pradesh, namely, Coastal Andhra, Rayalseema and Telangana can be treated as three sub areas.

If sampling is carried out in a series of stages, it is, of course, possible to combine probability and nonprobability sampling in one design. That is, one or more of the stages can be carried out according to probability sampling principles and the balance by nonprobability principles.

Say for example, there are 52 employment notified in unorganized sector and there are 20, 000 workers employed in this sector. Let us say, we wish to have proportionate stratified random sample of workers taking region as basis of stratification. Let us suppose that the workers in the state are distributed as is shown in Table 4.4.

**Table 4.5**
**Distribution of Workers in unorganised sector according to region**

| *Year* | *Population (No. of Workers)* | *Proportion of Workers in each sub-area* | *Percentage of Workers in each sub-area* |
|---|---|---|---|
| Coastal Andhra | 8,000 | .4 | 40 |
| Rayalseema | 2,000 | .1 | 10 |
| Telangana | 10,000 | .5 | 50 |
| **Total** | 20, 000 | 1.00 | 100 |

## Determination of Size of Sample

After selecting the method of sampling we need to determine the size of our sample. A good sample should have the characteristics of (i) Representativeness and (ii) Adequacy.

It may be mentioned that representativeness and adequacy do not automatically ensure accuracy of results. The sampling and data collection techniques need to be selected and employed carefully to obtain higher degrees of precision in results and generalizations about the population.

## Determination of Sample Size

Having decided the sampling method, the question we have to face is : What should be the sample size of our study? The size of sample is determined after considering a number of factors. Some of the important factors are listed below :

(1) The degree of accuracy,

(2) The degree of variability or diversity in the population, and

(3) The number of different variables examined simultaneously in the data analysis.

It is also to be kept in mind that :

(1) The more homogeneous the population, the smaller would be sample size.

(2) The larger the number of variables to be studied, the larger will be the sample size.

## Statistical Method of Determination of Size of Sample

In this method, the size of sample is determined by the following statistical formula :

$$N = T \times (1\text{-}T) / SEp2$$

Where N is sample size,

T is the estimated proportion of a characteristic in the population,

SEp is the standard error permitted in the sample.

Say for example, T = 0.5

SEp = 0.05

Putting these values, we get ;

$$N = 0.5 \times ( 1\text{-} 0.5 ) / (0 .05 \times 0.05 )$$
$$= .5 \times .5 / .25$$
$$= 100$$

We get a sample size N = 100

Let us take another example where we change the value of SEp to 0.01

$$N = 0.5 \times (1\text{-}0.5 ) / (0.01 \times 0.01)$$
$$= 0.5 \times 0.05 / 0.0001$$
$$= 0.25 / 0.0001$$
$$= 2500.$$

We get a sample size N = 250

It is to be noted that T ( the estimated proportion of population characteristic) has been taken as 0.5, presuming that the characteristic concerned has two sub categories, each probably accounting for 50 per cent of the distribution in the sample ( an example here would be the percentage of male and female workers).

The method raises three questions :

(1) How to determine size of the sample in case the value of T is not known?

(2) How to determine size of the sample if the characteristics selected have more than two sub categories?

(3) How to decide as to how much error in the estimate between the sample and population may be accepted?

It is because of the above complications most researchers find it difficult to determine the size of the sample using statistical method. .

Krejcie and Morgan (1970) have prepared a table based an improved formula in which no calculations are needed to determine the size of the sample. The table is reproduced here for your reference.

**Table 4.6**

**Table for Determining Needed Size *s* of a Randomly Chosen Sample from a Given Finite Population of *n* Cases such that the Sample Proportion *p* will be within ± 0.05 of the Population Proportion *p* with a 95 percent Level of Confidence**

| *Population Size* | *Sample Size* | *Population Size* | *Sample Size* | *Population Size* | *Sample Size* |
|---|---|---|---|---|---|
| 10 | 10 | 220 | 140 | 1200 | 291 |
| 15 | 14 | 230 | 144 | 1300 | 297 |
| 20 | 19 | 240 | 148 | 1400 | 302 |
| 25 | 24 | 250 | 152 | 1500 | 306 |
| 30 | 28 | 260 | 155 | 1600 | 310 |
| 35 | 32 | 270 | 159 | 1700 | 313 |
| 40 | 36 | 280 | 162 | 1800 | 317 |
| 45 | 40 | 290 | 165 | 1900 | 320 |

*(Contd.)*

*(Contd. Table 4.6)*

| *Population Size* | *Sample Size* | *Population Size* | *Sample Size* | *Population Size* | *Sample Size* |
|---|---|---|---|---|---|
| 50 | 44 | 300 | 169 | 2000 | 322 |
| 55 | 48 | 320 | 175 | 2200 | 327 |
| 60 | 52 | 340 | 181 | 2400 | 331 |
| 65 | 56 | 360 | 186 | 2600 | 335 |
| 70 | 59 | 380 | 191 | 2800 | 338 |
| 75 | 63 | 400 | 196 | 3000 | 341 |
| 80 | 66 | 420 | 201 | 3500 | 346 |
| 85 | 70 | 440 | 205 | 4000 | 351 |
| 90 | 73 | 460 | 210 | 4500 | 354 |
| 95 | 76 | 480 | 214 | 5000 | 357 |
| 100 | 80 | 500 | 217 | 6000 | 361 |
| 110 | 86 | 550 | 226 | 7000 | 364 |
| 120 | 92 | 600 | 234 | 8000 | 367 |
| 130 | 97 | 650 | 242 | 9000 | 368 |
| 140 | 103 | 700 | 248 | 10000 | 370 |
| 150 | 108 | 750 | 254 | 15000 | 375 |
| 160 | 113 | 800 | 260 | 20000 | 377 |
| 170 | 118 | 850 | 265 | 30000 | 379 |
| 180 | 123 | 900 | 269 | 40000 | 380 |
| 190 | 127 | 950 | 274 | 50000 | 381 |
| 200 | 132 | 1000 | 278 | 75000 | 382 |
| 210 | 136 | 1100 | 285 | 100000 | 384 |

**Note:** P is population size, N is sample size.

Let us take one example. If we want to know the sample size required to be representative of the opinions of 20,000 workers, refer table at P=20000. The sample size representative of the workers in this case will be 377. The table given above is applicable to any defined population.

Keeping in view certain factors like 'non-availability' or 'reluctance' of respondents, we decide to have a sample of, say, 400 workers ( 23 respondents in excess of the required size). First, we have to determine the proportion of workers in each sub-area (as shown in the second column). Then we have to calculate the composition of the sample taking each proportion of the stratifying characteristics in the population and multiplying it by the desired size of the sample. Thus, we multiply 400, the desired sample size by .4, the proportion of workers in Coastal Andhra in the population or (400) (.4) = 160

As such, we have to include 160 workers from Coastal Andhra in our sample. This procedure is repeated for sub areas as described below: (400) (.4) = 160 , (400) (.1) = 40, (400) (.5) = 200. The sample distribution is shown in Table 4.7

**Table 4.7**
**Distribution of Students by Proportion**

| *Year* | *Sample Break-up* | *Proportion* | *Percentage* |
|---|---|---|---|
| Coastal Andhra | 160 | .4 | 40 |
| Rayalseema | 40 | .1 | 10 |
| Telangana | 200 | . 5 | 50 |
| Total Sample (n) = | 400 | 1.00 | 100 |

After having determined the sample size from each subcategory, you can use simple random sampling using Tippet Number method as shown above for drawing the desired number of elements from each category.

## References


Abram, M. , (1950), *Social Surveys and Social Action,* London : Heinemann.

Ackoff, R.L. (1953) *The Design of Social Research,* Chicago: University of Chicago Press,

Bailey, Kenneth D. (1978). *Methods of Social Research*, London: The Free Press.

Baker, L. Therese. (1988). *Doing Social Research,* New York: McGraw Hill.

Black, James A. and Champion, (1976). Dean J. *Methods and Issues in Social Research* New York: John Wiley.

Buckingham, A and Saunders, (2004). P. *The Survey Methods Workbook.* Cambridge :Polity Press.

Festinger. L. and Katz. D. (eds.). (1953). *Research Methods in the Behavioral Sciences,*New York: The Dryden Press.

Gelles, R.J. (1978).*Methods for Studying Sensitive Family Topics.* American Journal of Orthopsychiatry, 48, 408-424.

Goode. W.J. and Hat. P.K. (1952). *Methods in Social Research,* New York: McGraw Hill.

Kerlinger. Fred R. (1964). *Foundations of Behavioral Research,* Delhi: Surjeet Publications.

Kidder, Louise H. (1981). *Research Methods in Social Relations,* New York: Holt.

Krejcie, R.V. and Morgan, D.W. (1970). "Determination of Sample Size" *Educational and Psychological Measurements, 30, 3.*

Lal Das, D.K. (2000), *Practice of Social Research : A Social Work Perspective,* Jaipur : Rawat Publications.

Lal Das, D.K. (2005), *Designs of Social Research,* Jaipur: Rawat Publications.

Miller. D.C. (1964). *Handbook of Research Design and Social Measurement* New York : David Mckey Co.

Monette, Duane R. et. al. (1986). *Applied Social Research: Tool for the Human Services* Chicago: Holt.

Moser. C.A. and Kalton. *Survey Methods in Social Investigation* London: Heinemann Educational Books, 1975.

Nachmias D and Nachmias C. (1981). *Research Methods in the Social Sciences*, New York: St. Martins press.

O'Leary Z. (2004). *The Essential Guide to Doing Research.* New Delhi : Vistaar Publications.

Ramachandran. P. (2000).*User Friendly Research and Statistics for Social Work.*

Secunderabad : Andhra Pradesh Social Service Society.

Rubin, Allen & Babbie E. (1989) .*Research Methodology for Social Work,* Belmont, California, Wadsworth.

Sellitz. G. et. al. (1973). *Research Methods in Social Relations New* York: Holt. Rinehart and Winston (3rd edition.

Suchman, E.A. (1953).*The Principles of Research Design*. In John T Dobyet. al., An Introduction to Social Research , New York : The Stackpole.

Wilkinson, T.S. and Bhandarkar, P.L. *Methodology and Techniques of Social Research*: Bombay: Himalayan, 1977.

# 5

# Selection of Tools of Data Collection

## Introduction

One of the important stages of research process is data collection. In order to collect the requisite data for any research study, you have to devise appropriate tools and use suitable measuring instruments. There are several tools of data collection, varying in design, operation, complexity of features, and interpretation. In certain situations you may select a standardized scale from books on research instruments/social measurements. In other situations you may find that existing tools of data collection do not suit your purpose or objective of research and, therefore, you may like to modify them or develop your own. Each tool of data collection is appropriate for collecting a particular type of data which lends itself to a particular type of analysis and interpretation for drawing meaningful conclusions and generalisations. For this, you need to familiarise yourself with the nature, merits and limitations of various tools of data collection. In this chapter we focus on sources of data, measurement in social research and the characteristics, types, uses and limitations of some commonly used tools of data collection.

## Sources of Data

Before we decide the tool of data collection, it is essential that we should have some idea about from which source do we gather data/ information about the phenomenon under study.

The two main sources of data in social science research are 'people' and 'paper'. The responses of questions put to people constitute the major sources of data in social research. This source is labeled as primary source of data. A large amount of data is already available in the form of 'paper' sources. This includes documents, historical records, diaries, biographies, statistical records etc. The 'paper' sources are commonly known as secondary sources of data or 'available data source'.

When a researcher decides to collect data through primary source he/she has three options, namely, questionnaire, observation, and interview. In case he/she opts for secondary source of data he/she uses the method of content analysis (For details about the Method of Content Analysis readers are advised to refer Books for Further Reading).

**The Concept of Measurement**

The concept of measurement refers to the process of describing abstract concepts in terms of specific indicators by assigning numbers to these indicants in accordance with rules. Measurement of social phenomena has become an essential prerequisite because of a number of reasons. One of the important reasons for measuring social phenomena is to allow the researcher the opportunity of using these phenomena in hypotheses to determine the effects of a set of variables on others. (Black and Champion, 1976)

Let us consider the hypothesis: "the adults who are lower in their self-esteem will tend to become chronic absentees to adult literacy classes than the adults with higher self-esteem" (a social psychological component of personality). Testing of this hypothesis needs a formal theoretical scheme where 'self-esteem' would be related systematically to 'absenteeism' in a causal fashion. One part of the testing process would consist of determining rank of absentees of the adults from the attendance records. We would match those adults with another group of adults randomly; selected from the same village who are regular in attending their classes. To ensure comparable samples of "absentees" and "regulars", the groups could be matched according to several other characteristics such as age, sex, year of education, socio-economic background, education and occupation of parents and others.

Other part of testing of hypothesis requires assessment of socio-psychological variable 'self-esteem'. How do we determine that a particular adult learner who is a chronic 'absentee' or 'regular' has more or less of this trait than the others? We cannot test the hypothesis mentioned above, until and unless we can quantify the variable 'self-esteem'. To test the hypothesis it is essential that the variable 'self-esteem' must be measured empirically. We must be able to say that adults vary according to this variable, and further more; we should specify the degree to which each adult possesses this variable. Only then we will be able to test our hypothesis. Measurement allows the researcher the opportunity of using variables in hypothesis to determine their effects on others.

Let us examine the following questions?

(1) Do you save money? Yes/No, (2) If yes, how much?

(3) "Child labour in our country must be banned".

Strongly Agree/Agree/Undecided/ Disagree / Strongly Disagree

The first question measure one aspect by determining the presence or absence of a characteristic 'saving habit' among child labour. The second question tries to measure in a more specific way involving the amount saved which tries to determine the degree of intensity of saving. Finally, a reaction or comment to a statement is in a sequence of responses, which in turn can be converted into scores and would measure the phenomena in question more specifically.

**Levels of Measurements**

Social phenomena can be measured in various ways, such as by asking questions or noting/observing behaviour. Measurement also differs from one another in terms of the level of measurement. Levels of measurement refer to a set of rules that define permissible mathematical functions that can be performed on numbers/scores produced by a measure. There are four levels of measurement, namely; nominal, ordinal, interval and ratio.

**Nominal Level of Measurement**

Nominal level of measurement is the lowest and most simple level of measurement. When a variable is classified into several nominal subclasses it is said that the variable in question is measured on a nominal level. For example, the variable sex has two nominal subclasses; male and female. Similarly, religions have many subclasses, if not infinite, among which are included Hindu, Muslim, Christian and Sikhs.

Numbers assigned to nominal subclasses at this level of measurement represent serial order only. The numbers do not have mathematical values. Hence, no mathematical function is possible with nominal data. For example let us consider the classification of nominal data as shown below:

(1) Hindu (2) Muslim (3) Christian

In this example suppose we add 1 and 2 we will get 3. Which would be equivalent of saying that a Hindu plus a Muslim equals a Christian. This is not true. In other words 1, 2 and 3 here represent first categories of respondents who are Hindus, second categories of respondents who are Muslims and third categories of respondents belonging to Christianity. Another example of nominal level of measurement is getting information about marital status in the following format:

Marital Status :

1. Unmarried ( ) 2. Married ( )
3. Divorcee ( ) 4. Widow ( )

## Ordinal Level of Measurement

When the relative positions of objects or persons with respect to some characteristics are defined, measurements are possible on ordinal levels. The fundamental requirement of an ordinal level of measurement is that one is able to determine the order of positions of objects or persons in terms of characteristics under study. Ordinal level measurements are considered of higher level than nominal level because in addition to being mutually exclusive (feature of nominal level of measurement) the categories have a fixed order. Level of education, for example, constitutes an ordinal variable and measures levels of education on ordinal scales.

Following illustration shows level of education divided into ordinal categories. In ordinal level of measurement, the numbers are used not only to differentiate subclasses, but also to determine less than or greater than relationship between them. For example, see the responses given to the level of education:

Level of Education :

1. Graduate ( ) 2. Intermediate ( ) 3. High School ( )
4. Middle School ( ) 5. Primary ( ) 6. Illiterate ( )

The responses have numbers ranging from 1 to 6 and are designed to identify ordinal differences between level of education. Each level is assigned a particular number relative to others and it can be determined readily that graduate level of education is higher than intermediate. However, there is no attempt to say that an equal distance will be found between all numbers. We cannot say that the same distance exists between 1 and 2 as exists between 3 and 4.

## Interval Level of Measurement

Interval level between the categories of measurement have equal spacing in addition to the characteristics of nominal level (mutually exclusive) and ordinal level (having fixed order). In interval measures the positions are not only ordered either in ascending order (lower, middle and higher) or in descending order (higher, middle and lower) but the intervals of measurement are also equal. In other words, the distance between the positions is equal, such as the degrees of a temperature scales. The examples of true interval scales are Fahrenheit and Celsius temperature scales. The units of measurement of both the scales are degree and are based on equal spacing characteristics of interval level of measurement.

In an interval scale an equal distance between units will be found. That means, 2 are same distance from 3 as 6 are from 5 and so on. For example, in thermometer having Celsius as unit of measurement, 60 degrees is 10 degrees more than 50 degrees. However, we cannot compare the ratios of two temperatures. It would be erroneous to infer that 100-degree is twice as hot as 50 degrees. This is because; interval scale does not have an absolute zero.

In social science research, we have very few measures clearly of interval level. One such measure that is relevant to social sciences is measurement of intelligence by intelligent quotient (IQ) tests. Units of measurement on IQ test are specific and each point on the scale is mutually exclusive. In addition the distances between IQ scores of 90 and 100 and 100 and 110 are equal. However, since the zero point on the interval scale is arbitrary, we cannot say that a person with an IQ of 130 is twice as intelligent as a person with an IQ of 65.

**Ratio Level of Measurement**

For example, income can be measured at ratio level of measurement because it has an absolute zero (no income, at least in money terms, not in term of economic status). Hence, a person with monthly income of Rs. 1,500 has thrice as much as a person earning Rs. 500. Most of the function can be performed on data measurement on interval scales.

However, one has to keep in mind that income, as ratio measure is only an indicator of the amount of money available to a person not as the measure of person's socio-economic status. For example, a difference between Rs. 1,00,000 and Rs. 1,10,000 does not necessarily indicate a change in socio-economic status equivalent to that between Rs. 20,000 and Rs. 30,000. It should be finally, noted that the variables capable of being measured at high levels are always better than the variables capable of being measured at lower levels.

Ratio level of measurement is the highest level of measurement. This level of measurement has all the characteristics of interval level of measurement except that the zero point is absolute in this case rather than arbitrary as in interval level of measurement. This means the ratio level of measurement contains the characteristics of nominal level of measurement (mutually exclusive) ordinal level of measurement (fixed order) and interval level of measurement (equal spacing, in addition to an absolute zero).

In social research we rarely come across a situation where ratio level of measurement is warranted mostly because it is really difficult to arrive at absolute zero while measuring social phenomena. However, to understand the ratio level of measurement we will consider the measurement of income with which researchers are likely to deal with. Though there is considerable controversy on whether 'no income' at all can be considered as absolute zero points of the scale, and whether there is equal spacing between the units, we will consider the measurement of income on this scale for the sake of better understanding.

This brief discussion on social measurement would help researcher to frame question keeping in mind the responses at different levels of measurement. It also helps in applying statistics and analyzing data because choice of statistical procedures more or less depends on level of measurement (please refer Appendix B).

## Tools of Data Collection

There are several tools of data collection, varying in design, operation, complexity of features, and interpretation. Each tool is appropriate for collecting a particular type of data or information which lends itself to a particular type of analysis and interpretation for drawing meaningful conclusions and generalisations.

Basically, following three methods are employed in collecting data from primary sources:

1. Questionnaire 2. Observation 3. Interview

## Questionnaire

Questionnaire is a commonly used tool for collecting a variety of data. A questionnaire may include a series of questions pertaining to psychological, social, educational, or any such issues.

They may pertain to studies of economic or social problems, measurement of opinion on public issues or events, studies of administrative policies and changes, studies on the cost of living, consumer expenditure, child welfare, and numerous other issues.

A questionnaire is a popular means of collecting different kinds of data in research. It is widely used in social research to obtain information about certain conditions and practices, and to inquire into opinions of individuals.

## Administration of Questionnaire

A questionnaire is administered personally either individually or to a group of individuals or is mailed to them to save a great deal of time and money in travel. In the former situation, the person administering the tool has an opportunity to establish rapport with the respondents, to explain the purpose of the study to the respondents and to explain the meaning of questions which may not be clear to them. In the latter situation, mailed questionnaire is mostly used when the individuals cannot be contacted personally.

## Characteristics of a Good Questionnaire

(1) A good questionnaire must translate the objectives of a study into specific questions, the answers to which will provide the data necessary to obtain the objectives and test the hypotheses. Each question should relate the corresponding objective so that the response obtained can be analysed and interpreted accordingly. The research objectives and specifications of the data required must precede the construction of questionnaire.

(2) The questionnaire must motivate the respondents to communicate the required information. It is essential to include a courteous and carefully constructed covering letter to explain the purpose and importance of the study. The covering letter should assure the respondent that delicate information will be held in strict confidence.

(3) The language of a good questionnaire must be simple and directed towards producing uniformity of understanding among the respondents. The words used in a questionnaire should be clear and unambiguous and within the easy grasp of the average intelligent of the respondents under study. The syntax should be clear and straightforward. Vague words, phrases and expressions should be avoided. Technical terms should be used only if the inquiry is directed to a select group which is well-versed in the technical language used. Proverbs and quotations should be avoided. Adjectives, such as 'bad', 'good', 'fair' and the like do not

lend themselves to quantitative measurements nor qualitative analysis unless they are used for comparisons on a rating scale.

(4) The respondent's frame of reference influences his/her answers. Complex questions are undesirable and often result in misleading data. Questions on controversial issues should be broken down into components, so that the researcher can determine the respondent's feeling about various aspects of the problem, including those which he/she refuses to comment upon. A series of specific questions is needed so as to uncover degrees of intensity of feeling or attitude. For example, questions to understand people's attitude towards the reservation policy have to be broken into issues like equality, equity, equal opportunities, etc.

(5) The required answers should be within the informational domain of the respondents. For example a question 'Do you read Reader's Digest' may not bring the desired responses as many respondents may not know about this magazine.

(6) A questionnaire should not be longer than necessary. The total number of questions must not be too large to tire or bore the respondents. If too many questions are asked and the respondent becomes tired, the questions at the end of the series may not be well answered. If it is necessary to include a large number of questions, it is advisable to have separate questionnaires.

**Limitations of Questionnaires**

(1) A questionnaire cannot be used with children and illiterates.

(2) The return of the mailed questionnaires is often very poor. As a result of this poor response, the data obtained are sometimes of limited validity. The respondents who return the questionnaires may not be representative of the entire group. It will make the sample a biased one and thus vitiate the findings.

(3) Sometimes respondents may not like to respond in writing to questions of personal and confidential nature or to questions involving controversial issues. It is sometimes difficult to formulate the questions on certain complex and delicate problems.

(4) There is no check on the respondent who misinterprets a question or gives incomplete or indefinite response.

5) Sometimes the respondent may modify his/her earlier/ original responses to the questions when he/she finds that his/her responses to latter questions are contradicting the previous ones.

## Sources of Available Tools of Data Collection

In many situations you may select a questionnaire from a list of available tools of data collection-commonly known as standardised scales. These scales are compiled by several authors in the form of books. Scales are also available on websites. Some important sources of available standardised scales are shown in the following box :

**Box 5.1 Sources of Standardised Scales**

**Books :**

American Psychiatric Association .1987. *Diagnostic and Statistical Manual of Mental Disorders* (Revised Edition 3), Washington, D.C.

Kimberly, K. *Encyclopaedia of Social Measurement*, University of Texas at Dallas;Academic Press

Miller , D.C. 1991.*Handbook of Research Design and Social Measurement*, New Delhi : Sage Publications.

Pareek, Udai and Rao , T. Venkateshwara. 1992. *First Handbook of Psychological and Social Instruments.* New Delhi : Concept Publishing Company.

Pestonjee, D.M. 1993. *Second Handbook of Psychological and Social Instruments*. New Delhi : Concept Publishing Company.

Pestonjee, D.M. 1997. *Third Handbook of Psychological and Social Instruments*.New Delhi : Concept Publishing Company.

In other situations you may find that existing research tools do not suit your purpose or objective of research and, therefore, you may like to modify them or develop your own.

## Content of Questions

Questionnaire enlists questions, which translate the research objectives into specific questions. The question must also encourage the respondent so that the necessary data is obtained. It is to these two ends that the question becomes the focus around which the questionnaire is constructed. One of the major issues involved in formulating the question is its content. The major issues on which questions may be concerned are facts, opinions, attitudes, respondents' motivation, and their level of acquaintance with a research problem. By and large, questions can be classified into two general categories, namely, (1) factual questions and (2) opinion and attitude questions.

## Factual Questions

Factual questions are asked to elicit information from the respondents regarding their background, such as sex, age, marital

**Box 5.2 Factual Questions**

**1. What is your age? : ________________**
**(As on 1st October, 2007)**

**2. What is your marital status? :**

| | |
|---|---|
| **1. Married** | ( ) |
| **2. Unmarried** | ( ) |
| **3. Widow** | ( ) |
| **4. Divorcee** | ( ) |

**3. What is your Salary/Wages : __________**

**4. What is your level of education? (please check one)**

| | |
|---|---|
| **1. Graduate** | ( ) |
| **2. Intermediate** | ( ) |
| **3. High School** | ( ) |
| **4. Middle School** | ( ) |
| **5. Primary** | ( ) |
| **6. Illiterate** | ( ) |
| **7. Any other** | ( ) |

status, education or income. The following is an example of such a question:

Other kinds of factual questions are intended to elicit information on the profile of the respondents (sex, work experience, place of residence, nativity etc.).

It looks easier to design factual questions. However, many a times factual questions pose the researcher with problems. In a survey many respondents misunderstood religion as a 'faith / belief' and reported that they do not believe in religion. Similarly, in other research study pertaining to socio-economic status, many failed to mention income out of milch animals, kitchen garden and poultry because they did not consider it as a source of income. Further, most probably, the sources of income are either wages or cash value of crops.

These two examples point to failure of communication system between the researcher and the respondents. A researcher is required to have a clear definition of the concept and is also required to communicate exactly the same to avoid such problems.

## Opinion and Attitude Questions

The concept "attitude" refers to the sum total of a person's inclination, prejudices, ideas, fears, and convictions about any specific topic. Opinions, on the other hand, are the verbal expression of attitudes (Thurstone, 1928, p. 33). Thus, a statement such as "Child labour should be banned" would reflect an opinion that is against child labour, but an attitude towards child labour would mean a more specific orientation of what a person feels and thinks about child labour.

Attitudes can be described by their content (what the attitude is about), by their direction (positive, neutral, or negative feelings about the object or issue in question), and by their intensity (an attitude may be held with greater or lesser vehemence). To one person, child labour may be just of passing interest; to another, it may be of great significance and that person may be ready to join anti-child labour movements.

Questions about opinions and attitudes present more problems in construction than questions about facts. Comparatively, it is simpler to obtain accurate data, for example, whether or not a person is married or single. It can be assumed that the respondent knows whether he or she is married or not. However, questions on opinions or attitudes, the assumption that the respondents know cannot always be made. For example, respondents may not have either positive or negative attitude towards child labour, or if they do, it might be largely latent ( Moser and Kalton, 1975, p. 317). Moreover, as there are various aspects or dimensions of attitudes, the respondent may agree with one aspect and disagree with another. This is the reason why attitudes cannot be measured by a single question. For example, if a respondent strongly agrees with the statement "Child labour should be banned," this does not imply a broad anti-child labour attitude. This person's agreement may be due to personal circumstances; for instance, the person who may be unemployed thinks that child labour would harm his or her prospect of employment. By using a set of statements, one can reduce the effects of one-aspect responses.

Finally, answers to opinion and attitude questions are more sensitive to changes in wording, emphasis, and sequence than are those to factual questions. This reflects, in part, the multidimensionality of many attitudes. Questions presented in different ways sometimes reflect different aspects of the attitude and thus result in different answers.

**Formats of Questions**

The format of the question and the response categories accompanying the questions are other aspects, which need attention of the researchers. Four types of question formats are discussed in the following sections: (1) Dichotomous questions, (2) open-ended questions, (3) closed-ended questions and (4) contingency questions.

**Dichotomous Questions**

Questions which have two and only two answers are called dichotomous Questions.

> **Box 5.3 Dichotomous Question :**
>
> **Q : Are you married ?**
> **(1) Yes (2) No**

**Open-Ended Questions**

Questions in a questionnaire can be either open-ended or closed-ended. Open-ended questions are not followed by any kind of specified responses, and the respondents' responses are recorded in full. For instance, the question

> **Box 5.4 Open-Ended Questions**
>
> **Q : "What do you personally feel are the most important issues related to child labour which the government should try to take care of?"**

**Closed-Ended Questions**

In closed-ended question, respondents are offered a set of answers from which they are asked to choose the one that most closely represents their views. For example, to measure sex discrimination against women in the unorganised sector, the following closed-ended question may be asked:

> **Box 5.5 Closed-Ended Questions**
>
> **"Equal remuneration should be given to men and women for same work or work of similar nature."**
> **Strongly agree**
> **Agree**
> **Indifferent**
> **Disagree**
> **Strongly disagree**

**Multiple Choice Questions**

The advantage of the open-ended question is that it does not force the respondent to adapt to predetermined responses: having understood the question, one can express one's ideas freely, spontaneously and in one's own language. If the answers to open-ended questions are not clear, the researcher may probe, that is, ask the respondent to explain further or to give reasons for something stated earlier.

### Multiple Choice Questions

In multiple choice questions, respondents are offered a set of answers from which they are asked to choose the one that most closely represents their views. For example :

**Box 5.6 Multiple Choice Questions**

**Which one of the following is the reason for continuing the present job?**

| | | | |
|---|---|---|---|
| **(a)** | **Nature of work** | **(b)** | **Duration of work** |
| **(c)** | **Wages/Salary** | **(d)** | **Promotion** |

### Multiple Response Questions

In multiple response questions, respondents are allowed to give a combination of answers from a set of answers. For example:

**Box 5.7 Multiple Response Question**

**Why do you work?**

**(1) To supplement the family income.**
**(2) To have independent income of one's own.**
**(3) To achieve a position or status of one's own.**
**(4) To utilize plenty of spare time.**
**(5) To be away from the unhappy atmosphere of home.**
**(6) To escape from domestic work and get freedom to mix with people.**

**In this case, a respondent can say that he works because :**
**(1) To supplement the family income and (2) to achieve a position or status of one's own. Contingency Questions**

### Contingency Questions

Frequently questions that are relevant to some respondents may be irrelevant to others. For example, the question "Check the most important reasons why you are not going to college" obviously applies only to those intermediate students who are not planning to go to college at all. It is often necessary to include questions that might apply only to some respondents and not to others. Some questions may be relevant only to females and not to males: others will only apply to respondents who are self-employed, and so on.

When a question is applicable to only a sub - group of the sample it is known as contingency question. A contingency question is a special case of a closed-ended question and it is one that applies only to a subgroup of respondents. The relevance of the question to this subgroup is determined by the answer of respondents to a preceding question. For example, in a research study the preceding question was, "Are you aware of the Act?" The contingency question could be, "If yes, what do you know about it?" The relevance of the second question to the respondent is contingent upon his or her response to the preceding question. Only respondents who responded "Yes" to the preceding question will find the contingency question relevant. Therefore, the response categories of the preceding questions will be 1.Yes (answer the following question); 2. No (skip to question 3).

**Box 5.8 Contingency Questions**

**Q. "Are you aware of the Act?"**
**(1) Yes (2) No**
**Contingency Questions**
**Q "If yes , what do you know about it ?"**
**( If no, skip to the next Question )**

## Response Format

In this section we will discuss some of the formats of response categories of closed-ended questions. The general format is to present all possible responses and have the respondent check the appropriate response. The respondent can either encircle his or her answer or check a box or a blank as in the following examples:

**Box 5.9 Response Format**

**Q. What is your marital status?**

| | | |
|---|---|---|
| **Married** | ☐ **Married** | **1. Married** |
| **Single** | ☐ **Single** | **2. Single** |
| **Divorced** | ☐ **Divorced** | **3. Divorced** |
| **Widowed** | ☐ **Widowed** | **4. Widowed** |

## Attitude /Rating Scales

One of the most common formats for questions asked in social research is the rating scale. The rating scale is used whenever

**Box 5.10 Attitude of the Employer**

**Q.1 The employers prefer male employees because women employees take more sick leaves and quit more readily.**
**(1) Agree ( ) (2) Undecided ( )(3) Disagree ( )**

**Q 2. The employers feel that women employees can't cope with stressful situations like men can and as such don't give us work like men.**
**(1) Agree ( ) (2) Undecided ( )(3) Disagree ( )**

**Q.3. Women employees are not given responsible positions because most women are too emotional to be able to handle positions of great responsibility.**
**(1) Agree ( ) (2) Undecided ( )(3) Disagree ( )**

**Q.4 The employer takes advantage of women employees and sexually exploits us.**
**(1) Agree ( ) (2) Undecided ( )(3) Disagree ( )**

respondents are asked to make a judgment in terms of sets of ordered categories, such as "agree," "favourable," or "very often." For example:

### Matrix Questions

The matrix question is a method for organizing a set of questions that have the same response patterns. The following is an example of matrix questions.

**Box 5.11 Matrix Questions**

Q. "In my work place the following welfare services are provided."

| | | Yes | No | If yes then what do you think about it? Satis-factory | Fairly Satis | Unsatis-factory |
|---|---|---|---|---|---|---|
| (1) | Crèches and Day Nurseries | ( ) | ( ) | - | - | - |
| (2) | Maternity Benefits | ( ) | ( ) | - | - | - |
| (3) | Canteen (common) | ( ) | ( ) | - | - | - |
| (4) | Canteen (separate) | ( ) | ( ) | - | - | - |
| (5) | Rest place (common) | ( ) | ( ) | - | - | - |
| 6) | Rest place (Separate) | ( ) | ( ) | - | - | - |
| 7) | Toilet (separate) | ( ) | ( ) | - | - | - |

### Sequence of Questions

Once the format of questions is decided, a researcher has to consider the order in which questions are to be placed in the questionnaire. Two general patterns of question sequence have been found to be most appropriate for motivating respondents to cooperate: the *funnel sequence* and the *inverted funnel sequence.*

It should be kept in mind that questions that are presented first in the questionnaire should put the respondent at ease; and if an interviewer is present; they should help in creating rapport between the researcher and the respondent. Thus, the question in the beginning should be easy to answer, interesting, and it should not deal with sensitive issues. For example, questions about drinking habit or sex life of respondents, if placed at the beginning, in all possibilities will demotivate the respondents to answer the subsequent questions. It is also suggested that such questions be placed later, for they reduce the respondent's initial motivation to cooperate.

### Questions to be Avoided

#### Leading Questions

A question worded in such a manner that it appears to the respondent that the researcher expects a certain answer, is commonly known as leading question. A question designed to elicit general opinion about work satisfaction might read, "How do you feel about your work?" The same question worded in a leading form might read, "Are you satisfied with your work?" This question makes it easier for respondents to answer *yes* than *no.* In answering *yes,* they are agreeing with the words of the question and are not contradicting the researcher.

**Box 5.12 Leading Questions**

**Q. Are you satisfied with your work?**
**Q. Should child labour be banned?**
**Q. Do you support Indian National Congress?**

As far as possible leading questions are to be avoided if one is looking for objective responses. In some situations, particularly, where leading questions may serve the research objective, leading questions with suitable wordings are used with extra care.

#### Threatening Questions

Threatening questions refer to behaviours that are illegal or contra-normative or behaviours that are socially deviant and are not discussed in public. For example, questions that inquire about the respondent's gambling habits, about their drinking habits, child abuse or sexual behaviours are referred as threatening questions. Often it is necessary to include such questions in studies, which the respondent may find embarrassing and thus difficult to answer.

Though it is suggested to avoid threatening questions as far as possible, in cases where it is necessary to include such questions it is advised to use a long introduction to the question (or may be indirect question) rather than asking short questions (or direct questions); by an open-ended rather than a closed-ended format; and, to a lesser extent, by letting the respondents pick their own words to talk about the sensitive issues. For example, to know about respondent's drinking behaviour the following question may be asked :

**Box 5.13 Threatening Questions in Indirect Form**

**Q. "In the past one year, how often you could not control yourself to become intoxicated while drinking?"**

Respondents may be asked to classify their responses into one of the following categories:

Once in three month
Once a month
Once a week
Several times a week
Daily

**Double-barreled Questions**

When two or more than two questions are included in one question it is termed as double-barreled questions. The following question, included in a survey, is an example:

**Box 5.14 Double-barreled Question**

**Q. "Women should stay at home and take care of their children and other family members and stop taking up employment outside."**

**- Agree - Undecided -Disagree**

The above statement includes two separate questions that are joined by the conjunction 'and'. Such questions might confuse respondents who agree with one aspect of the question – stay at home and take care of children and other family members and not with the other – stop taking employment outside. Many questions that includes 'and' is very likely doubled-barreled, hence, it is suggested not to include such questions.

### Instructions

While constructing a questionnaire it is utmost necessary that the instructions must go with each question or with a set of questions. Instructions are required to all such questions that are not self-explanatory. It may be general instruction such as "circle the appropriate category" or very specific instructions that explain how to rank order a set of priorities. The instructions are usually written for the interviewer and thus are often short and concise.

### Constructing a Questionnaire

There are many stages involved in the construction of a questionnaire, beginning with the research problem and going through the process of formulating the questions and considering the format and the type of questions to be used.

To illustrate the various stages of construction of questionnaire first we will consider our research problem, the objectives and the hypotheses. We have decided to study: **"Sex Discrimination against Women at Work in Unorganised Sector in Andhra Pradesh".** The specific objectives of the study are:

1. To assess the nature and extent of discrimination on the basis of sex against women at work
2. To determine the extent of disparities in wages/salary (wage differential) of male and female employees for work of similar nature, and
3. To identify the important correlates of sex discrimination and wage disparities.

The following variables were identified:

**Independent Variables:**

Age, Marital Status, Type of Family, Level of Education, Castes, Nativity, Income, Religion, and Designation.

**Dependent Variables :**

Sex Discrimination and
Wage Disparities

Before we discuss about the construction of tools of data collection, it is essential that we should decide about from which source we gather data about the phenomenon under study. It is clear from the objectives, hypotheses and variables that we have to collect data from primary source for all the variables except "wage disparities". To determine wage disparities it would be better to collect data about wages from secondary source-that is Acquaintance Registers of the organizations. A male sample and a female sample were selected in each of the three regions of the state in the study. The major sources of data for this study would be the responses of questions put to respondents-women and men workers.

Two questionnaires – one for male workers and other for female workers are required for the proposed study. The questionnaires should contain attitudinal questions probing the respondent's perceptions of sex discrimination, the respondent's interpersonal relationships, their attitude toward wage differentials, and their perception of the equality between the sexes.

The questionnaire may start off with respondent number for the person being interviewed as well as his/her personal background followed by opinion questions on perceived discrimination. The next part of the questionnaire consists of wage disparities and attitude questions towards wage differentials. To illustrate the process of construction of questionnaire a sample questionnaire addressed to female respondents is reproduced below:

**Cover Page :**

**Box 5.15 Sample Questionnaire**

**Questionnaire (For Female Employees)**

RESPONDENT NO: | | | |

Sex Discrimination against Women at Work in Unorganised Sector in Andhra Pradesh

Ms Uthara

M.A. (Social Work) Final Year

DR. Mayank Shrinivasan

Senior Faculty Member

COLLEGE OF SOCIAL WORK

HYDERABAD- 500 004.

## PART A :PERSONAL INFORMATION

1. Name :
2. Age in Years :

**Data with regard to Independent Variables :**

**Box 5.15 Sample Questionnaire Continues.......**

**PERSONAL INFORMATION**

| | | | | |
|---|---|---|---|---|
| 1. | Nativity | : | Coastal Andhra | ( ) |
| | | | Rayalseema | ( ) |
| | | | Telangana | ( ) |
| 2. | Age in Years | : | ________________ (as on 1st October, 2007) | |
| 3. | Designation | : | | |
| 4. | Establishment | : | | |
| 5. | Level of Education | : | 1. Graduate | ( ) |
| | | | 2. Intermediate | ( ) |
| | | | 3. High School | ( ) |
| | | | 4. Middle School | ( ) |
| | | | 5. Primary | ( ) |
| | | | 6. Illiterate | ( ) |
| | | | 7. Any other | ( ) |
| 6. | Marital Status | : | 1. Unmarried | ( ) |
| | | | 2. Married | ( ) |
| | | | 3. Divorcee | ( ) |
| | | | 4. Widow | ( ) |
| 7. | Caste | : | 1. O.C | ( ) |
| | | | 2. B.C | ( ) |
| | | | 3. S. C. | ( ) |
| | | | 4. S.T. | ( ) |
| 8. | Religion | : | 1. Hindu | ( ) |
| | | | 2. Muslim | ( ) |
| | | | 3. Christian | ( ) |
| | | | 4. Any other | ( ) |

**Data related to Women at Work :**

**Box 5.15 Sample Questionnaire Continues.......**

9. Since how long are you working ____________________
(completed years)
10. Were you working before :
(1) In the same job ( )
(2) In some other job ( )
(3) N. A. ( )
11. If in some other, what was the job? ____________________
12. When did you take up the present job? ____________________
13. Why did you change? ____________________

**Measurement of Perceived Sex Discrimination (Objective 1) : (Self Perception)**

**Box 5.15 Sample Questionnaire Continues.......**

14. Does employer make any discrimination while recruitment.
(1) Yes ( ) (2) No ( ) (3) Not sure ( )
15. Does your employer make any discrimination against you with respect of men employees on the basis of:

| | Yes | No |
|---|---|---|
| (1) Nature of work | ( ) | ( ) |
| (2) Duration of work | ( ) | ( ) |
| (3) Wages | ( ) | ( ) |
| (4) Promotion | ( ) | ( ) |
| (5) ____________________ (If any other, specify) | ( ) | ( ) |

16. The employers prefer male employees because we take more sick leave and quit more readily.
(1) Agree ( ) (2) undecided ( ) (3) Disagree ( )
17. The employers feel that we can't cope with stressful situations like men can and as such don't give us work like men.
(1) Agree ( ) (2) undecided ( ) (3) Disagree ( )
18. We are not given responsible positions because of their belief that most women are too emotional to be able to handle positions of great responsibility.
(1) Agree ( ) (2) undecided ( ) (3) Disagree ( )
19. The employer takes advantage of us being women and sexually exploits us.
(1) Agree ( ) (2) undecided ( ) (3) Disagree ( )

**Data to Determine Wage Disparities(Objective 3) : Measurement of Perceived Sex Discrimination (Objective 1):**

**Box 5.15 Sample Questionnaire Continues.......**

14. What is your monthly salary/wages now? Rs. ____________
( Data to be collected from Acquaintance Registers of the organizations.)
15. Is there any difference of wages between you and a male worker having same?
kind of work as you?
(1) Yes ( ) (2) No ( ) (3) Not sure ( )
(In case the answer to Q. No. 17 is 'No' or 'Not sure', ask Q. No. 21)

**Box 5.15 Sample Questionnaire Continues.......**

16. What do you feel about it?
17. Equal remuneration should be given to men, women workers for same work or work of similar nature. ( )
18. It doesn't make much of a difference even if we are not paid equal wages as men. ( )
19. Equal remuneration should not be given to men and women workers for same work or work of a similar nature. ( )
20. How much is the difference?
(1) A great difference ( ) (2) A little difference ( )

**(Perception of Discrimination by Others)**

**Box 5.15 Sample Questionnaire Continues.......**

*ATTITUDE OF EMPLOYER*

20. The employers prefer male employees because we take more sick leaves and quit more readily.
(1) Agree ( ) (2) undecided ( ) (3) Disagree ( )
21. The employers feel that we can't cope with stressful situations like men can and as such don't give us work like men.
(1) Agree ( ) (2) undecided ( ) (3) Disagree ( )
22. We are not given responsible positions because of their belief that most women are too emotional to be able to handle positions of great responsibility.
(1) Agree ( ) (2) undecided ( ) (3) Disagree ( )
23. The employer takes advantage of us being women and sexually exploits us.
(1) Agree ( ) (2) undecided ( ) (3) Disagree ( )

**Box 5.15 Sample Questionnaire Continues.......**

*ATTITUDE OF FELLOW MALE EMPLOYEES*

24. Our male colleagues resent working with us as equal to them.
    (1) Agree ( ) (2) undecided ( ) (3) Disagree ( )
25. The subordinate male employees hate talking orders from us.
    (1) Agree ( ) (2) undecided ( ) (3) Disagree ( )
26. the men feel that we are no good at work and hence want we to be paid less than they did.
    (1) Agree ( ) (2) undecided ( ) (3) Disagree ( )
27. The men look down upon us because of their belief that a woman's role is that of a homemaker and a mother rather than an employee.
    (1) Agree ( ) (2) undecided ( ) (3) Disagree ( )
28. The fellow male employee sexually exploits us.
    (1) Agree ( ) (2) undecided ( ) (3) Disagree ( )

**Wage Disparities ( Objective 2)**

**Box 5.15 Sample Questionnaire Continues.......**

29. Since how long are you working ____________________
    (completed years)
30 If in some other, what was the job? ________________
    (Designation)
31. When did you take up the present job? ______________
32. Why did you change? __________________________
33. If you were working before 1976, what was your monthly? salary/wages then? Rs.______________

**Box 5.15 Sample Questionnaire Continues.......**

34. What is your monthly salary/wages now? Rs. __________
35. Is there any difference of wages between you and a male worker having same kind of work as you?
    (1) Yes ( ) (2) No ( ) (3) Not sure ( )
    (In case the answer to Q.No.18 is 'No' or 'Not sure', ask Q.No.21)

**Box 5.15 Sample Questionnaire Continues.......**

36. What do you feel about it?
37. Equal remuneration should be given to men, women workers for same work or work of similar nature. (    )
38. It doesn't make much of a difference even if we are not paid equal wages as men. (    )
39. Equal remuneration should not be given to men and women workers for same work or work of a similar nature. (    )
    How much is the difference?
    (1) A great difference (    ) (2) A little difference (    )

## Interview

In preceding section you read about one of the important tools of data collection, namely, questionnaires, and its strengths and limitations. This section is a continuation of the previous section. In this section we shall discuss a few more tools of data collection such as, interviews, observations, and documents. Each of these tools and techniques has a specific role in the process of collecting data and has its own uses and limitations.

Interview is a process of communication or interaction in which the subject or interviewee gives the needed information verbally in a face-to-face situation. In a research situation it may be seen as an effective, informal conversation, initiated for a specific purpose as it focusses on certain areas. The main objective may be the exchange of ideas and experiences and eliciting of information. Through interview schedule, the researcher can explain more explicitly the purpose of the investigation.

## Types of Interview

Interviews may be classified according to the purpose for which they are used and according to their design and structure.

For purposes of research, an interview may be used, as a tool for gathering data required by the researcher to test a hypothesis or to solve his/her problems. This type of interview is called 'research interview'.

Interviews may vary in design and structure. In some situations, an interviewer may interview one individual at a time. It is called an 'individual interview'. In a 'group interview', a group of individuals is interviewed at one and the same time.

Interviews are also classified as 'structured' and 'unstructured'. A 'structured interview' is one in which the whole situation is carefully structured and the major areas of inquiry are mapped out. However, the interviewee is given considerable freedom to express his/her description of the situation. In this type of interview, the interviewer uses a highly standardised tool and a set of pre-determined questions.

'Unstructured interview' is one where the interviewer does not follow a list of predetermined questions. The interviewees are encouraged to relate their concrete experiences with no or little direction from the interviewer, to dwell on whatever events seem significant to them, to provide their own definition of their social situations and series of questions to be asked and the procedure to arrange the form and timing of the questions. He/She can rephrase the questions, modify them and add new questions to his/her list.

## Techniques of Interviewing

Although the interview as a research tool can be modified according to the needs of the research situation, there are certain techniques that need to be understood. These techniques deal with preparation for the interview, conducting the interview and recording the information gathered.

### (1) Preparation for the Interview

It is necessary to plan carefully for an interview. The interviewer must decide exactly what kind of data the interview should yield, whether the structured or unstructured type of interview will be more useful and how the results of interview should be recorded. It is advisable to try out the interview on some persons before using it for actual investigation. This is helpful in revealing the deficiencies or shortcomings that need to be corrected before the interview is carried out. The interviewer must have a clear idea of the sort of information he/she needs, and may accordingly prepare a list of questions in the form of a "schedule". Interview schedule is a device consisting of a set of questions, which are asked and filled by an interviewer in a face-to-face situation with the interviewee. Since it is administered personally, it provides the researcher an opportunity to establish a rapport with the respondents. This helps the researcher to explain the nature and purpose of investigation and to make the meaning of the questions clear to the respondents in case they misinterpret a question or give incomplete or indefinite responses. The schedule also economises time and expenses of investigation. The procedure of constructing a schedule is same as that of a questionnaire.

### (2) The Process of Interview

In the process of an interview, a cordial relationship between the interviewer and interviewee is most essential. A good rapport helps the interviewee to feel at ease and express himself/herself willingly. In order to establish a good rapport, the interviewer should greet the interviewee in a friendly manner so as to get settled in a relaxed manner. As an interviewer you should observe the following rules in order to elicit effective responses:

(i) Ask only one question at a time.
(ii) Repeat a question if necessary.
(iii) Try to make sure that the interviewee understands the questions.
(iv) Listen carefully to the interviewee's answer.
(v) Observe the interviewee's facial expressions, gestures, and tone or voice so as to derive meanings from his/her body language.
(vi) Allow the interviewee sufficient time to answer the question, but do not let the interview drag on and on.
(vii) Avoid suggesting answers to questions.
(viii) Do not show signs of surprise, shock, anger or other emotions if unexpected answers are given.
(ix) Maintain a neutral attitude with respect to controversial issues during the interview.
(x) Take note of answers that seem to be vague, ambiguous, or evasive.
(xi) Use tact and skill in getting the subject back to an area of inquiry if he/she has strayed too far from the original question.
(xii) In the unstructured interview, ask additional questions to follow up clues or to obtain additional information.

### (3) Recording of the Interview

The recording of the interview is obviously an essential step in interviewing. The interviewer may use a schedule, a structured format, rating scale or a tape recorder to record the responses of the interviewee. The use of a tape recorder during the conduct of the interview not only eliminates the omissions, distortions, elaboration, and other modifications of data usually found in written interview responses, but it also provides an objective basis for evaluating the adequacy of the interview data in relation to the performance of the interviewee. The use of a tape-recorder also permits the interviewer to devote full attention to the interviewee and save much of the time which he/she would otherwise use in writing down the responses during or after the interview. However, if a tape-recorder is not available, the interviewer has to take notes to record the responses.

**Uses of the Interview**

(i) An interview provides an opportunity to the interviewer to ask questions on various areas of inquiry. It permits greater depth in responses, which is not possible through any other means.

(ii) An interview is an independent tool of research for gathering information pertaining to feelings, attitudes or emotions. Since an interview is a highly flexible tool in the hands of skillful interviewers, it allows a more liberal atmosphere than in the use of other techniques of investigation. Questions not readily grasped by interviewees can be rephrased or repeated with proper emphasis and explanations when necessary.

**Limitations of the Interview**

In spite of many merits of the interview method, it is not without demerits that jeopardize its value, even when it is used as a supplementary research technique.

(i) Interview is a time consuming technique.

(ii) The effectiveness of the interview depends greatly upon the skill of the interviewer which everyone does not ordinarily possess. .

(iii) It is difficult to avoid subjectivity on the part of the interviewer.

(iv) An interview is a difficult process because even in the presence of a skilled interviewer some interviewees do not respond freely, frankly and accurately.

(v) Since memory and retention are highly selective processes, interviewees generally provide accurate and vivid accounts of the most recent experiences, or of situations that they encounter most frequently. Painful or embarrassing experiences are forgotten or consciously avoided by the interviewees.

**Observation**

Observation may be defined as a process in which one or more persons observe some real-life situation and record pertinent occurrences. Observation is a technique used to classify and record in a planned manner the individual responses to real life situations.

**Types of Observation**

Observation may be classified into two types:
(a) Participant Observation (b) Non-participant Observation

**Participant observation**

In the process of 'participant observation' the observer becomes one of the group members and participates in some activity or the other of the group. The observer may play any one of the several roles in observation, with varying degrees of participation, as a visitor, an attentive listener, an eager learner, or as a participant observer.

**Non-participant observation:**

In the process of 'non-participant observation', the observer takes a position where his/her presence is not felt by the group. He/She may follow closely the behaviour of an individual or characteristics of one or more groups.

In this type of observation, a one-way 'vision screen' permits the observer to see the subject but prevents the subject from seeing the observer.

Observations may also be classified into the following two categories:
(i) Structured observation, and (ii) Unstructured observation.

**Structured Observation**

Structured observation is formal in character and is designed to provide systematic description to test causal hypothesis. It is executed in controlled situations like classrooms or workshop settings. This type of observation starts with relatively specific formulations. There is not much choice with respect to the content of observation. The observer sets up in advance the categories of behaviour in terms of which he/she wishes to analyse the problem, and keeps in mind the time limit within which he/she has to make the observation.

**Unstructured observation**

Unstructured observation is associated with participant observation and is often an exploratory exercise. In unstructured observation the observer considers aspects of behaviour in terms of their contexts or situations of which they are a part.

**Stages in the Process of Observation**

As a research technique, observation needs proper planning, expert execution, and adequate recording and interpretation.

(i) Planning for observation

Planning for observation includes definition of specific activities or units of behaviour to be observed; the nature of the groups of subjects to be observed; the scope of observation–individual or group; determination of the length of each observation period; and deciding about the tools to be used in making the observation and recording.

(ii) The Process of Observation

The process of observation includes:

(a) Proper arrangement of specific conditions for the subjects to be observed, (b) Assuming proper role for observing, (c) Focussing attention on the specific activities or behaviour under observation, and (d) Proper handling of recording instruments.

(iii) Recording and Interpreting the Observation

Recording of the data through observation should take place either simultaneously or soon after the observation. In the former case, the observer goes on recording his/her observation simultaneously with the occurrence of the phenomenon observed. In the latter case, the observer undertakes to record his/her observations not simultaneously with the actual event, but immediately after he/she has observed for a certain period of time while the details are still fresh in his/her mind. In viewing, classifying and recording behaviour, the observer must take utmost care to minimize the influence of his/her biases, prejudices, attitudes and values on the observation recording. The observer should know what he/she is looking for in a given situation and should carefully and objectively record the relevant data. Subjectivity on the part of an observer may partly be due to his/her emotional involvement, his/her selective perceptions and memory. In order to overcome these biases, various electronic appliances/instruments are used to obtain more accurate records of events. The use of cameras, tape-recorders, stopwatches, binoculars, audiometer, one-way vision screens, mirrors, etc., allows behaviour to be measured to a degree of accuracy which cannot be achieved by the unaided human observer. It is worthwhile to develop an "observation schedule" like an interview schedule for making and recording observations. The specific behaviours to be observed and recorded should be listed in this schedule.

### Documents

Documents are records which describe a process of personal/group development, or the occurrence of an event. It describes the process of personal/group development or the occurrence of an event in accordance with legal or administrative regulations attached to that event. The documents and records are useful in bringing together data for a given time period for scientific analysis.

The content of the documents records are reviewed in terms of the research problem before they are actually used by the researcher. Since the data comes ready-made as the content of the document, they do not depend on a specific investigator or research team's accessibility to the field.

### Types of Documents

Documents are, generally, classified into following categories.

### Personal Letters

Personal letters constitute the most frequently available type of expressive documents. The value of letters as expressive documents varies with the cultural background of the writers. Nonetheless, the writer communicates freely his/her views and emotions in personal letters.

### Life Histories/case Histories

Life or case histories in the form of diaries, biographies and autobiographies have been used extensively by historians. They have been identified as the "personal documents par excellence" by psychologists. However, they have not been used much in social or psychological research.

### Official Records

Official records provide useful information about the time and occurrence of an event in accordance with legal administrative regulations attached to that event. Such data cover a very wide range comprising extensive records of events, namely, births, deaths, marriages, divorces, institutional attendance (school, college, distance education centre etc.), performance in psychological and educational test, crimes, court actions, prison records, registration, voting, social security payments and benefits, illness/hospital data, production/business records, memberships, census data etc.

### Journals

Information about new ideas and developments often appear in journals long before they appear in books. In fact, they are the best sources for reports on recent researches in the area of social sciences. Journals provide updated treatment to current questions and issues in social sciences. They also publish articles of local interest that never appear in the book form. Journals are the best sources for determining contemporary opinion and status, present or past.

## Reference

Bailey, Kenneth D. (1978). *Methods of Social Research*, London: The Free Press.

Baker, L. Therese. (1988). *Doing Social Research,* New York: McGraw Hill.

Black, James A. and Champion, (1976). Dean J. *Methods and Issues in Social Research* New York: John Wiley.

Buckingham, A and Saunders, (2004). P. *The Survey Methods Workbook.* Cambridge : Polity Press.

Festinger. L. and Katz. D. (eds.). (1953). *Research Methods in the Behavioural Sciences,* New York: The Dryden Press.

Goode. W.J. and Hat. P.K. (1952). *Methods in Social Research,* New York: McGraw Hill.

Kerlinger. Fred R. (1964). *Foundations of Behavioural Research,* Delhi : Surjeet Publications.

Kidder, Louise H. (1981). *Research Methods in Social Relations,* New York: Holt.

Lal Das, D.K. (2000), *Practice of Social Research : A Social Work Perspective,* Rawat Publications, Jaipur.

Lal Das, D.K. (2005), *Designs of Social Research,* Jaipur: Rawat Publications.

Miller. D.C. (1964). *Handbook of Research Design and Social Measurement* New York : David Mckey Co.

Monette, Duane R. et. al. (1986). *Applied Social Research: Tool for the Human Services* Chicago: Holt.

Moser. C.A. and Kalton. *Survey Methods in Social Investigation* London: Heinemann Educational Books, 1975.

Nachmias D and Nachmias C. (1981). *Research Methods in the Social Sciences*, New York: St. Martins press.

O'Leary Z. (2004).*The Essential Guide to Doing Research*. New Delhi : Vistaar Publications.

Ramachandran, P. (2000). *Research and Statistics for Social Work.* Secnderabad : Andhra Pradesh Social Service Society

Rubin, Allen and Babbie E. (1989) .*Research Methodology for Social Work*, Belmont, California, Wadsworth.

Sellitz. G. et. al. (1973). *Research Methods in Social Relations* New York: Holt Rinehart and Winston (3rd edition).

Thurstone, L. and Chave, E. (1929). *The Measurement of Attitude,* Chicago: University of Chicago press.

Wilkinson, T.S. and Bhandarkar, P.L. *Methodology and Techniques of Social Research*: Bombay: Himalayan, 1977.

Young. P.V. (1953) *Scientific Social Surveys and Research* Englewood Cliff. N.J. Prentice Hall .

# 6

# Data Processing

## Introduction

In previous chapter, we discussed about methods and tools of data collection. Once data are collected the researcher turns his focus of attention on its processing. In this chapter we will discuss about one of the important stages of the research process, i.e. data processing.

## Processing of Data

Processing of data is a link between data collection and data analysis. A researcher has to make his/her plan for each and every stage of the research process. As such, a good researcher makes a perfect plan of processing and analysis of data. To some researchers data processing and analysis is not a very serious activity. They feel many a time that data processing is a job of a computer assistant. As a consequence, they have to be contended with the results given by computer assistant which may not help them to achieve their objectives. To avoid such situations, it is essential that data processing must be planned in advance and instructed to assistants accordingly. In this unit we will discuss about data processing and data analysis. Data processing refers to certain operations such as editing, coding, computing of the scores, preparation of master charts, tabulation, etc.

## Editing of Data

After collection of filled in questionnaires/interview schedules, editing of entries therein are not only necessary but also useful in making subsequent steps simpler. Many a times, a researcher or the assistant either miss entries in the questionnaires or enter responses, which are not legible. This sort of discrepancies can be resolved by editing the schedule meticulously. Another problem comes up at the time of tabulation of data when researcher asks for tabulation of responses from consecutive questions. In cases where data are not edited there has to be inconsistency in the tabulations, the researcher has to be very particular about, contingency questions where category 'not applicable' exists. In the process of editing, the researcher has to be very careful about contingency questions having 'not applicable' as a response.

## Coding of Data

Responses to questions may be either 'numeral' or 'verbal'. Say for example, the responses to question on "age" would be numerals like , 24, 26, 34, ... etc. where as the responses to question on "gender" would be verbal , like 'male' or 'female'. When responses are likely to be numerals , commonly known as "actual" we need not give "codes" to it because it can be counted and tabulated. In the code book we write 'actual' in the response column and put '—
—' in 'codes' column. For the variable 'gender' the responses could be either 'male' or 'female', as such we give code '1' for 'male' and '2' for 'female'. The code book is , generally, presented in the following format.

**Box 6.1 Coding of Responses**

Q. 1 Age : 24

Q. 2 Gender : Male☐ Female☐

CODE BOOK

| Q.No. | Var. No. | Information Sought | Responses | Codes |
|---|---|---|---|---|
| 1 | 1 | Age | Actual | -------- |
| 2 | 2 | Gender | Male<br>Female | 1<br>2 |

You need to give 'numbers' to 'response carefully. The coding scheme will vary according to the type of questions. Coding of 'actual' data has been explained in the sub-sequent sections of this chapter entitled **"Data Processing through SPSS-Transform-Recode".**

A close-end question which is generally pre-coded , can be just included in the code book. See the following example:

Q. 3 Marital Status : 1. Unmarried
2. Married
3. Divorcee
4. Widow

Since, the question is already coded; you can include it in the code book as shown below:

**Box 6.2 Coding of Closed-end Question**

Q. 3 Marital Status : 1. Unmarried
2. Married
3. Divorcee
4. Widow

CODE BOOK

| *Q.No.* | *Var. No.* | *Information Sought* | *Responses* | *Codes* |
|---|---|---|---|---|
| 3 | 3 | Marital Status | Unmarried<br>Married<br>Divorce<br>Widow | 1<br>2<br>3<br>4 |

Coding of open-end questions involves operations such as classification of major responses and developing a response category of 'others' for responses which were not given frequently. Say for example, a question on 'Occupation' has following responses:

| *Sl.No.* | *Response* | *Frequencies* | *Percentage* |
|---|---|---|---|
| 1. | Agricultural Labour | 264 | 52.8 |
| 2. | Farm labour | 136 | 27.2 |
| 3. | Daily Wage Labour | 64 | 12.8 |
| 4. | Farmer | 16 | 3.2 |
| 5. | Tailor | 4 | .8 |
| 6. | Carpenter | 3 | .6 |
| 7. | Coolly | 3 | .6 |
| 8. | Kirana Shop | 1 | .2 |
| 9. | Vegetable Shop | 1 | .2 |
| 10. | Toddy Taper | 1 | .2 |
| 11. | Watchman | 1 | .2 |
| 12. | Peon | 1 | .2 |
| 13. | Clerk | 1 | .2 |
| 14. | Teacher | 1 | .2 |
| 15. | Cycle Mechanic | 1 | .2 |
| 16. | Maistry | 1 | .2 |
| 17. | Driver | 1 | .2 |
|  | Total | 500 | 100.0 |

There are three major responses, namely, Agricultural Labour, Farm labour, and Daily Wage Labour. The remaining responses are smaller proportion. Therefore you need to develop a new a response category of 'others' for responses which were not given frequently. Then the above distribution would appear as shown below:

| *Sl.No.* | *Response* | *Frequencies* | *Percentage* |
|---|---|---|---|
| 1. | Agricultural Labour | 264 | 52.8 |
| 2. | Farm labour | 136 | 27.2 |
| 3. | Daily Wage Labour | 64 | 12.8 |
| 4. | Others | 36 | 7.2 |
| | Total | 500 | 100 |

The classification of responses is primarily based on similarities or differences among the responses. Usually, in the case of open-end questions, to classify responses, researcher looks for major characteristics of the responses and puts it accordingly.

**Box 6.3 Recategorisation of Responses**

Q. 3 Occupation

CODE BOOK

| *Q.No.* | *Var. No.* | *Information Sought* | *Responses* | *Codes* |
|---|---|---|---|---|
| 4 | 4 | Occupation | Agricultural Labour<br>Farm labour<br>Daily Wage Labour<br>Others | 1<br>2<br>3<br>4 |

In case of attitude scales, researcher has to keep in mind, the direction or weightage of responses. For example, a response 'strongly agree' is coded as 'five'. The subsequent codes would be in order. Therefore, if there are responses like 'agree', 'undecided', 'disagree' and 'strongly disagree' they have to be coded as four, three, two, and one. Say for example, an item of an attitude scale which has responses on 5 point scale:

"Equal remuneration should be given to men and women for same work or work of similar nature."

Strongly agree
Agree
Indifferent
Disagree
Strongly disagree

**Box 6.4 Coding of Attitude Scale Responses**

**Q.** "Equal remuneration should be given to men and women for same work or work of similar nature."

Strongly agree
Agree
Indifferent
Disagree
Strongly disagree

CODE BOOK

| *Q.No.* | *Var. No.* | *Information Sought* | *Responses* | *Codes* |
|---|---|---|---|---|
| 4 | 4 | Equal remuneration should be given to men and women | Strongly agree<br>Agree<br>Undecided<br>Disagree<br>Strongly disagree | 1<br>2<br>3<br>4<br>5 |

The matrix questions have to be coded taking into consideration each cell as one variable. For example, if the column of matrix represents employment status, namely, 'permanent' and 'temporary' and row represents employers or type of employer, namely, government and private, the first cell would represent a variable 'government- permanent'. The second cell would represent 'government-temporary' and so on.

**Box 6.5 Coding of Matrix Question**

Q. Nature of Job :

| *Employer* | *Permanent* | *Temporary* | *Ad-hoc* | *Daily Wage* |
|---|---|---|---|---|
| Government | | | | |
| Semi-Government | | | | |
| Private | | | | |

CODE BOOK

| *Q.No.* | *Var. No.* | *Information Sought* | *Responses* | *Codes* |
|---|---|---|---|---|
| 21 | 26 | Nature of Job | Government- Permanent<br>Government-Temporary<br>Government-Ad-hoc<br>Government-Daily Wage | 1<br>2<br>3<br>4 |
| | 27 | Nature of Job | Semi-Government-Permanent<br>Semi-Government-Temporary<br>Semi-Government-Ad-hoc<br>Semi-Government-Daily Wage | 1<br>2<br>3<br>4 |
| | 28 | Nature of Job | Private- Permanent<br>Private -Temporary<br>Private -Ad-hoc<br>Private -Daily Wage | 1<br>2<br>3<br>4 |

In multiple response questions, respondents are allowed to give a combination of answers from a set of answers. For example:

**Box 6.6 Coding of Multiple Response Question**

**Q. Why do you work? (Multiple Response)**

**(1) To supplement the family income.**
**(2) To have independent income of one's own.**
**(3) To achieve a position or status of one's own.**
**(4) To utilize plenty of spare time.**
**(5) To be away from the unhappy atmosphere of home.**
**(6) To escape from domestic work and get freedom to mix with people.**

**In this case, a respondent can say that he works because :**

**(1) To supplement the family income and (2) to achieve a position or status of one's own.**

CODE BOOK

| *Q.No.* | *Var. No.* | *Information Sought* | *Responses* | *Codes* |
|---|---|---|---|---|
| 21 | 26 | Reason of doing a job | **To supplement the family income.** | 1 |
| | | | **To have independent income of one's own.** | 2 |
| | | | **To achieve a position or status of one's own** | 3 |
| | | | **To utilize plenty of spare time.** | 4 |
| | | | **To be away from the unhappy atmosphere of home.** | 5 |
| | | | **To escape from domestic work and get freedom to mix with people.** | 6 |
| | | | 1+2 | 7 |
| | | | 1+3 | 8 |
| | | | 1+4 | 9 |
| | | | 1+2+3 | 10 |
| | | | 1+2+3+4 | 11 |

## Contingency Questions

Contingency question is applicable to only a sub - group of the sample. As such, responses to a contingency question invariably include a special category known as "Not Applicable". For example:

**Box 6.7 Contingency Questions**

Q. 1 "Are you married?"
Yes / No
(If 'no' skip to question 3).

Q. 2 "If yes, what is your husband?"
Teacher
Engineer
Doctor
Lawyer
Not Applicable

CODE BOOK

| *Q.No.* | *Var. No.* | *Information Sought* | *Responses* | *Codes* |
|---|---|---|---|---|
| 21 | 26 | "Are you married?" | Yes<br>No | 1<br>2 |
| | 27 | Occupation of husband | Teacher<br>Engineer<br>Doctor<br>Lawyer<br>Not Applicable | 1<br>2<br>3<br>4<br>9 |

In order to demonstrate the points discussed above a section of a code book used in a study is reproduced in Table 6.1

**TABLE 6.1**
**CODE BOOK**

| *Q.No.* | *Variable No.* | *Information Sought* | *Responses* | *Code* |
|---|---|---|---|---|
| 2 | V1 | Age | Actual | - |
| 3 | V2 | Designation | Worker<br>Supervisor<br>Manager | 1<br>2<br>3 |
| 4 | V3 | Establishment | Public<br>Private | 1<br>2 |

*(Contd.)*

*(Contd.Table 6.1)*

| *Q.No.* | *Variable No.* | *Information Sought* | *Responses* | *Code* |
|---|---|---|---|---|
| 5 | V4 | Level of Education | Graduate<br>Intermediate<br>High School<br>Middle School<br>Primary<br>Illiterate<br>Other | 1<br>2<br>3<br>4<br>5<br>6<br>7 |
| 6 | V5 | Marital Status | Married<br>Unmarried<br>Widow<br>Divorce | 1<br>2<br>3<br>4 |
| 36 | V35 | Nature of work | Yes<br>No | 1<br>2 |
| | V36 | Duration of work | Yes<br>No | 1<br>2 |
| | V37 | Wages | Yes<br>No | 1<br>2 |
| | V38 | Promotion | Yes<br>No | 1<br>2 |
| 43 | V42 | Attitude of Employer Preference for male employees | Agree<br>Undecided<br>Disagree | 1<br>2<br>3 |

**Preparing a Master Chart**

After a code book is prepared, the data can be transferred either to a master chart or directly to computer through a statistical package. Going through master chart to computer is much more advantageous than entering data directly to computers because one can check the wrong entries in the computer by comparing 'data listing' as a computer output and master chart. Entering data directly to computer is disadvantageous, as there is no way to check wrong entries, which will show inconsistencies in tabulated data at the later stages of tabulation. A sample of master chart prepared in accordance with the code book is presented in Table 6.2.

**TABLE 6.2**
**MASTER CHART**

| *Respondent Number* | *Variable Labels* | | | | | | | | | |
|---|---|---|---|---|---|---|---|---|---|---|
| | *Age* | *Designation* | *Establishment* | *Level of Education* | *Marital Status* | *Nature of Work* | *Duration of Work* | *Wages* | *Promotions* | *Attitude of Employer* |
| | *Variable Number* | | | | | | | | | |
| | V1 | V2 | V3 | V4 | V5 | V6 | V7 | V8 | V9 | V10 |
| 1 | 23 | 3 | 4 | 2 | 2 | 3 | 4 | 1220 | 3 | 4 |
| 2 | 28 | 2 | 3 | 4 | 1 | 5 | 5 | 1547 | 3 | 3 |
| 3 | 23 | 4 | 4 | 4 | 2 | 1 | 4 | 1922 | 1 | 3 |
| 4 | 28 | 1 | 3 | 3 | 1 | 2 | 5 | 1847 | 2 | 5 |
| 5 | 23 | 3 | 4 | 2 | 2 | 1 | 7 | 2922 | 1 | 1 |
| 6 | 24 | 3 | 1 | 1 | 3 | 1 | 1 | 1220 | 1 | 1 |
| 7 | 22 | 3 | 1 | 1 | 3 | 1 | 2 | 1547 | 1 | 1 |
| 8 | 24 | 2 | 1 | 1 | 3 | 1 | 2 | 1922 | 2 | 1 |
| 9 | 45 | 2 | 2 | 1 | 3 | 1 | 2 | 1847 | 2 | 2 |
| 10 | 35 | 3 | 1 | 2 | 2 | 2 | 1 | 2922 | 3 | 3 |
| 11 | 36 | 1 | 2 | 2 | 2 | 3 | 2 | 1847 | 4 | 4 |
| 12 | 34 | 2 | 3 | 1 | 1 | 2 | 3 | 2922 | 4 | 3 |

*(Contd.)*

*(Contd. Table 6.2)*

| *Respondent Number* | *Variable Labels* | | | | | | | | | |
|---|---|---|---|---|---|---|---|---|---|---|
| | *Age* | *Designation* | *Establishment* | *Level of Education* | *Marital Status* | *Nature of Work* | *Duration of Work* | *Wages* | *Promotions* | *Attitude of Employer* |
| | *Variable Number* | | | | | | | | | |
| | V1 | V2 | V3 | V4 | V5 | V6 | V7 | V8 | V9 | V10 |
| 13 | 35 | 2 | 4 | 2 | 2 | 2 | 4 | 1220 | 3 | 2 |
| 14 | 46 | 1 | 3 | 3 | 1 | 1 | 4 | 1547 | 3 | 1 |
| 15 | 45 | 2 | 3 | 3 | 1 | 2 | 5 | 1922 | 2 | 1 |
| 16 | 23 | 1 | 4 | 3 | 2 | 3 | 5 | 1847 | 1 | 1 |
| 17 | 22 | 3 | 1 | 1 | 3 | 1 | 2 | 1547 | 1 | 1 |
| 18 | 24 | 2 | 1 | 1 | 3 | 1 | 2 | 1922 | 2 | 1 |
| 19 | 45 | 2 | 2 | 1 | 3 | 1 | 2 | 1847 | 2 | 2 |
| 20 | 35 | 3 | 1 | 2 | 2 | 2 | 1 | 2922 | 3 | 3 |

**Tabulation of Data**

The data entered in a master chart are simple figures without any form or structure. Data are in a raw state for they have not gone through any treatment. This mass of data is known as ungrouped data or raw data. Before we analyse and interpret the data we need to process the data further in tabular form. This stage of processing of data is known as 'tabulation'. To understand the process of tabulation we will consider a part of our master chart (TABLE 6.2) where data relating to age, gender and perceived sex discrimination have been entered.

**TABLE 6.3**
**MASTER CHART**

| *RESPONDENT NUMBER* ↓ | *AGE* | *GENDER (1=MALE, 2=FEMALE)* | *PERCEIVED SEX DISCRIMINATION (1=LOW, 2=MODERATE, 3=HIGH)* |
|---|---|---|---|
| | **V1** | **V2** | **V3** |
| **1** | **23** | **1** | **3** |
| **2** | **28** | **1** | **3** |
| **3** | **23** | **2** | **3** |
| **4** | **28** | **1** | **2** |
| **5** | **23** | **2** | **1** |
| **6** | **24** | **2** | **1** |
| **7** | **22** | **2** | **1** |
| **8** | **24** | **1** | **2** |
| **9** | **45** | **1** | **3** |

*(Contd.)*

*(Contd.Table 6.3)*

| *RESPONDENT NUMBER* ↓ | *AGE* | *GENDER (1=MALE, 2=FEMALE)* | *PERCEIVED SEX DISCRIMINATION (1=LOW, 2=MODERATE, 3=HIGH)* |
|---|---|---|---|
| **10** | **35** | **2** | **3** |
| **11** | **36** | **1** | **1** |
| **12** | **34** | **1** | **2** |
| **13** | **35** | **1** | **1** |
| **14** | **46** | **2** | **3** |
| **15** | **45** | **2** | **3** |
| **16** | **23** | **2** | **3** |
| **17** | **22** | **1** | **2** |
| **18** | **24** | **1** | **2** |
| **19** | **45** | **2** | **3** |
| **20** | **35** | **2** | **2** |

We may present the data pertaining to age as shown in the following table. This is known as ungrouped data.

**TABLE 6.4**
**AGE OF 20 RESPONDENTS**

| *Respo. No.* | *Age* | *Respondent. No.* | *Age* |
|---|---|---|---|
| 1 | 23 | 11 | 60 |
| 2 | 28 | 12 | 38 |
| 3 | 23 | 13 | 39 |
| 4 | 28 | 14 | 40 |
| 5 | 23 | 15 | 51 |
| 6 | 24 | 16 | 37 |

*(Contd.)*

*(Contd.Table 6.4)*

| *Respo. No.* | *Age* | *Respondent. No.* | *Age* |
|---|---|---|---|
| 7 | **22** | 17 | 40 |
| 8 | **24** | 18 | 72 |
| 9 | **45** | 19 | 39 |
| 10 | **35** | 20 | 50 |

Ungrouped data presented in this manner are not capable of being rapidly or easily interpreted. Only a vague impression may be obtained by its perusal. To comprehend data easily we need to process data further and present it as grouped data. A first step in such a grouping would be achieved by representing the repetitions of age by tallies. For grouping the data first we prepare a tally sheet as shown below:

**TABLE 6.5**
**TALLY SHEET SHOWING THE AGE OF 20 RESPONDENTS**

| *Age* | *Tallies* | *Total* |
|---|---|---|
| 22 | II | 2 |
| 23 | IIII | 4 |
| 24 | III | 3 |
| 25 | | |
| 26 | | |
| 27 | | |
| 28 | II | 2 |
| 29 | | |
| 30 | | |
| 31 | | |
| 32 | | |
| 33 | | |
| 34 | I | 1 |
| 35 | III | 3 |
| 36 | I | 1 |

*(Contd.)*

*(Contd.Table 6.5)*

| *Age* | *Tallies* | *Total* |
|---|---|---|
| 37 | | |
| 38 | | |
| 39 | | |
| 40 | | |
| 41 | | |
| 42 | | |
| 43 | | |
| 44 | | |
| 45 | III | 3 |
| 46 | I | 1 |
| | Total | 20 |

To understand the data rapidly we present the data pertaining to age as shown in the following table. This is known as 'Frequency Table or 'Univariate Table'.

**TABLE 6.6**
**DISTRIBUTION OF RESPONDENTS BY AGE**

| *Age* | *No. of Respondents (f)* |
|---|---|
| **22** | **2** |
| **23** | **4** |
| **24** | **3** |
| **28** | **2** |
| **34** | **1** |
| **35** | **3** |
| **36** | **1** |
| **45** | **3** |
| **46** | **1** |
| **Total** | **20** |

In order that data may be more readily comprehensible grouping further reduces the bulk of this data. Such grouping is achieved by representing the age in intervals as shown below:

**TABLE 6.7**
**AGE OF RESPONDENTS**

| *Age in Years* | *No. of Respondents (f)* |
|---|---|
| 22-27 | 9 |
| 28-33 | 2 |
| 34-39 | 5 |
| 40-45<br>46-51 | 3<br>1 |
| Total | 20 |

### Categorisation

Here it is important to note that categorisation must be arrived at with the help of statistical techniques. Since statistical techniques have not been discussed yet we have taken arbitrary group interval of five years. Categorisation based on statistical techniques helps researcher to justify the frequency distribution.

### Constructing a Bivariate Table

A bivariate table is one in which two variables have been cross-classified. It consists of rows and columns, where the categories of one variable are labels for the rows and the categories of the second variable are labels for the columns. Usually, the independent variable is the row variable and the dependent variable is the column variable. As an illustration of how a bivariate table is constructed, let us consider part of our master chart (Table 6.2).

**TABLE 6.8**
**MASTER CHART (PARTIAL )**

| *Respondent. No.* | *Gender 1=Male, 2=Female* | *Perceived Sex Discrimination 1=Low, 2=Moderate 3=High* |
|---|---|---|
| 1 | 1 | 3 |
| 2 | 1 | 3 |
| 3 | 2 | 3 |

*(Contd.)*

*(Contd.Table 6.8)*

| *Respondent. No.* | *Gender 1=Male, 2=Female* | *Perceived Sex Discrimination 1=Low, 2=Moderate 3=High* |
|---|---|---|
| 4 | 1 | 2 |
| 5 | 2 | 1 |
| 6 | 2 | 1 |
| 7 | 2 | 1 |
| 8 | 1 | 2 |
| 9 | 1 | 3 |
| 10 | 2 | 3 |
| 11 | 1 | 1 |
| 12 | 1 | 2 |
| 13 | 1 | 1 |
| 14 | 2 | 3 |
| 15 | 2 | 3 |
| 16 | 2 | 3 |
| 17 | 1 | 2 |
| 18 | 1 | 2 |
| 19 | 2 | 3 |
| 20 | 2 | 2 |

A part of master chart lists 20 respondents by their gender and perceived sex discrimination scores. These observations have been tallied and classified by their joint position on gender and perceived sex discrimination into the appropriate cells in Table 6.9. For example, the first cell of the table (1, 3) represents male (1) respondents who have perceived high sex discrimination (3).

**TABLE 6.9**
**GENDER AND PERCEIVED SEX DISCRIMINATION**
**(Dummy Table with Tallies)**

| | *Perceived Sex discrimination* | | | |
|---|---|---|---|---|
| *Gender* | *High (3)* | *Moderate (2)* | *Low (1)* | *Total* |
| Male (1) | (1,3) III = 3 | (1,2) IIIII = 5 | (1,1) II = 2 | 10 |
| Female (2) | (2,3) IIIII I = 6 | (2,2) I = 1 | (2, 1) III = 3 | 10 |
| Total | 9 | 6 | 5 | 20 |

(1,3) = Cell Code = Males who have perceived 'High Sex Discrimination".

(1,2) = Cell Code = Males who have perceived 'Moderate Sex Discrimination".

(1,1) = Cell Code = Males who have perceived 'Low Sex Discrimination".

(2,3) = Cell Code = Females who have perceived 'High Sex Discrimination".

(2,2) = Cell Code = Females who have perceived 'Moderate Sex Discrimination".

(2,1) = Cell Code = Females who have perceived 'Low Sex Discrimination".

The Table 6.9 is a 2-by-3 table because it has two rows and three columns, each representing a category of either variable gender or the variable sex discrimination. The third row represents the column totals; and the fourth column, the row totals

To comprehend the data rapidly we present the table as shown below:

**TABLE 6.10**
**GENDER AND PERCEIVED SEX DISCRIMINATION**

| *Gender* | *Perceived Sex discrimination* | | | *Total* |
|---|---|---|---|---|
| | *High* | *Moderate* | *Low* | |
| Male | 3 | 5 | 2 | 10 |
| Female (2) | 6 | 1 | 3 | 10 |
| Total | 9 | 6 | 5 | 20 |

## Data Processing through Computer

In preceding sections we have discussed how we can process our data manually. A number of softwares are available for processing of data through computer. One such software is Statistical Package for Social Sciences (SPSS). It is a powerful data processing and analysis software specially tailored to the requirements of social science researchers and widely used by them. SPSS uses descriptive menus and simple dialog boxes to do most of the work for you. It provides online 'Help' in several ways :

1. Help Menu : Every SPSS window has a help menu on the 'Menu Bar'.
2. 'Dialog Box' context menu help : Click the right mouse button in a dialog box and select *What's This*?
3. Dialog Box 'Help' buttons : Most dialog boxes have a 'Help' button that take you directly to a help topic for that dialog box.
4. SPSS tutorial : Choose tutorial on the help menu in any SPSS window to access the online, introductory tutorial.

If you are unfamiliar with statistical procedures , the 'Statistics Coach' can help you get started by prompting you with simple questions , non-technical language , and visual examples that help you select the basic statistical feature that are best suited to your data. We will be using SPSS for Windows 11.0 to demonstrate data processing and analysis for the study referred above.

## Basic Steps in Data Analysis

Step I : Define your data.
Step II : Get your data entered into SPSS Data Editor.
Step III : Select the variables for the analysis.
Step IV : Select a procedure from the menus to calculate Statistics.
Step V : Run the procedure and look at the results.

## Starting the SPSS Session

**Click** the **Start** button and select **SPSS 11.0** from **Program Menu** or **Double Click** the **icon** of **SPSS.11 on the Desk Top.**

SPSS 11.0 for Windows.lnk

When you start an **SPSS** session, the **Untitled-SPSS Data Editor** opens automatically.

## SPSS Data Editor

The **Untitled-SPSS Data Editor** provides a spreadsheet for entering and editing data and creating data files.

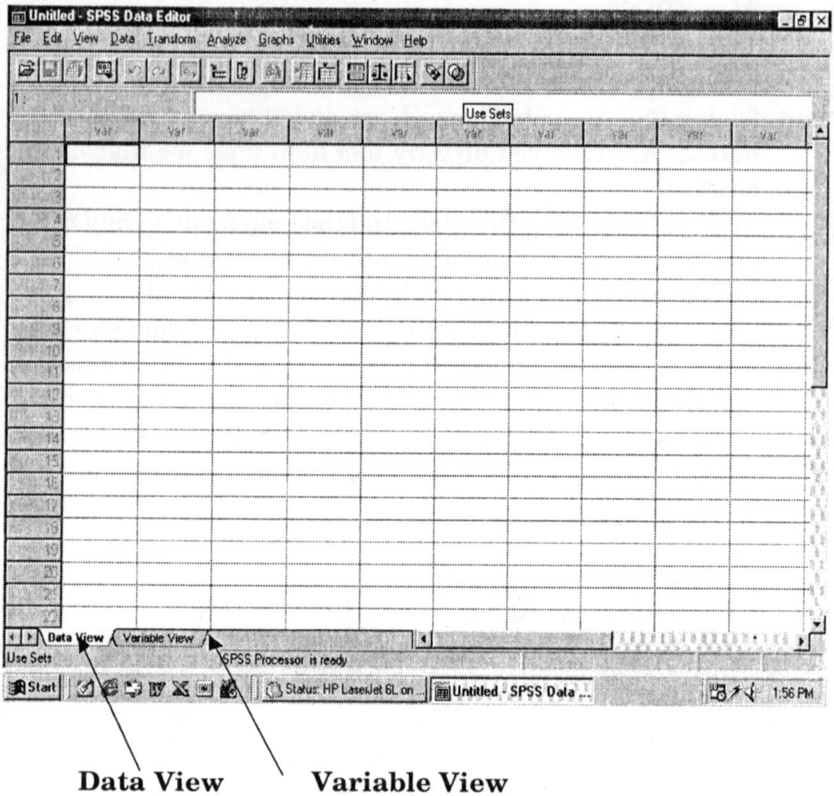


**Important features of the Data Editor**:

- First column represents Respondent Numbers (1, 2, 3, .....by default).
- First row represents Variable Numbers (var- by default).
- At the bottom left corner there are two buttons : 'Data View' and 'Variable View'
- Data View shows the data file and Variable View shows details about variables.

Untitled-SPSS Data Editor displays a window with a prompt:

What would you like to do?

? Run the Tutorial
? Type in Data
? Open an existing file

More Files
? Open another type of file

If you like to enter data select **O K** Type in Data' and click button.

**Define Variable**

Once you prepare your Code Book, you need to include it in the program for further action to be taken. The process of including the code book is known as "Define Variable".

To define variable click at 'Variable View' (see the figure above).

The **Untitled-SPSS Data Editor** provides a spreadsheet for defining data. Next, Click in the first column and type variable name, Label and Values as shown below :

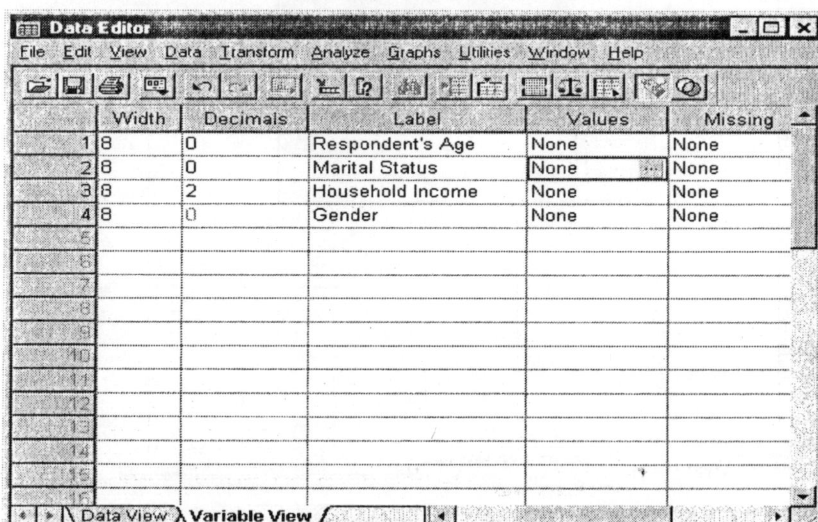

Value labels provide a method for mapping your variable values to a string label. In the case of this example, there are two acceptable values for the *marital* variable. A value of 0 means that the subject is single, and a 1 means that he or she is married.

Select the **Values** cell for the **marital** row and click the button to open the Value Labels dialog box.

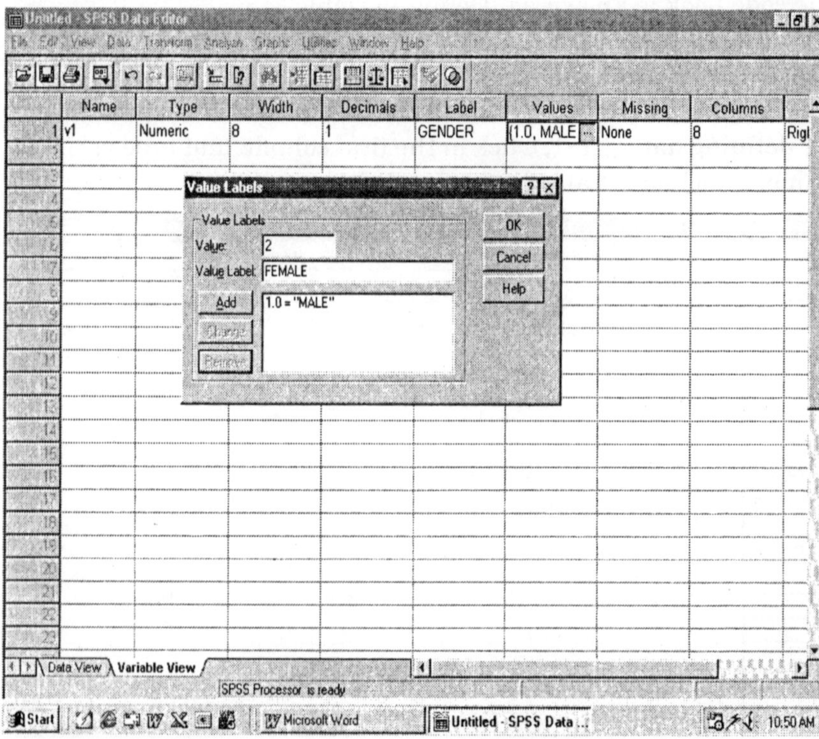

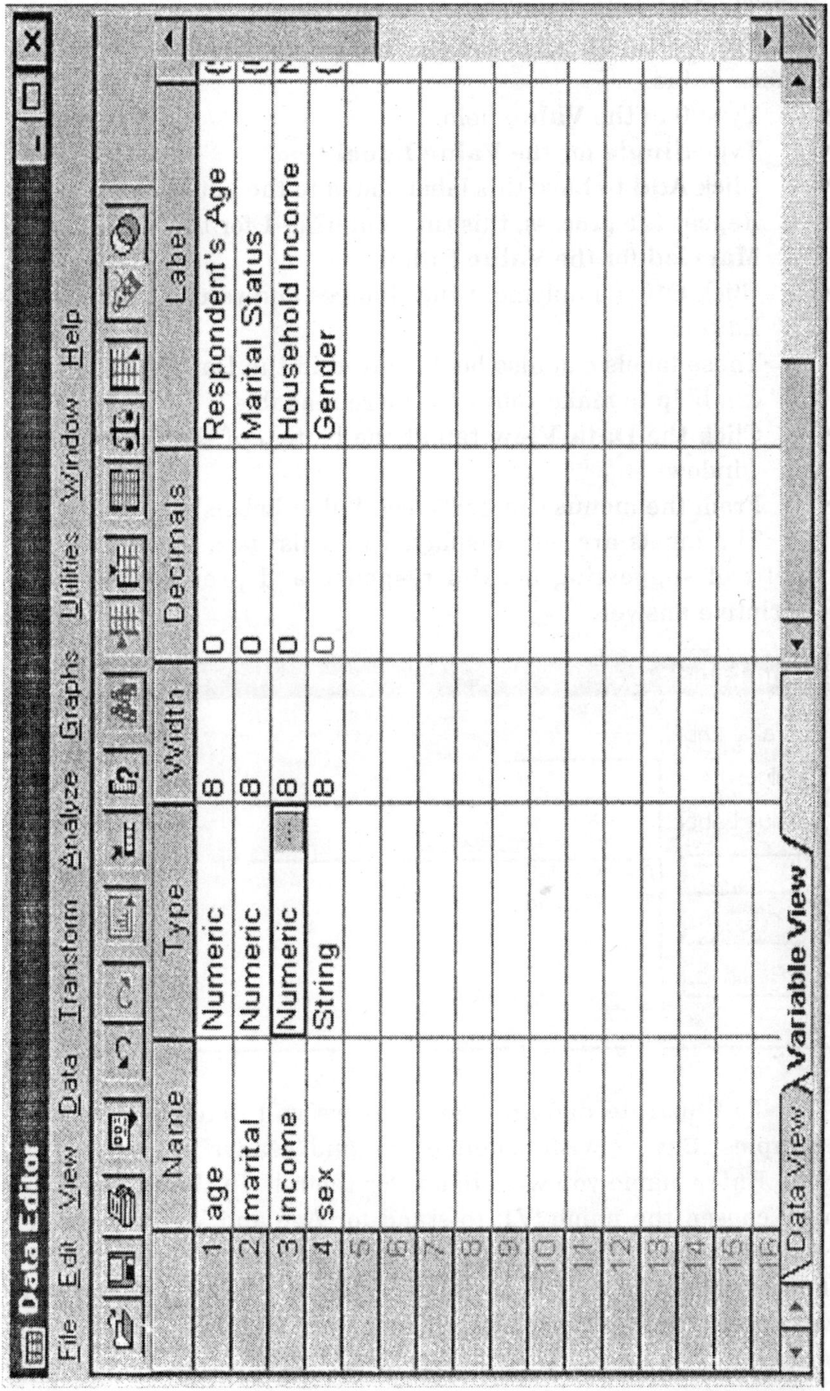
Data Editor
File Edit View Data Transform Analyze Graphs Utilities Window Help
Name Type Width Decimals Label
1 age Numeric 8 0 Respondent's Age
2 marital Numeric 8 0 Marital Status
3 income Numeric 8 0 Household Income
4 sex String 8 0 Gender
Data View
Variable View

The **Value** is the actual numeric value.

The **Value Label** is the string label applied to the specified numeric value.

- Type **0** in the **Value** field.
- Type **Single** for the **Value Label**.
- Click **Add** to have this label added to the list.
- Repeat the process, this time entering **1** for the **Value** and **Married** for the **Value Label**.
- Click **OK** to implement the changes and return to the Data Editor.
- These labels can also be displayed in the Data View, which can help to make your data more readable.
- Click the **Data View** tab at the bottom of the Data Editor window.
- From the menus choose: 'View  Value Labels'

The labels are now displayed in a list box, which has the benefit of suggesting a valid response and providing a more descriptive answer.

To illustrate defining variables we will take up one more examples . Say we wish to define 'age' and 'gender' .

Enter  name you wish to use for the cell. In the example we have chosen the name 'V1' to stand for Age and V2 for Gender. Next, click on the label cell then type "Age" and then "Gender" in the variable label cell. Then click on the Values cell, a dialog box will appear, in that type value & value label and then click on Add button.

| | Name | Type | Decimal | Width | Label | Values |
|---|---|---|---|---|---|---|
| 1 | V1 | | | | Age | |
| 2 | V2 | | | | Gender | Click → Here |

For example, **type** "1" in the value box, then **click** the value label box and **type** "Male" and finally **click** the **"Add"** button. Repeat for the other value of the variable. Once you have finished assigning value labels, **click** on **continue button.** (See the figure below)

Dialog Box : Value Label

**Value** **1**

**Value Label** **Male**

**Add**

**1.00 = "Male"**

- In case you need to change the labels you can always return to this dialog box.
- The **change button** can be used to change a value label.
- The **remove button** can be used to remove a value label.
- The **cancel button** can be used to cancel your labeling work and help button can be used to access the SPSS on line help Now go ahead and define the remaining variables.

**Entering Data**

To enter data click on **Data View.**

The **Untitled-SPSS Data Editor** provides a spreadsheet for entering data and creating data files.

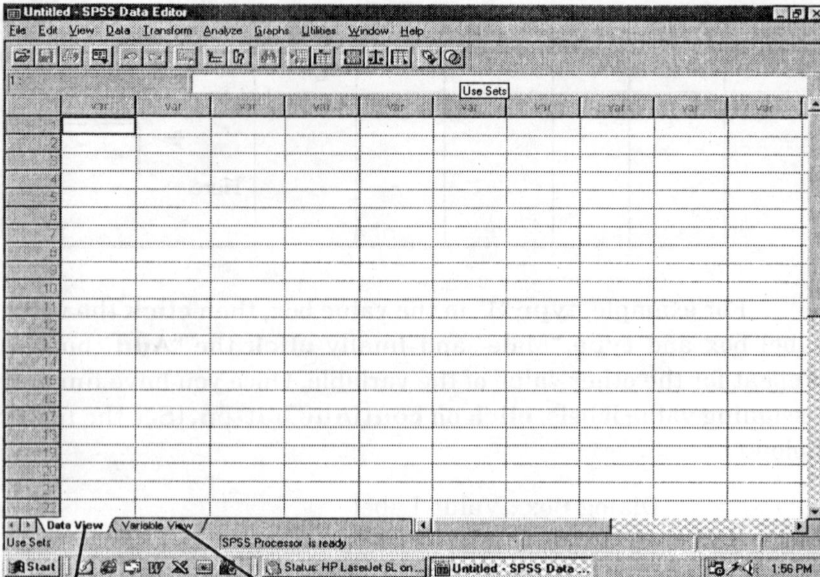


**Data View** **Variable View**

Select a cell in the **Data Editor**

Enter the data value. The value is displayed in the cell of the **Data Editor**

Press [ → ] and select another cell to enter data value.

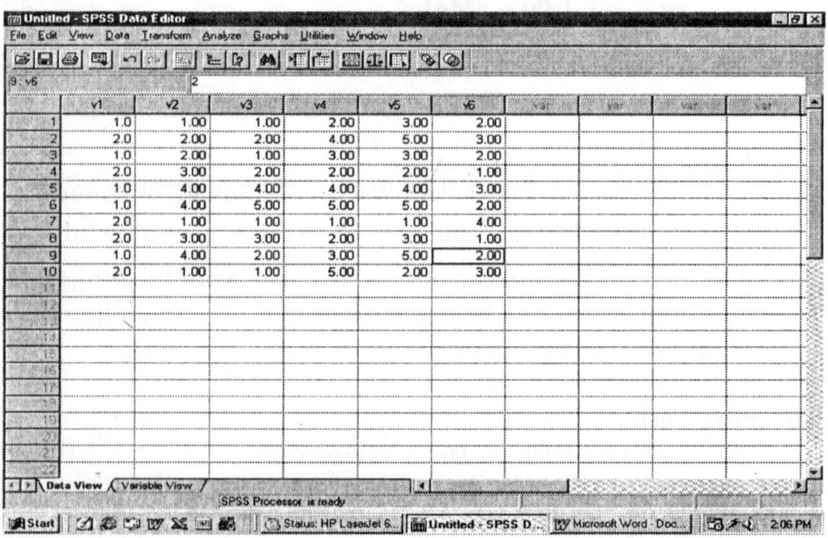

For example, to enter the data simply move the cursor to the upper-left-hand corner and enter 1 for the first respondent's gender "male", then Press and move the cursor one cell to the right to enter data value, say, enter 1 for the level of education "illiterate", and so on. On the screen you will see like Figure 4.

Saving Data and Creating a SPSS File

To save data,

From the menus choose:

File

**Save**

Because these data have not been saved previously you will see a dialogue box prompting you to **enter a file name**. **Type** in the name **"attitude"** and **click** the **OK** button. **SPSS** will then save the data to this file. (SPSS will automatically attach the **.sav** extension if you do not type it in.)

Data Verification

To verify the data:

From menu, choose

**Analyse**

Reports

**Case Summaries**

**Dialog Box- Summarize Cases**

Transfer Variables from Left Box to Right Box and click OK.

**Taking Print Out**

To take print out :

From menu, choose

**File**

**Print**

Tally the data values in print out with your Master Chart.

**Data Editing**

Go to the Cell representing Respondent Number and the variable.

Say for example, fourth respondent is male (1) but you have entered Female (2).

Go to the cell and now enter 1, the data value will be corrected. Make all other corrections. Save the corrections.

**Transform Data**

**Recode** : Recode into Different Variables reassigns the values of existing variables or collapses ranges of existing values into new values for a new variable. For example, you could collapse salaries into a new variable containing salary-range categories.

Suppose we want to regroup the data values for age (actual). First of all we have to find out the Quartile Values of 'age' (which will serve as criteria for regrouping) for the 'age'.

To get quartile values :

From menu, choose

**Analyze**

Descriptive Statistics

Frequencies

Select 'age' and transfer it to the Right Box. Click **Statistics** button.

Select Quartiles [√] from Percentile Values given in the left top corner of the Dialog Box .

Click Continue.

Click OK.

**Note down Q1 (25%) and Q3 (75%) values.**

**Say for example, the values are :Q1 = 21 Q3 = 46**

**To recode 'age'**

Choose Transform from the menu :

Recode Into ⟶ different variable

You get Recode - Into different variable-Dialog Box

Highlight 'age' and transfer it to the Input-Output Variable Box where you will find it is asking for New Variable name.

Age ?

Go to output variable and type Name and Label of the new variable.

Name

| V100 | | Change |

**Label**

| Age Regrouped |
|---|

Click Change.

Click Old and New Variable button.

Recode into Different Variable – Old and New Values Dialog Box.

A. Old Values [21]

Lowest through [1]

New Value

Click 'add'. [Lowest through 21 ⟶ 1]

B. Old Value

Range [22] through [46]

New Value [2]

Old ⟶ New

Click [Add] [22 thru 46]

C. Old Value

Range [47] through highest.

New Value [3]

Click Continue.

Click OK.

V1 ⟶ will be recoded and regrouped accordingly.

To see the regrouped data :

From menu, choose

**Analyze**

Descriptive Statistics

Frequencies

Highlight 'age regrouped' 'v100' and transfer it to the Right Box,

Click OK. You will get a frequency table of 'age regrouped'.

**Compute** : It computes values for a variable based on numeric transformations of other variables.

To Compute :
Choose 'Transform' from the 'menu' :
Transform
Compute

Compute Dialog Box

| **Target Variable** | = | **Numeric Expression** |
|---|---|---|
| V200 | | |

Transfer 1st (Statement) Variable from Left Box to Numeric Expression Box and

Click [ + ] button.

Transfer 1st (Statement) Variable from Left Box to Numeric Expression Box and

Click [ **OK** ] button.

Continue till all the statements are transferred to Numeric Expression Box

## References

Baker, L. Therese. (1988).*Doing Social Research,* New York: McGraw Hill.

Black, James A. and Champion, (1976). Dean J. *Methods and Issues in Social Research* New York: John Wiley.

Brace. N. et.al. (2003). *SPSS for Psychologists.* New York : Pal grave Macmillan.

Buckingham, A and Saunders, (2004). P. *The Survey Methods Workbook.* Cambridge :Polity Press.

Craft, J.L. (1990). *Statistics and Data Analysis for Social Workers.* Illinois: F.E. Peacock Publishers

Kerlinger. Fred R. (1964). *Foundations of Behavioral Research,* Delhi : Surjeet Publications.

Kidder, Louise H. (1981). *Research Methods in Social Relations,* New York: Holt.

Monette, Duane R. et. al. (1986). *Applied Social Research: Tool for the Human Services* Chicago: Holt.

Nachmias D and Nachmias C. (1981). *Research Methods in the Social Sciences*, New York: St. Martins press.

O'Leary Z. (2004).*The Essential Guide to Doing Research*. New Delhi : Vistaar Publications

Rubin, Allen & Babbie E. (1989). *Research Methodology for Social Work*, Belmont, California, Wadsworth.

Wilkinson, T.S. and Bhandarkar, P.L. *Methodology and Techniques of Social Research*: Bombay: Himalayan, 1977.

# 7

# Data Analysis

## Introduction

In previous chapter, we discussed about data processing. Once data processing is over the researcher turns his focus of attention on its analysis. In this chapter we will discuss about data analysis; another important stage of the research process.

## The Purpose

The main purpose of data analysis is to examine associations / relationships between the variables. Analysis of data is made with reference to the objectives of the study and research questions if any. It is also designed to test the hypothesis. Analysis of data involves re-categorisation of variables, tabulation, interpretation, explanation and causal inferences. The ultimate goal of data analysis is to draw meaningful inferences and generalisation.

## Setting Up the Analytic Model

Data analysis starts with setting up of analytic model based on objectives and hypotheses of the study. That is, before we begin the analysis of data we have to look back to the objectives and hypotheses of our research study and set up analytic models. These models are diagrammatic presentation of variables and their interrelationships.

**In Chapter II we identified the following objectives and hypotheses :**

**Objectives of the Study**

The specific objectives of the study are :

1. To assess the nature and extent of discrimination on the basis of sex against women at work
2. To explore the factors responsible for sex discrimination against women at work.
3. To determine the extent of disparities in wages/salary (wage differential) of male and female employees for work of similar nature, and
4. To identify the important correlates of wage differential.

**Hypotheses**

1. Personal characteristics (say age) and sex discrimination against women at work are likely to be associated.
2. There may be a direct association between regional development, wage disparities and level of sex discrimination.

The variables in the objectives and hypotheses stated above are age, wage disparities, regional development and sex discrimination. The bivariate relationships between the variables can be diagrammatically presented as follows :

**Bivariate Analytic Models**

**Model 1**

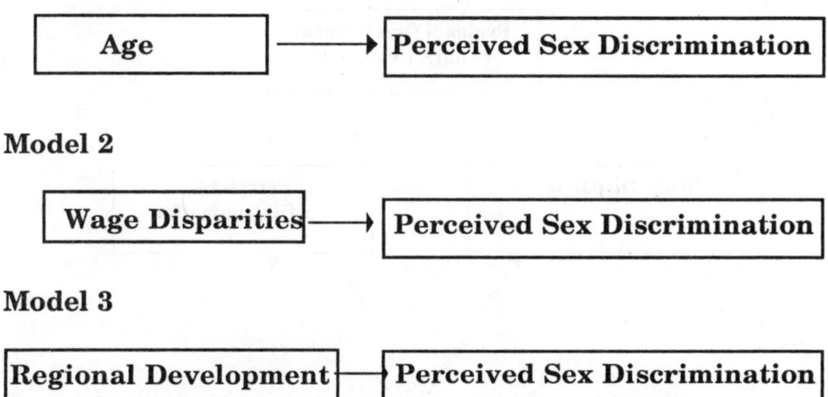


**Figure 7.1 Bivariate Analytic Models**

## Trivariate Analytic Model

For trivariate analysis, variables which show significant bivariate association is selected as third variable (control variables). The original bivariate association is reexamined with each variable as third variable. This can be illustrated as follows :

**Model 1**

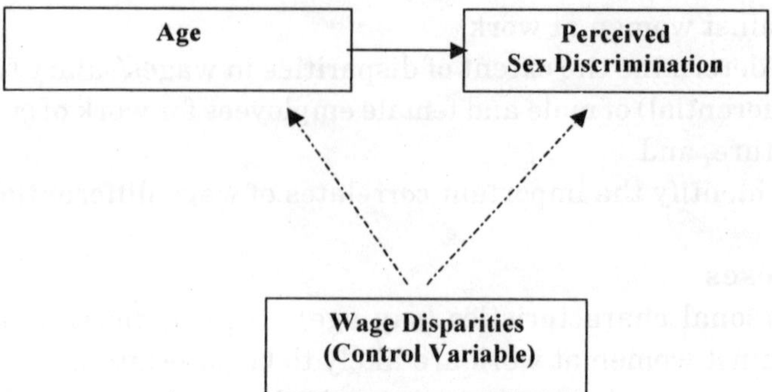


**Model 2**

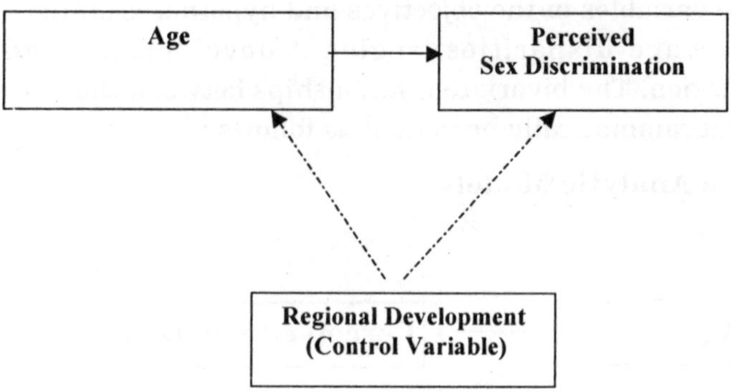


**Model 3**

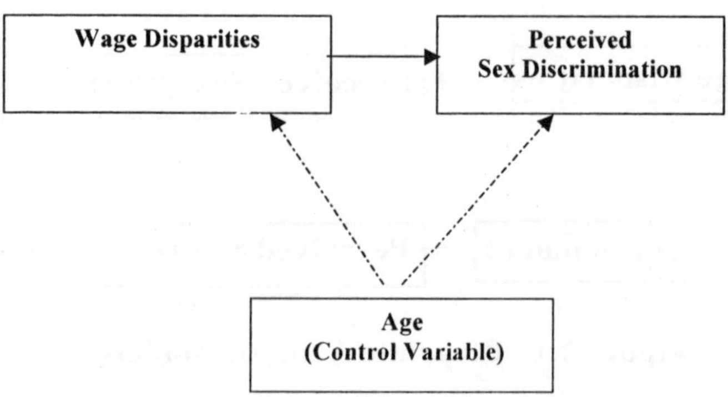

**Model 4**

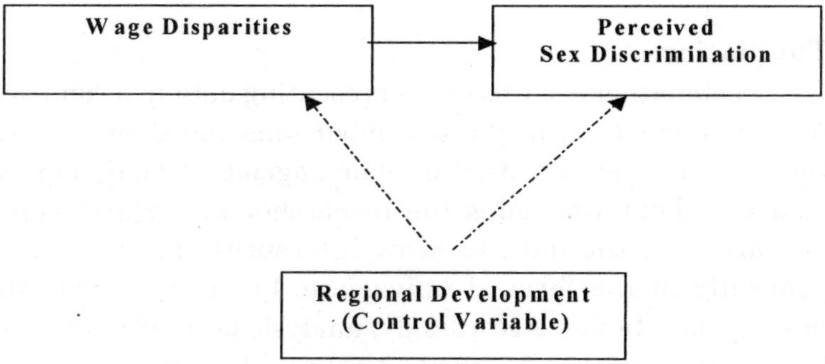


**Model 5**

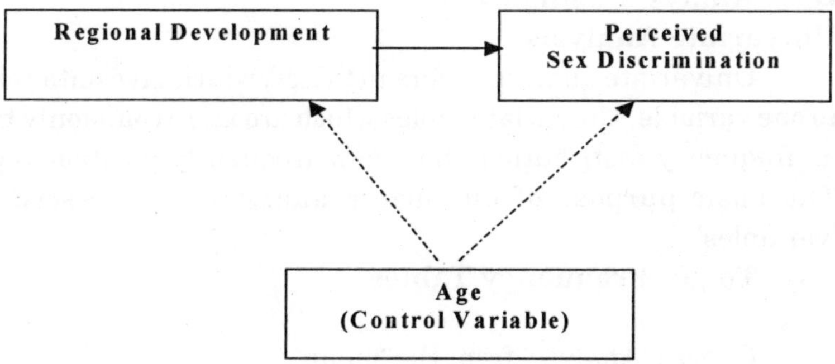


**Model 6**

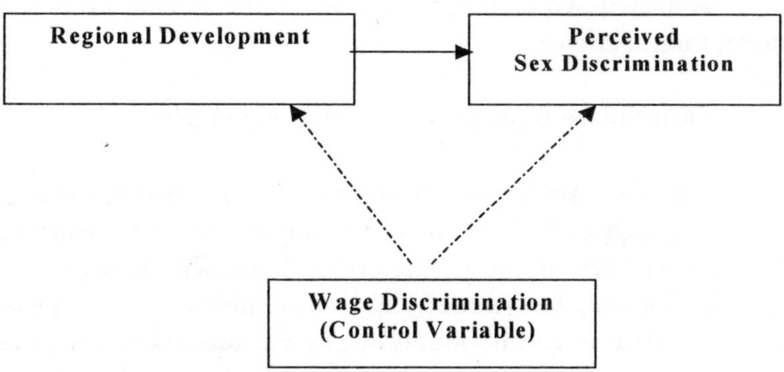


**Figure 7.2 Trivariate Analytic Models**

With the analytic models described above, you can proceed to analyse the data as discussed in the following sections.

**Tabulation**

Tabulation is a process of presenting data in a compact form in such a way as to facilitate comparisons and show the involved relations. In other words, it is an arrangement of data in rows and columns. This also helps the researcher to perform statistical operation on the data to draw inferences. Tabulation can be generally in the form of univariate, bivariate, trivariate and multivariate tables. Accordingly, analysis proceeds in the form of univariate analysis, bivariate analysis, trivariate analysis and multivariate analysis.

**Data Analysis Using SPSS**

**Univariate Analysis**

Univariate analysis refers to tables, which give data relating to one variable. Univariate tables which are more commonly known as frequency distribution show how frequently an item repeats. The basic purpose of univariate analysis is to describe the 'variables'.

**To get Frequency Tables**

Choose 'Analyze' from the 'menu' :

Analyze

A drop down menu will appear on the screen. From the drop down menu, choose :

Descriptive Statistics ——→ Frequencies

Usually, frequency distribution tables are prepared to examine each of the independent and dependent variables. The frequency distributions are generally shown with parentages. The distribution may be symmetrical or asymmetrical. These properties of a distribution can be found out by various measures of central tendencies. However, researcher is required to decide which is most suited for this analysis. To know how much is the variation; the researcher has to calculate measures of dispersion.

**Click 'Frequencies' to get 'Frequencies Dialog** Box'

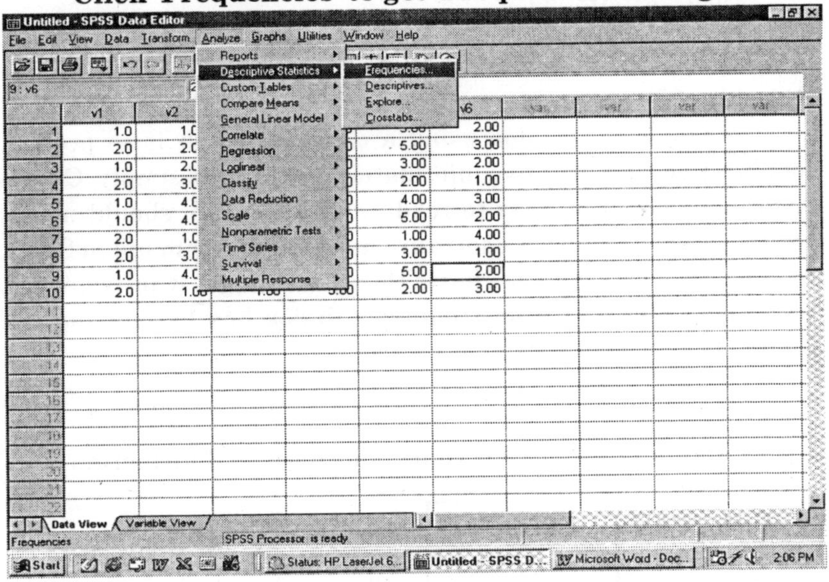

Select the variables from the 'Left Box' for frequency distribution. Move the list of selected variables into the 'Right Box' by **Clicking the** button with the picture of the arrow.

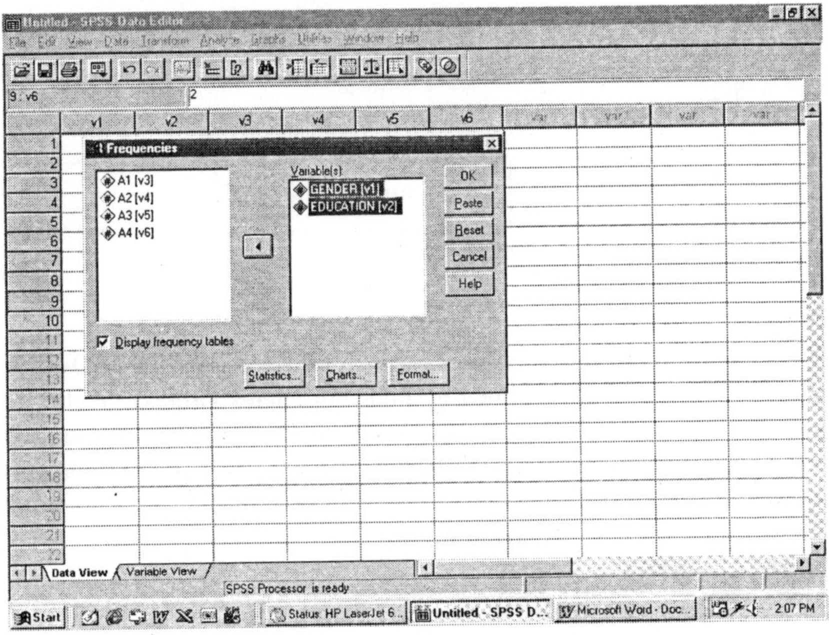

Click **OK**

## Graphical Presentation of Data

A major reason for using a chart or graph is to present comparative , quantitative information quickly and simply. Charts or graphs should be easy to read , and, therefore, should not be very complex. Graphs or charts are an optional command in SPSS. In case you wish to have charts then you can get it in two ways. You can get charts from frequency dialog box by clicking the command "Chart".

To get Charts :

**Click chart** for bar chart, pie-charts and histogram.

Chart

Frequencies : Chart Dialog Box

Chart Type | Continue

☐ Bar Chart

☐ Pie Chart

☐ Histogram | With normal Curve

Click **OK**

Now **click** the **OK** button, it automatically opens an Output – SPSS Viewer Window showing the Frequencies Tables and charts.

Alternatively, you can select 'Graphs' from the menu in that you will see types of charts. Select the 'chart' you wish to have and then the variable.

To obtain Graphs from menu:

Choose 'Graphs' from the 'menu' and click :

A drop down menu will appear on the screen. From the drop down menu, choose :

Pie..... → Pie Dialog Box | Select Define
↓
Transfer the variables

Now **click** the **OK** button, it automatically opens an Output – SPSS Viewer Window showing the charts .

**SPSS Output**

**Statistics**

| | | *Age* | *Wage Disparities* | *Regional Develop-ment* | *Perceived Discrimi-nation* |
|---|---|---|---|---|---|
| N | Valid | 400 | 400 | 400 | 400 |
| | Missing | 0 | 0 | 0 | 0 |
| Mean | | 38.7100 | 123.2500 | 21.5725 | 8.8125 |
| Std. Error of Mean | | 7.31000 | .04428 | .03729 | .03195 |
| Median | | 1.0000 | 3.0000 | 1.0000 | 9.0000 |
| Mode | | 1.00 | 3.00 | 1.00 | 9.00 |
| Std. Deviation | | .079676 | .88570 | .74574 | .63903 |
| Variance | | .69348 | .78446 | .55613 | .40836 |
| Range | | 2.00 | 2.00 | 2.00 | 2.00 |
| Minimum | | 1.00 | 1.00 | 1.00 | 8.00 |
| Maximum | | 3.00 | 3.00 | 3.00 | 10.00 |
| Percentitles | 25 | 38.0000 | 115.0000 | 13.0000 | 8.0000 |
| | 50 | 39.0000 | 126.0000 | 23.0000 | 9.0000 |
| | 75 | 59.0000 | 167.0000 | 37.0000 | 9.0000 |

**Frequency Table**

**AGE**

| | | Frequency | Percent | Valid Percent | Cumulative Percent |
|---|---|---|---|---|---|
| Valid | Young | 222 | 55.5 | 55.5 | 55.5 |
| | Middle Aged | 97 | 24.3 | 24.3 | 79.8 |
| | Old | 81 | 20.3 | 20.3 | 100.0 |
| | Total | 400 | 100.0 | 100.0 | |

**WAGE DISPARITIES**

| | | Frequency | Percent | Valid Percent | Cumulative Percent |
|---|---|---|---|---|---|
| Valid | Low | 119 | 29.8 | 29.8 | 29.8 |
| | Medium | 62 | 15.5 | 15.5 | 45.3 |
| | High | 219 | 54.8 | 54.8 | 100.0 |
| | Total | 400 | 100.0 | 100.0 | |

**PERCEIVED DISCRIMINATION**

| | | Frequency | Percent | Valid Percent | Cumulative Percent |
|---|---|---|---|---|---|
| Valid | Low | 126 | 31.5 | 31.5 | 31.5 |
| | Medium | 223 | 55.8 | 55.8 | 87.3 |
| | High | 51 | 12.8 | 12.8 | 100.0 |
| | Total | 400 | 100.0 | 100.0 | |

The format of SPSS outputs needs some modifications. There are a number of conventions relating to the format of tables. Keeping these conventions in mind the SPSS outputs of hypothetical data are presented in tabular forms. Tables 7.1, 7.2 and 7.3 present two independent variables and one dependent variable.

**TABLE 7.1**
**AGE OF THE RESPONDENTS**

| *Age (In years)* | *Distribution of Respondents* | |
|---|---|---|
| | *Frequencies* | *Percentage* |
| Young (18-38) | 222 | 55.5 |
| Middle (39-58) | 97 | 24.3 |
| Old (59-78) | 81 | 20.3 |
| Total | 400 | 100.0 |

**TABLE 7.2**
**WAGE DISPARITIES**

| *Wage Disparities* | *Distribution of Respondents* | |
|---|---|---|
| | *Frequencies* | *Percentage* |
| High | 119 | 29.8 |
| Medium | 62 | 15.5 |
| Low | 219 | 54.8 |
| Total | 400 | 100.0 |

**TABLE 7.3**
**RESPONDENTS BY REGIONAL DEVELOPMENT**

| *Regional Development* | *Distribution of Respondents* | |
|---|---|---|
| | *Frequencies* | *Percentages* |
| High | 233 | 58.3 |
| Medium | 105 | 26.3 |
| Low | 62 | 15.5 |
| Total | 400 | 100.0 |

**TABLE 7.4**
**PERCEIVED DISCRIMINATION**

| *Perceived Discrimination* | *Distribution of Respondents* | |
|---|---|---|
| | *Frequencies* | *Percentages* |
| Low | 126 | 31.5 |
| Medium | 223 | 55.8 |
| High | 51 | 12.8 |
| Total | 400 | 100.0 |

A frequency distribution of a single variable is the frequency of observation in each category of a variable. For example, an examination of the frequency distribution in Table 7.1 would provide a description of the number of respondents in different age groups. The tables have four rows, the first three being the categories of variables, which appear in the left hand columns and the right hand columns show the number of observation in each category. The last rows are the totals of all frequencies appearing in tables.

To analyse the data it is necessary to convert the frequencies into figures that can be interpreted meaningfully. Frequencies expressed in comparable numbers are called proportions or percentages. A proportion is obtained by dividing the frequency of a category by the total number of responses in the distribution. Proportions when multiplied by 100 become a percentage. For example, the relative weight of the category 'Young' in Table 7.1 can be expressed by the proportion 222/400=.555 or by the percentage 222/400x100=55.5 per cent. These figures indicate that about 56 out of every 100 respondents in the group are 'young'. Proportions and percentages permit the comparison of two or more frequency distributions.

Let us consider the frequency distribution (Tables 7.2, 7.3 and 7.4) which describes the wage disparities, regional development and perceived discrimination of respondents.

While distribution of respondents by 'wage disparities' displayed in Table 7.2 clearly shows the predominance of respondents having 'low' wage disparities whereas, distribution of respondents by 'regional development' in Table 7.3 indicates the predominance of respondents from 'high' regional development. Table 7.4 presents distribution 0f respondents by levels of perceived discrimination. It clearly shows that comparatively larger number of respondents perceived 'high' sex discrimination than those who perceived 'low' sex discrimination.

In case of nominal variables categories can be listed in any arbitrary order. Thus, the variable "Religion" may be described with the category 'Hindu' or the category 'Christian' listed first. However, the categories of ordinal, interval and ratio variables are arranged in order.

The sample out put charts of SPSS is shown below in Figure 7.3.

AGE

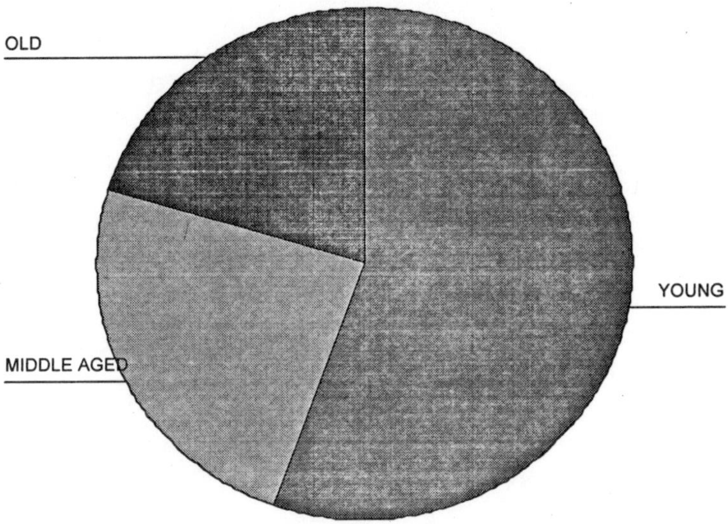


WAGE DISPARITIES

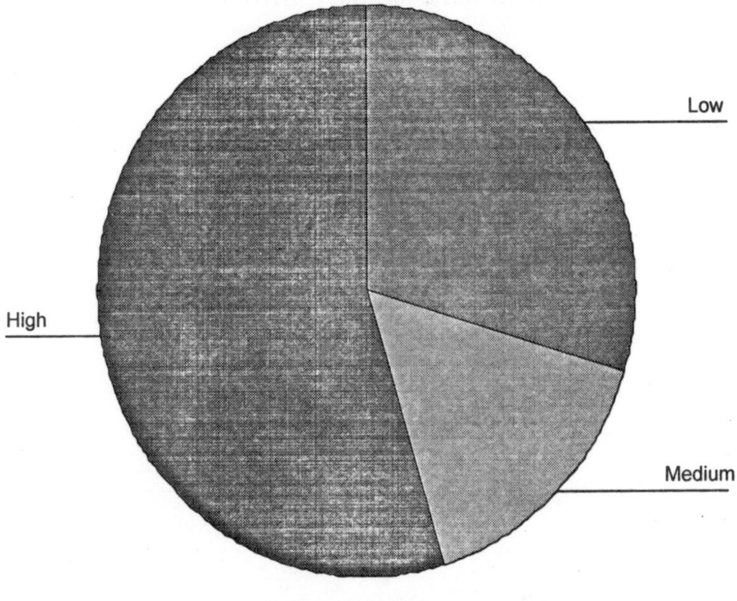

REGIONAL DEVELOPMENT

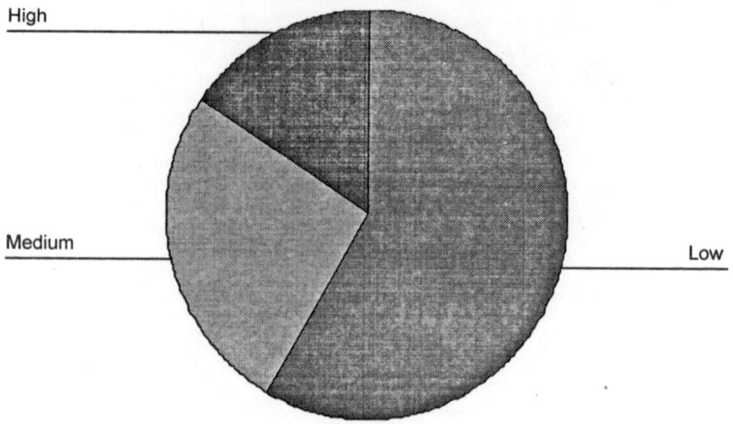


PERCEIVED DISCRIMINATION

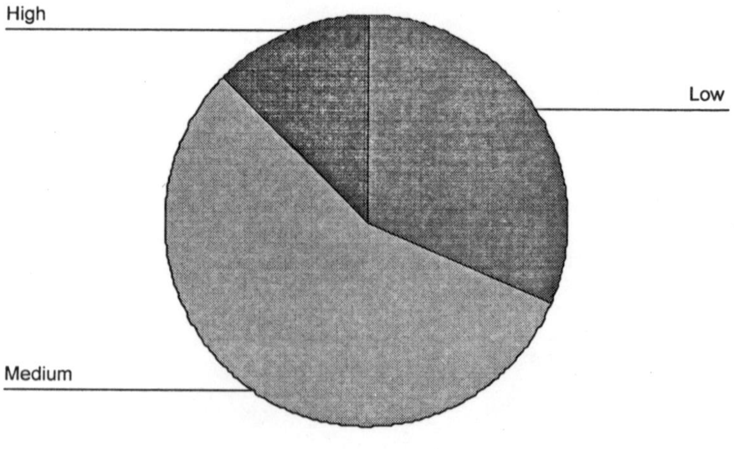

**Bar Chart**

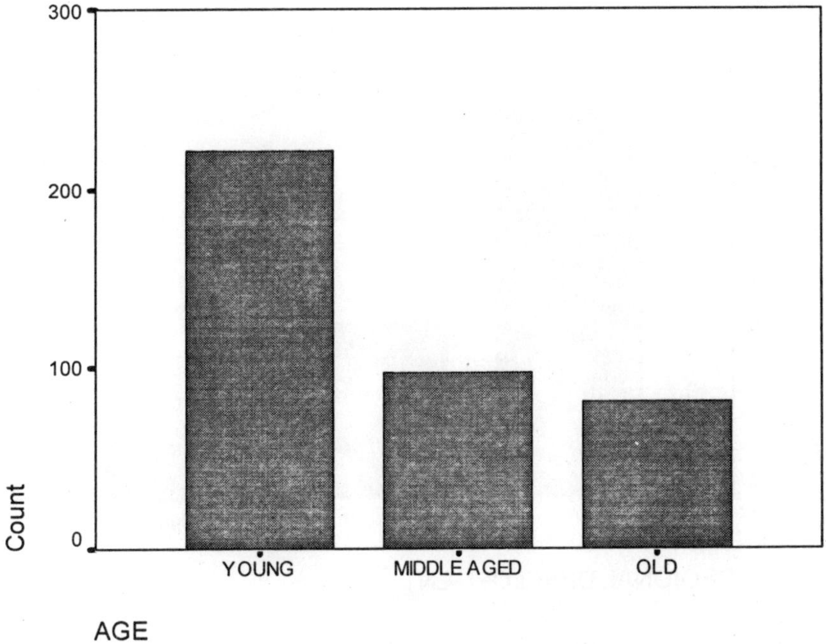
300
200
100
0
Count
YOUNG
MIDDLE AGED
OLD
AGE

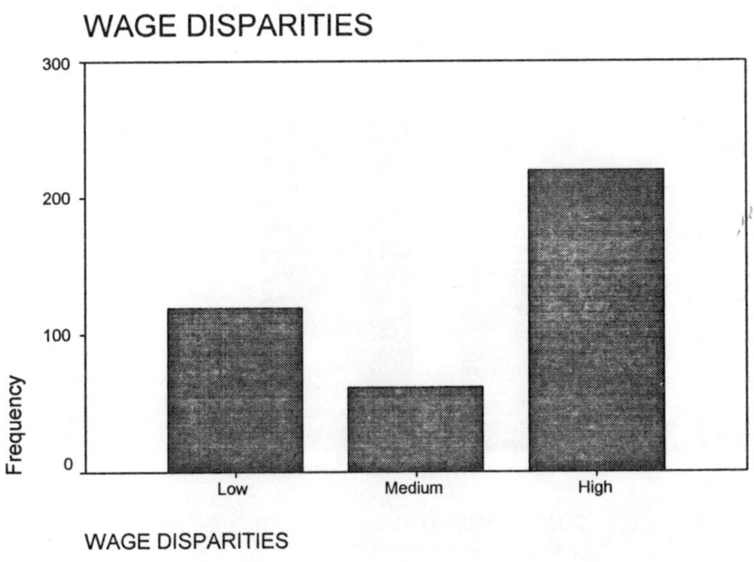
WAGE DISPARITIES
300
200
100
0
Frequency
Low
Medium
High
WAGE DISPARITIES

REGIONAL DEVELOPMENT

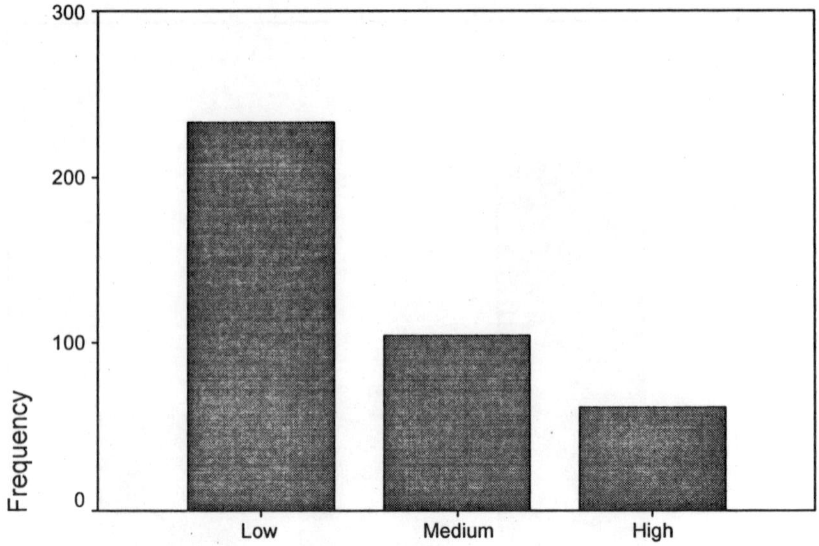


REGIONAL DEVELOPMENT

PERCEIVED DISCRIMINATION

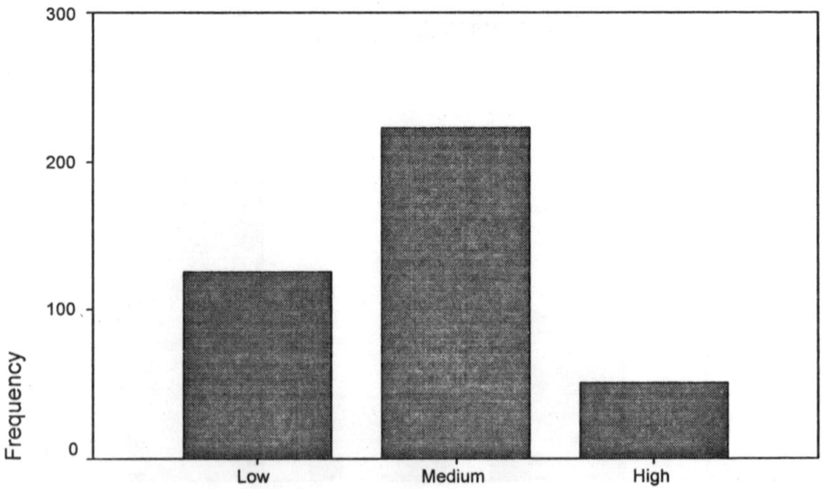


PERCEIVED DISCRIMINATION

**Histogram**

AGE

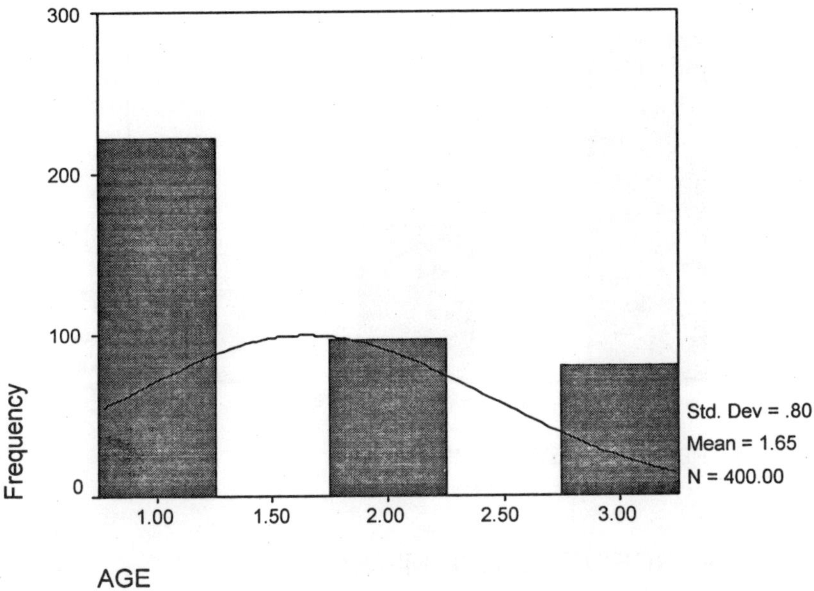


WAGE DISPARITIES

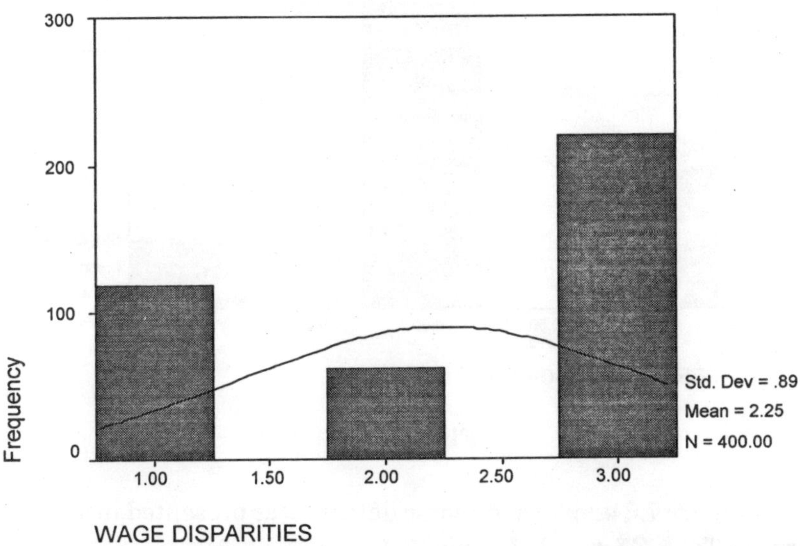

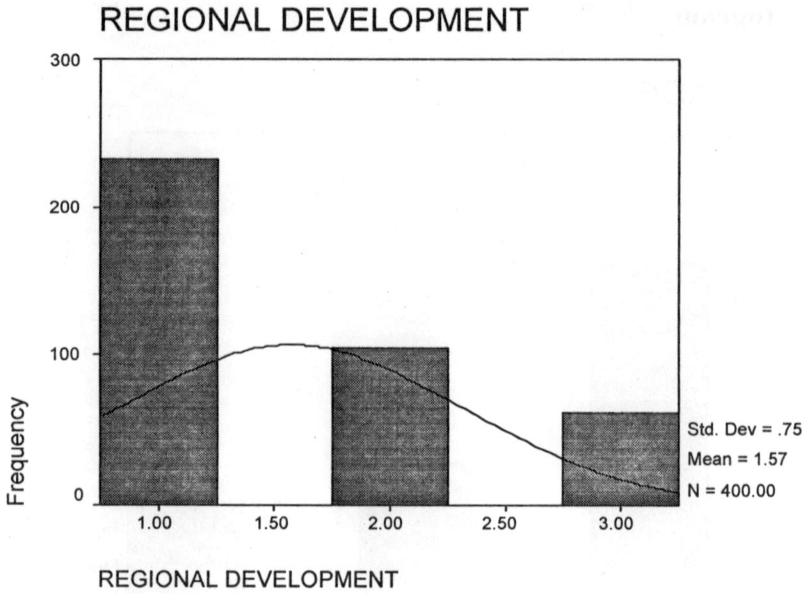


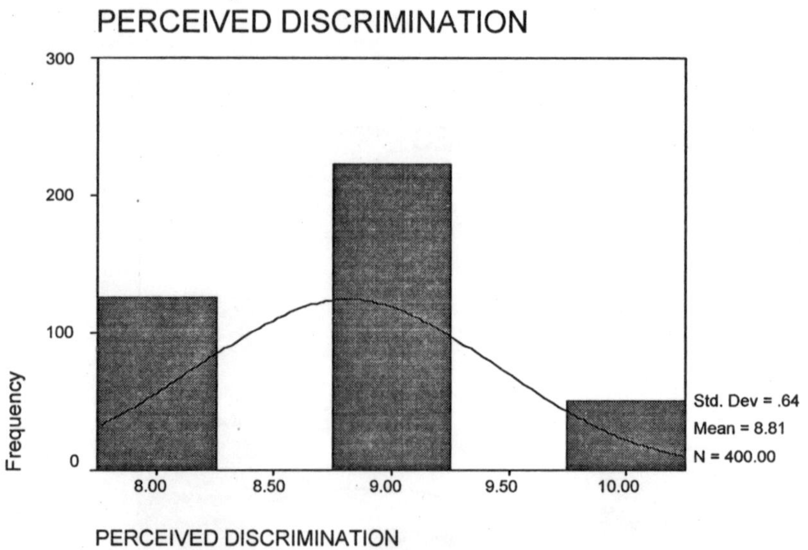


**Figure 7.3**

Figure 7.3 displays the same data as was presented in tabular form in Tables 7.1, 7.2, 7.3, and 7.4.

**Bivariate Analysis**

If you are interested in knowing the associations/relationships between the variables you have to cross tabulate the data pertaining to the variables. A bivariate table/cross table presents data of two variables.

**To obtain crosstables:**

• **From menu, choose :**

**Analyse**

↓

**Descriptive Statistics** ⟶ Frequencies<br>Descriptives<br>**Crosstab**

Click **Crosstab.**

**You get Crosstab Dialog Box**

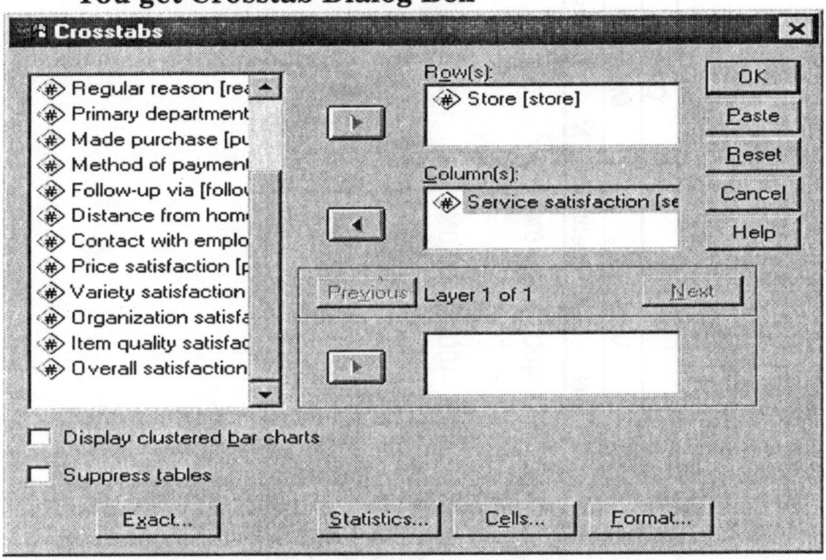


Highlight the variable (say 'age') and transfer it to the **ROW** Box.

Highlight another variable (say 'perceived sex discrimination') and transfer it to the **COLUMN** Box.

- Click **Cell** button.
- Select **Row ( percentage)** from the Dialog Box .
- Click **Continue.**
- Click **OK.**

**A sample output of a Crosstable is shown below:**

**Crosstabs**

**Case Processing Summary**

| | Cases | | | | | |
|---|---|---|---|---|---|---|
| | Valid | | Missing | | Total | |
| | N | Percent | N | Percent | N | Percent |
| AGE * PERCEIVED DISCRIMINATION | 400 | 100.0% | 0 | .0% | 400 | 100.0% |
| WAGE DISPARITIE * PERCEIVED DISCRIMINATION | 400 | 100.0% | 0 | .0% | 400 | 100.0% |
| REGIONAL DEVELOPMENT * PERCEIVED DISCRIMINATION | 400 | 100.0% | 0 | .0% | 400 | 100.0% |

**AGE * PERCEIVED DISCRIMINATION Crosstabulation**

| | | | PERCEIVED DISCRIMINATION | | | Total |
|---|---|---|---|---|---|---|
| | | | Low | Medium | High | |
| AGE | YOUNG | Count | 80 | 106 | 36 | 222 |
| | | % within AGE | 36.0% | 47.7% | 16.2% | 100.0% |
| | MIDDLE AGED | Count | 33 | 54 | 10 | 97 |
| | | % within AGE | 34.0% | 55.7% | 10.3% | 100.0% |
| | OLD | Count | 13 | 63 | 5 | 81 |
| | | % within AGE | 16.0% | 77.8% | 6.2% | 100.0% |
| Total | | Count | 126 | 223 | 51 | 400 |
| | | % within AGE | 31.5% | 55.8% | 12.8% | 100.0% |

**WAGE DISPARITIES * PERCEIVED DISCRIMINATION Crosstabulation**

| | | | PERCEIVED DISCRIMINATION | | | Total |
|---|---|---|---|---|---|---|
| | | | Low | Medium | High | |
| WAGE DISPARITIES | Low | Count | 69 | 33 | 17 | 119 |
| | | % within WAGE DISPARITIES | 58.0% | 27.7% | 14.3% | 100.0% |
| | Medium | Count | 24 | 34 | 4 | 62 |
| | | % within WAGE DISPARITIES | 38.7% | 54.8% | 6.5% | 100.0% |
| | High | Count | 33 | 156 | 30 | 219 |
| | | % within WAGE DISPARITIES | 15.1% | 71.2% | 13.7% | 100.0% |
| Total | | Count | 126 | 223 | 51 | 400 |
| | | % within WAGE DISPARITIES | 31.5% | 55.8% | 12.8% | 100.0% |

**The Principle of Covariation**

Before we analyse and interpret the data presented above we have to understand the phenomenon 'covariation'. Covariation simply means two variables go together. In other words we can say that two variables covary because specific categories of one variable go with specific categories of the other variable.

The phenomenon of covariation is demonstrated in Tables 7.5, 7.6, and 7.7 as shown below. These tables summarise hypothetical data on two variables: 'social class' and 'perceived sex discrimination'.

**TABLE 7.5**
**SOCIAL CLASS AND PERCEIVED SEX DISCRIMINATION**
(Perfect Association)

| *Social Class* | *Perceived Sex Discrimination* | | | *TOTAL* |
|---|---|---|---|---|
| | *High* | *Moderate* | *Low* | |
| Upper | 0 | 0 | 100 | 100 |
| Middle | 0 | 100 | 0 | 100 |
| Lower | 100 | 0 | 0 | 100 |
| Total | 100 | 100 | 100 | 300 |

**TABLE 7.6**
**SOCIAL CLASS AND PERCEIVED SEX DISCRIMINATION**
( Moderate Association )

| *Social Class* | *Perceived Sex Discrimination* | | | *TOTAL* |
|---|---|---|---|---|
| | *High* | *Medium* | *Low* | |
| Upper | 0 | 20 | 80 | 100 |
| Middle | 30 | 70 | 0 | 100 |
| Lower | 70 | 10 | 20 | 100 |
| Total | 100 | 100 | 100 | 300 |

**TABLE 7.7**
**SOCIAL CLASS AND PERCEIVED SEX DISCRIMINATION**
( Near Zero Association)

| *Social Class* | *Perceived Sex Discrimination* | | | *TOTAL* |
|---|---|---|---|---|
| | *High* | *Medium* | *Low* | |
| Upper | 35 | 35 | 30 | 100 |
| Middle | 25 | 25 | 50 | 100 |
| Lower | 40 | 40 | 20 | 100 |
| Total | 100 | 100 | 100 | 300 |

Table 7.5 illustrates a pattern of perfect association of variables. It is observed that all upper social class respondents perceived low sex discrimination. All respondents belonging to middle social class perceived moderate sex discrimination and all respondents belonging to lower social class perceived high sex discrimination. The two variables co-vary because specific categories of the variable "social class" go with specific categories of the variable "perceived low sex discrimination".

The same pattern recurs in Table 7.6 , but to a lesser extent because not all members of a given social class belong to the same level of perceived low sex discrimination. Yet it can still be said that most respondents of a particular social class perceived a particular level of sex discrimination.

When variables are not associated , it is said that they are independent of each other, that is , that they do not "go together". Table 7.7 illustrates this point. There is no clear pattern for any social class in the table. Upper class respondents can perceive high, moderate, or low sex discrimination , because they are more or less equally distributed among the levels of sex discrimination; the same goes for the respondents belonging to middle and lower social class. One cannot say anything about a person's level of perception of sex discrimination on the basis of his or her social class.

Tables 7.5, 7.6, and 7.7 are examples of crosstables. Crosstables consist of the categories of two variables and their joint frequencies. Its components are displayed in the crosstables presented in the above tables. Each table has two dimensions , one per variable. The variables are divided into a number of categories, for example, the variable "social class" has been divided into the categories "upper", "middle", and "lower", and the variable "perceived sex discrimination " into "high" "moderate" and "low". "The cells of the table constitute an intersection between two categories. The frequencies in each cell are of those observations that have two characteristics in common. For example , Table 7.7 shows 35 upper caste respondents who perceived low sex discrimination.

### Percentaging Bivariate Tables

A common way of analysing bivariate table and comparing its univariate distributions to assess association is by expressing its frequencies as percentages. Percentaging tables are appropriate whenever the variables are nominal, but the use of percentages is predominant even when the variables being analysed are ordinal or interval.

**TABLE 7.8**
**GENDER AND PERCEIVED SEX DISCRIMINATION**

| *Gender* | *Perceived Sex discrimination* | | | *Total* |
|---|---|---|---|---|
| | *High* | *Moderate* | *Low* | |
| Male | 3 | 5 | 2 | 10 |
| Female | 6 | 1 | 3 | 10 |
| Total | 9 | 6 | 5 | 20 |

### Analysis of Data presented in Crosstables

Keeping the conventions and format in mind the SPSS outputs are presented in Crosstable with row percentages as shown below :

**TABLE 7.9**
**AGE AND PERCEIVED SEX DISCRIMINATION**

| *Age* | *Perceived Sex Discrimination* | | | *Total* |
|---|---|---|---|---|
| | *Low* | *Medium* | *High* | |
| Young (18-21) | 80 (36.0) | 106 (47.7) | 36 (16.2) | 222(100.0) |
| Middle (22-46) | 33(34.0) | 54( 55.7) | 10 ( 10.3) | 97(100.0) |
| Old (47-60) | 13 (16.0) | 63( 77.8) | 5 ( 6.2) | 81(100.0) |
| Total | 126 (31.5) | 223 (55.7) | 51 (12.8) | 400(100.0) |

The Principle of Table Reading

1. Look for the title : The title describes the information that is contained in the table. In Table 7.9 the title tells about differences in perceived sex discrimination between age groups of respondents.
2. Determine in which direction the percentages have been computed. In Table 7.9, the percentages have been computed across the rows.
3. Make comparisons. Comparing the percentage differences in the table is a quick method for assessing the extent of a relationship between the variables. Comparisons are always made in a direction opposite to the one in which the percentages have been computed. If the percentages have been computed across the rows, as in the Table 7.9, then we compare percentages down the column.

Table 7.9 presents data with regard to two variables namely 'age' and the 'level of perceived sex discrimination'. First row presents data with regard to 'young' respondents. The second row presents data about respondents who are in the 'middle age' group last row represents respondents who are 'old'. Similarly, the first column gives data pertaining to respondents who have perceived 'low' discrimination. The second column presents data of respondents who have perceived 'medium' sex discrimination and the last column represents the respondents who perceived 'high' sex discrimination. For example, the first cell (in the left-hand corner) represents 36 respondents who were 'young' and 'perceived high sex discrimination'.

The association between two variables can be explained either by comparing the percentages of respondents column wise in case the percentages are calculated row wise or can also be examined by various statistical techniques depending upon the level of measurement of the data.

In this chapter we will discuss the analysis of data by comparing the percentages of respondents column wise. Bivariate analysis of data by various statistical techniques will be discussed in the next chapter.

It is evident from Table 7.9 that about one-third (31.5 per cent) of the respondents perceived 'low sex discrimination'. Among them comparatively, more younger respondents (36 per cent) perceived low sex discrimination than those respondents who were either in middle age group (34.0 percent ) or old-age group (16 per cent). It may be concluded that there is difference in perceived sex discrimination in different age groups of the respondents.

**TABLE 7.10**
**WAGE DISPARITIES AND PERCEIVED SEX DISCRIMINATION**

| *Wage Disparities* | *Perceived Sex Discrimination* | | | *TOTAL* |
|---|---|---|---|---|
| | *High* | *Medium* | *Low* | |
| Low | 17(14.3) | 33(27.7) | 69(58.0) | 119(100.0) |
| Medium | 4(6.5) | 34(54.8) | 24(38.7) | 62(100.0) |
| High | 30(13.7) | 156(71.2) | 33(15.1) | 219(100.0) |
| Total | 51(12.7) | 223 (55.8 ) | 126 (31.5) | 400 (100.0) |

Table 7.10 shows that comparatively, a larger number of respondents who had 'low' wage disparities (58.0 per cent) have perceived 'low' sex discrimination than those respondents who had 'high' disparities (15.5 per cent).

**TABLE 7.11**
**REGIONAL DEVELOPMENT AND PERCEIVED SEX DISCRIMINATION**

| *Regional Development* | *Perceived Sex Discrimination* | | | *TOTAL* |
|---|---|---|---|---|
| | *High* | *Medium* | *Low* | |
| Low | 36(15.5) | 117(50.2) | 80(34.3) | 233(100.0) |
| Medium | 10(9.5) | 62(59.0) | 33(31.5) | 105(100.0) |
| High | 5(8.0) | 44(71.0) | 13(21.0) | 62(100.0) |
| Total | 51(12.7) | 223 (55.8 ) | 126 (31.5) | 400 (100.0) |

Table 7.11 shows that comparatively, a larger number of respondents from 'low' regional development have perceived 'high' sex discrimination than respondents from 'high' regional development.

## Graphical Presentation of Data in Crosstables

Data in crosstables are presented through interactive charts. The sample out put of interactive pie diagrams produced by SPSS is shown below in Figure 7.4.

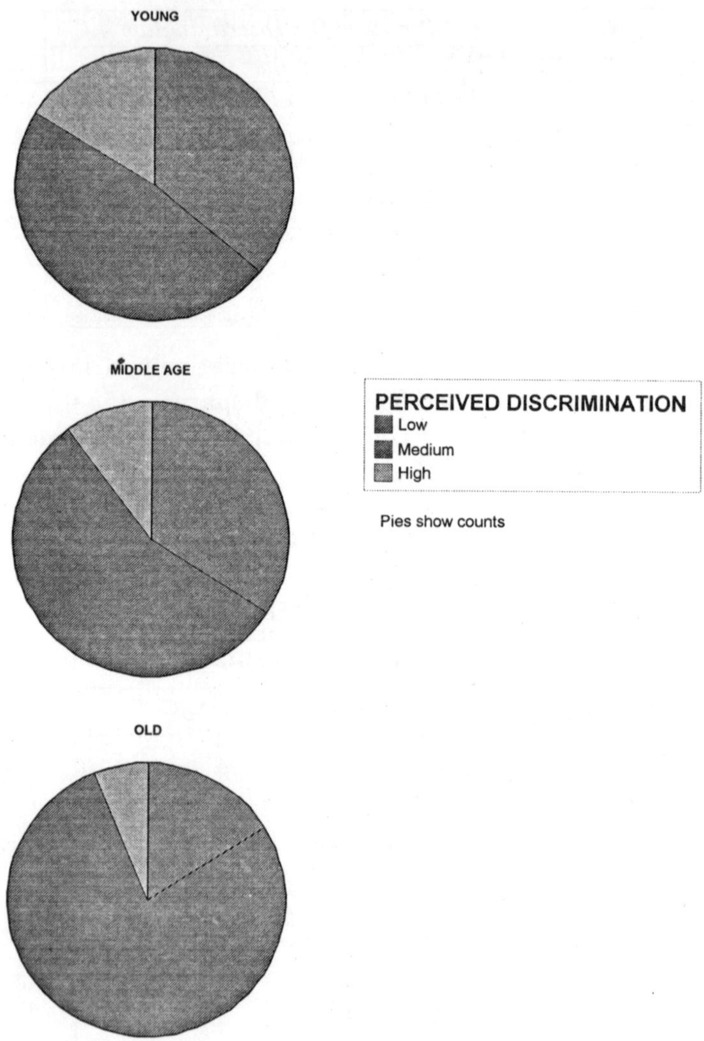

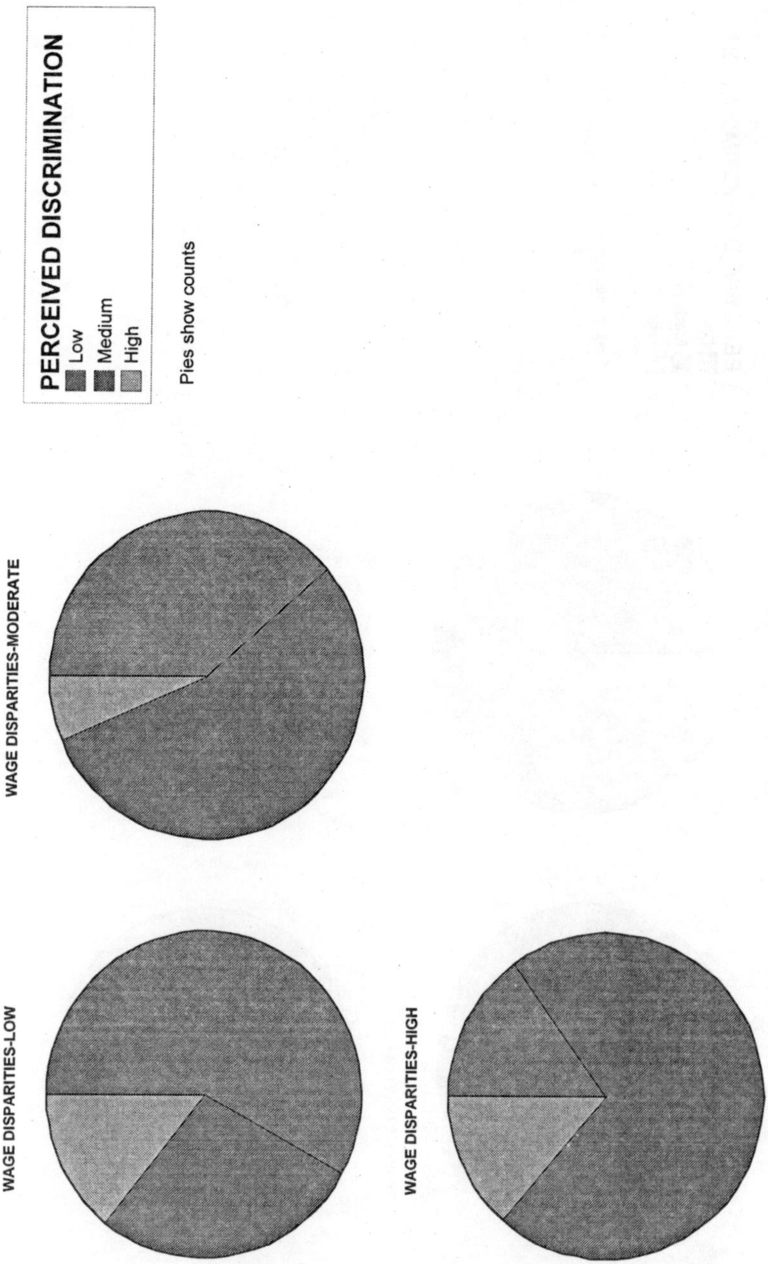
PERCEIVED DISCRIMINATION
Low
Medium
High
Pies show counts
WAGE DISPARITIES-MODERATE
WAGE DISPARITIES-LOW
WAGE DISPARITIES-HIGH

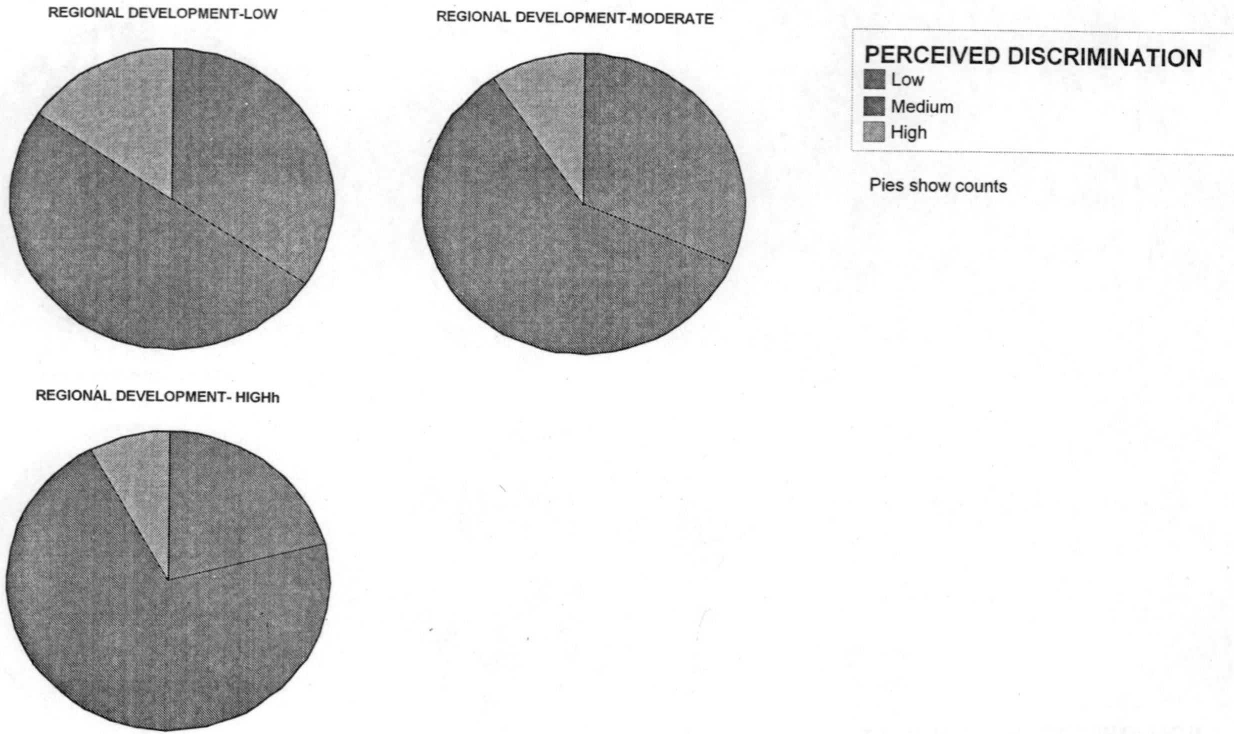


**Figure 7.4 : Pie Charts Showing association between two Variables**

**Trivariate Analysis**

In the preceding sections we discussed bivariate analysis of data. This section deals with the analysis of association between more than two variables. It plays a very significant role in drawing conclusions. Bivariate analysis of data is followed by trivariate analysis of data for cause- effect analysis. The purpose of trivariate analysis is to substantiate the findings of bivariate analysis and to examine if there is cause –effect relationship between the variables. The bivariate analysis establishes association and its direction. To draw the causal inference one has to reexamine the bivariate associations by controlling the effect of other variables into the analysis.

While analyzing bivariate association between 'wage disparities' and 'perceived sex discrimination' ; we found that the variables are positively associated. That is higher the wage disparities higher the 'perceived sex discrimination'.

If we wish to interpret the result at this juncture we would say that there is a relationship between the variables and that as 'wage disparities' increases/decreases the level of perception of sex discrimination will increase/decrease. However, it is also possible that increase/decrease in the level of perceived sex discrimination is not due to 'wage disparities ' but rather to 'regional development'. That is respondents from highly developed region generally perceive low sex discrimination just because they get higher wages since 'regional development' adversely affect 'wage disparities'. In other words, the association between 'wage disparities' and 'perception of sex discrimination' is due to the fact that the both the variables 'wage disparities' and 'perception of sex discrimination' are associated with a third variable, 'regional development'.

Bivariate association may be observed because of two reasons: it may be observed just due to chance, or it may exist due to a third variable which is yet to be revealed. Above all, the change in the dependent variable may be explained by more than one single independent variable. In both the cases, reexamination of the bivariate association by controlling the effect of third variable serves the purpose of clarifying and elaborating the original association.

Trivariate analyses serve three important functions in social research ; control, elaboration and prediction. Firstly, whenever the experimental control is not possible, trivariate analysis is used to examine the bivariate association to see if the association is due to the third variable. Secondly, bivariate association is clarified by introducing a third variable. Finally, trivariate analysis helps to identify more independent variables to account for the variation in the dependent variable.

### Variable as a Control

If the two variables are associated it is not necessary that there is cause and effect relationship between the two variables. It is essential that the effects of other variables are ruled out as alternative explanation of the association.

In the example cited above we have said that both the variables ; 'wage disparities' and 'perception of sex discrimination' may be associated with a third variable, 'regional development'. As such, it is possible that the joint association leads to a statistical association that has no causal significance. The original bivariate association between 'wage disparities' and 'perception of sex discrimination' is called spurious.

Therefore, it is mandatory for a researcher to reveal such variables and substantiate the bivariate association. It is the basic principle of all research studies and is achieved by a process called 'control'.

In experimental research designs the subjects are divided into two groups : experimental group and control group, by using the process of randomization. This assures that all the extraneous variables are controlled and the groups differ only with regard to their exposure to the independent variable. However, it is rather difficult to manipulate groups before the study in quasi-experimental research designs. As such, statistical techniques are used as method of control in quasi-experimental and survey research designs. The statistical techniques are used during data analysis. There are two methods of statistical control : (1) crosstabulation, and (2) partial correlation. In the first method data are crosstabulated and subgroups are compared. In the second method – partial correlation - a statistical procedure is used to nullify the effects of extraneous variables.

**Cross Tabulation as a Method of Control**

In this method the sample is divided into subgroups according to the categories of the controlled variable. The variables which show an association with independent and dependent variables are selected as control variables. The original bivariate association is reexamined within each subgroup.

There are three possibilities :

(1) the original bivariate association is not affected by the third variable,

(2) the original bivariate association is effected by the third variable and the association is disappeared, and

(3) the original bivariate association is partially affected.

While, when a third variable completely accounts for the bivariate association between the independent and dependent variable the association is referred as ***spurious*** whereas if a third variable does not accounts for the bivariate association between the independent and dependent variable the association is referred as ***non-spurious***.

To know if there is a third variable which is affecting the bivariate relationships between two variables, you need to reexamine the bivariate relationship by controlling the effects of a third variable. Let us reexamine Tables 7.5, 7.6 and 7.7. Data show that all the three independent variables, namely, 'age', 'wage disparities' and 'regional development' are associated with the dependent variable- perceived sex discrimination. To know whether there is effect of a third variable on the bivariate relationships you need to prepare the following partial tables:

(1) Age and Perceived Sex Discrimination-controlling the effect of Wage Disparities.

(2) Age and Perceived Sex Discrimination-controlling the effect of Regional Development.

(3) Wage Disparities and Perceived Sex Discrimination-controlling the effect of Age.

(4) Wage Disparities and Perceived Sex Discrimination-controlling the effect of Regional Development.

(5) Regional Development and Perceived Sex Discrimination-controlling the effect of Age.

(6) Regional Development and Perceived Sex Discrimination-controlling the effect of Wage Disparities.

We can generate these tables through SPSS as described below:

A trivariate table/partial table presents data of three variables.

**To obtain partial tables (trivariate tables):**

- **From menu, choose :**

**Analyse**

↓

**Descriptive Statistics** ⟶ **Frequencies**
**Descriptives**
**Crosstab**

**Click Crosstab.**
**You get Crosstab Dialog Box**

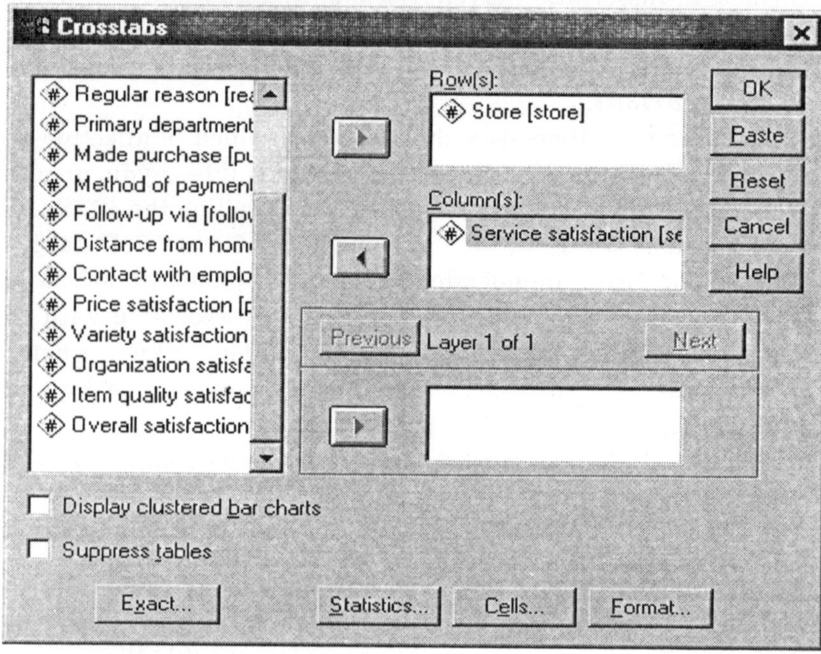


Highlight the variable (say 'age') and transfer it to the ROW Box.

Highlight another variable (say 'perceived sex discrimination') and transfer it to the COLUMN Box.

Highlight third variable-control variable (say Regional Development) and transfer it to **LAYER BOX** (the Third Box)

**Case Processing Summary**

| | Cases | | | | | |
|---|---|---|---|---|---|---|
| | Valid | | Missing | | Total | |
| | N | Percent | N | Percent | N | Percent |
| AGE * PERCEIVED DISCRIMINATION * WAGE DISPARITIE | 400 | 100.0% | 0 | .0% | 400 | 100.0% |
| AGE * PERCEIVED DISCRIMINATION * REGIONAL DEVELOPMENT | 400 | 100.0% | 0 | .0% | 400 | 100.0% |

**AGE * PERCEIVED DISCRIMINATION * WAGE DISPARITIES Crosstabulation**

| WAGE DISPARITIES | | | | PERCEIVED DISCRIMINATION | | | Total |
|---|---|---|---|---|---|---|---|
| | | | | Low | Medium | High | |
| Low | AGE | YOUNG | Count | 48 | 19 | 10 | 77 |
| | | | % within AGE | 62.3% | 24.7% | 13.0% | 100.0% |
| | | MIDDLE AGED | Count | 15 | 6 | 5 | 26 |
| | | | % within AGE | 57.7% | 23.1% | 19.2% | 100.0% |
| | | OLD | Count | 6 | 8 | 2 | 16 |
| | | | % within AGE | 37.5% | 50.0% | 12.5% | 100.0% |
| | Total | | Count | 69 | 33 | 17 | 119 |
| | | | % within AGE | 58.0% | 27.7% | 14.3% | 100.0% |
| Medium | AGE | YOUNG | Count | 18 | 25 | 3 | 46 |
| | | | % within AGE | 39.1% | 54.3% | 6.5% | 100.0% |
| | | MIDDLE AGED | Count | 4 | 7 | 1 | 12 |
| | | | % within AGE | 33.3% | 58.3% | 8.3% | 100.0% |
| | | OLD | Count | 2 | 2 | | 4 |
| | | | % within AGE | 50.0% | 50.0% | | 100.0% |
| | Total | | Count | 24 | 34 | 4 | 62 |
| | | | % within AGE | 38.7% | 54.8% | 6.5% | 100.0% |
| High | AGE | YOUNG | Count | 14 | 62 | 23 | 99 |
| | | | % within AGE | 14.1% | 62.6% | 23.2% | 100.0% |
| | | MIDDLE AGED | Count | 14 | 41 | 4 | 59 |
| | | | % within AGE | 23.7% | 69.5% | 6.8% | 100.0% |
| | | OLD | Count | 5 | 53 | 3 | 61 |
| | | | % within AGE | 8.2% | 86.9% | 4.9% | 100.0% |
| | Total | | Count | 33 | 156 | 30 | 219 |
| | | | % within AGE | 15.1% | 71.2% | 13.7% | 100.0% |

**AGE * PERCEIVED DISCRIMINATION * REGIONAL DEVELOPMENT Crosstabulation**

| REGIONAL DEVELOPMENT | | | | PERCEIVED DISCRIMINATION | | | Total |
|---|---|---|---|---|---|---|---|
| | | | | Low | Medium | High | |
| Low | AGE | YOUNG | Count | 66 | 69 | 31 | 166 |
| | | | % within AGE | 39.8% | 41.6% | 18.7% | 100.0% |
| | | MIDDLE AGED | Count | 9 | 23 | 5 | 37 |
| | | | % within AGE | 24.3% | 62.2% | 13.5% | 100.0% |
| | | OLD | Count | 5 | 25 | | 30 |
| | | | % within AGE | 16.7% | 83.3% | | 100.0% |
| | Total | | Count | 80 | 117 | 36 | 233 |
| | | | % within AGE | 34.3% | 50.2% | 15.5% | 100.0% |
| Medium | AGE | YOUNG | Count | 13 | 21 | 4 | 38 |
| | | | % within AGE | 34.2% | 55.3% | 10.5% | 100.0% |
| | | MIDDLE AGED | Count | 17 | 22 | 4 | 43 |
| | | | % within AGE | 39.5% | 51.2% | 9.3% | 100.0% |
| | | OLD | Count | 3 | 19 | 2 | 24 |
| | | | % within AGE | 12.5% | 79.2% | 8.3% | 100.0% |
| | Total | | Count | 33 | 62 | 10 | 105 |
| | | | % within AGE | 31.4% | 59.0% | 9.5% | 100.0% |
| High | AGE | YOUNG | Count | 1 | 16 | 1 | 18 |
| | | | % within AGE | 5.6% | 88.9% | 5.6% | 100.0% |
| | | MIDDLE AGED | Count | 7 | 9 | 1 | 17 |
| | | | % within AGE | 41.2% | 52.9% | 5.9% | 100.0% |
| | | OLD | Count | 5 | 19 | 3 | 27 |
| | | | % within AGE | 18.5% | 70.4% | 11.1% | 100.0% |
| | Total | | Count | 13 | 44 | 5 | 62 |
| | | | % within AGE | 21.0% | 71.0% | 8.1% | 100.0% |

**Case Processing Summary**

| | Cases | | | | | |
|---|---|---|---|---|---|---|
| | Valid | | Missing | | Total | |
| | N | Percent | N | Percent | N | Percent |
| WAGE DISPARITIES * PERCEIVED DISCRIMINATION * AGE | 400 | 100.0% | 0 | .0% | 400 | 100.0% |
| WAGE DISPARITIES * PERCEIVED DISCRIMINATION * REGIONAL DEVELOPMENT | 400 | 100.0% | 0 | .0% | 400 | 100.0% |

**WAGE DISPARITIES * PERCEIVED DISCRIMINATION * AGE Crosstabulation**

| AGE | | | | PERCEIVED DISCRIMINATION | | | Total |
|---|---|---|---|---|---|---|---|
| | | | | Low | Medium | High | |
| YOUNG | WAGE DISPARITIES | Low | Count | 48 | 19 | 10 | 77 |
| | | | % within WAGE DISPARITIES | 62.3% | 24.7% | 13.0% | 100.0% |
| | | Medium | Count | 18 | 25 | 3 | 46 |
| | | | % within WAGE DISPARITIES | 39.1% | 54.3% | 6.5% | 100.0% |
| | | High | Count | 14 | 62 | 23 | 99 |
| | | | % within WAGE DISPARITIES | 14.1% | 62.6% | 23.2% | 100.0% |
| | Total | | Count | 80 | 106 | 36 | 222 |
| | | | % within WAGE DISPARITIES | 36.0% | 47.7% | 16.2% | 100.0% |
| MIDDLE AGED | WAGE DISPARITIES | Low | Count | 15 | 6 | 5 | 26 |
| | | | % within WAGE DISPARITIES | 57.7% | 23.1% | 19.2% | 100.0% |
| | | Medium | Count | 4 | 7 | 1 | 12 |
| | | | % within WAGE DISPARITIES | 33.3% | 58.3% | 8.3% | 100.0% |
| | | High | Count | 14 | 41 | 4 | 59 |
| | | | % within WAGE DISPARITIES | 23.7% | 69.5% | 6.8% | 100.0% |
| | Total | | Count | 33 | 54 | 10 | 97 |
| | | | % within WAGE DISPARITIES | 34.0% | 55.7% | 10.3% | 100.0% |

| AGE | | | | PERCEIVED DISCRIMINATION | | | Total |
|---|---|---|---|---|---|---|---|
| | | | | Low | Medium | High | |
| OLD | WAGE DISPARITIES | Low | Count | 6 | 8 | 2 | 16 |
| | | | % within WAGE DISPARITIES | 37.5% | 50.0% | 12.5% | 100.0% |
| | | Medium | Count | 2 | 2 | | 4 |
| | | | % within WAGE DISPARITIES | 50.0% | 50.0% | | 100.0% |
| | | High | Count | 5 | 53 | 3 | 61 |
| | | | % within WAGE DISPARITIES | 8.2% | 86.9% | 4.9% | 100.0% |
| | Total | | Count | 13 | 63 | 5 | 81 |
| | | | % within WAGE DISPARITIES | 16.0% | 77.8% | 6.2% | 100.0% |

**WAGE DISPARITIES * PERCEIVED DISCRIMINATION * REGIONAL DEVELOPMENT Crosstabulation**

| REGIONAL DEVELOPMENT | | | | PERCEIVED DISCRIMINATION | | | Total |
|---|---|---|---|---|---|---|---|
| | | | | Low | Medium | High | |
| Low | WAGE DISPARITIES | Low | Count | 43 | 13 | 8 | 64 |
| | | | % within WAGE DISPARITIES | 67.2% | 20.3% | 12.5% | 100.0% |
| | | Medium | Count | 19 | 20 | 3 | 42 |
| | | | % within WAGE DISPARITIES | 45.2% | 47.6% | 7.1% | 100.0% |
| | | High | Count | 18 | 84 | 25 | 127 |
| | | | % within WAGE DISPARITIES | 14.2% | 66.1% | 19.7% | 100.0% |
| | Total | | Count | 80 | 117 | 36 | 233 |
| | | | % within WAGE DISPARITIES | 34.3% | 50.2% | 15.5% | 100.0% |
| Medium | WAGE DISPARITIES | Low | Count | 25 | 13 | 6 | 44 |
| | | | % within WAGE DISPARITIES | 56.8% | 29.5% | 13.6% | 100.0% |
| | | Medium | Count | 2 | 9 | 1 | 12 |
| | | | % within WAGE DISPARITIES | 16.7% | 75.0% | 8.3% | 100.0% |
| | | High | Count | 6 | 40 | 3 | 49 |
| | | | % within WAGE DISPARITIES | 12.2% | 81,6% | 6.1% | 100.0% |
| | Total | | Count | 33 | 62 | 10 | 105 |
| | | | % within WAGE DISPARITIES | 31.4% | 59.0% | 9.5% | 100.0% |

| REGIONAL DEVELOPMENT | | | | PERCEIVED DISCRIMINATION | | | Total |
|---|---|---|---|---|---|---|---|
| | | | | Low | Medium | High | |
| High | WAGE DISPARITIES | Low | Count | 1 | 7 | 3 | 11 |
| | | | % within WAGE DISPARITIES | 9.1% | 63.6% | 27.3% | 100.0% |
| | | Medium | Count | 3 | 5 | | 8 |
| | | | % within WAGE DISPARITIES | 37.5% | 62.5% | | 100.0% |
| | | High | Count | 9 | 32 | 2 | 43 |
| | | | % within WAGE DISPARITIES | 20.9% | 74.4% | 4.7% | 100.0% |
| | Total | | Count | 13 | 44 | 5 | 62 |
| | | | % within WAGE DISPARITIES | 21.0% | 71.0% | 8.1% | 100.0% |

**Case Processing Summary**

| | Cases | | | | | |
|---|---|---|---|---|---|---|
| | Valid | | Missing | | Total | |
| | N | Percent | N | Percent | N | Percent |
| REGIONAL DEVELOPMENT * PERCEIVED DISCRIMINATION * AGE | 400 | 100.0% | 0 | .0% | 400 | 100.0% |
| REGIONAL DEVELOPMENT * PERCEIVED DISCRIMINATION * WAGE DISPARITIES | 400 | 100.0% | 0 | .0% | 400 | 100.0% |

**REGIONAL DEVELOPMENT * PERCEIVED DISCRIMINATION * AGE Crosstabulation**

| AGE | | | | PERCEIVED DISCRIMINATION | | | Total |
|---|---|---|---|---|---|---|---|
| | | | | Low | Medium | High | |
| YOUNG | REGIONAL DEVELOPMENT | Low | Count | 66 | 69 | 31 | 166 |
| | | | % within REGIONAL DEVELOPMENT | 39.8% | 41.6% | 18.7% | 100.0% |
| | | Medium | Count | 13 | 21 | 4 | 38 |
| | | | % within REGIONAL DEVELOPMENT | 34.2% | 55.3% | 10.5% | 100.0% |
| | | High | Count | 1 | 16 | 1 | 18 |
| | | | % within REGIONAL DEVELOPMENT | 5.6% | 88.9% | 5.6% | 100.0% |
| | Total | | Count | 80 | 106 | 36 | 222 |
| | | | % within REGIONAL DEVELOPMENT | 36.0% | 47.7% | 16.2% | 100.0% |
| MIDDLE AGED | REGIONAL DEVELOPMENT | Low | Count | 9 | 23 | 5 | 37 |
| | | | % within REGIONAL DEVELOPMENT | 24.3% | 62.2% | 13.5% | 100.0% |
| | | Medium | Count | 17 | 22 | 4 | 43 |
| | | | % within REGIONAL DEVELOPMENT | 39.5% | 51.2% | 9.3% | 100.0% |
| | | High | Count | 7 | 9 | 1 | 17 |
| | | | % within REGIONAL DEVELOPMENT | 41.2% | 52.9% | 5.9% | 100.0% |
| | Total | | Count | 33 | 54 | 10 | 97 |
| | | | % within REGIONAL DEVELOPMENT | 34.0% | 55.7% | 10.3% | 100.0% |

| AGE | | | | PERCEIVED DISCRIMINATION | | | Total |
|---|---|---|---|---|---|---|---|
| | | | | Low | Medium | High | |
| OLD | REGIONAL DEVELOPMENT | Low | Count | 5 | 25 | | 30 |
| | | | % within REGIONAL DEVELOPMENT | 16.7% | 83.3% | | 100.0% |
| | | Medium | Count | 3 | 19 | 2 | 24 |
| | | | % within REGIONAL DEVELOPMENT | 12.5% | 79.2% | 8.3% | 100.0% |
| | | High | Count | 5 | 19 | 3 | 27 |
| | | | % within REGIONAL DEVELOPMENT | 18.5% | 70.4% | 11.1% | 100.0% |
| | Total | | Count | 13 | 63 | 5 | 81 |
| | | | % within REGIONAL DEVELOPMENT | 16.0% | 77.8% | 6.2% | 100.0% |

**REGIONAL DEVELOPMENT * PERCEIVED DISCRIMINATION * WAGE DISPARITIES Crosstabulation**

| WAGE DISPARITIES | | | | PERCEIVED DISCRIMINATION | | | Total |
|---|---|---|---|---|---|---|---|
| | | | | Low | Medium | High | |
| Low | REGIONAL DEVELOPMENT | Low | Count | 43 | 13 | 8 | 64 |
| | | | % within REGIONAL DEVELOPMENT | 67.2% | 20.3% | 12.5% | 100.0% |
| | | Medium | Count | 25 | 13 | 6 | 44 |
| | | | % within REGIONAL DEVELOPMENT | 56.8% | 29.5% | 13.6% | 100.0% |
| | | High | Count | 1 | 7 | 3 | 11 |
| | | | % within REGIONAL DEVELOPMENT | 9.1% | 63.6% | 27.3% | 100.0% |
| | Total | | Count | 69 | 33 | 17 | 119 |
| | | | % within REGIONAL DEVELOPMENT | 58.0% | 27.7% | 14.3% | 100.0% |
| Medium | REGIONAL DEVELOPMENT | Low | Count | 19 | 20 | 3 | 42 |
| | | | % within REGIONAL DEVELOPMENT | 45.2% | 47.6% | 7.1% | 100.0% |
| | | Medium | Count | 2 | 9 | 1 | 12 |
| | | | % within REGIONAL DEVELOPMENT | 16.7% | 75.0% | 8.3% | 100.0% |
| | | High | Count | 3 | 5 | | 8 |
| | | | % within REGIONAL DEVELOPMENT | 37.5% | 62.5% | | 100.0% |
| | Total | | Count | 24 | 34 | 4 | 62 |
| | | | % within REGIONAL DEVELOPMENT | 38.7% | 54.8% | 6.5% | 100.0% |

| WAGE DISPARITIES | | | | PERCEIVED DISCRIMINATION | | | Total |
|---|---|---|---|---|---|---|---|
| | | | | Low | Medium | High | |
| High | REGIONAL DEVELOPMENT | Low | Count | 18 | 84 | 25 | 127 |
| | | | % within REGIONAL DEVELOPMENT | 14.2% | 66.1% | 19.7% | 100.0% |
| | | Medium | Count | 6 | 40 | 3 | 49 |
| | | | % within REGIONAL DEVELOPMENT | 12.2% | 81.6% | 6.1% | 100.0% |
| | | High | Count | 9 | 32 | 2 | 43 |
| | | | % within REGIONAL DEVELOPMENT | 20.9% | 74.4% | 4.7% | 100.0% |
| | Total | | Count | 33 | 156 | 30 | 219 |
| | | | % within REGIONAL DEVELOPMENT | 15.1% | 71.2% | 13.7% | 100.0% |

Tables in SPSS outputs need modifications as per the conventions and format of research report. The modified tables are presented below: :

### TABLE 7.12
### AGE AND PERCEIVED SEX DISCRIMINATION (CONTROLLING FOR WAGE DISPARITIES)

| *Wage Disparities* | *Age* | *Perceived Sex Discrimination* | | | *Total* |
|---|---|---|---|---|---|
| | | *Low* | *Moderate* | *High* | |
| Low | Young | 48(62.3) | 19(24.7) | 10(13.0) | 77 (100.0) |
| | Middle Age | 15 (57.7 ) | 6 ( 23.1) | 5 (19.2 ) | 26(100.0) |
| | Old | 6 (37.5 ) | 8 ( 50.0) | 2 ( 12.5) | 16(100.0) |
| | Total | 69 (58.0 ) | 33( 27.7 ) | 17(14.3 ) | 119(100.0) |
| Moderate | Age | Low | Moderate | High | Total |
| | Young | 18 (39.1 ) | 25 ( 54.3) | 3 ( 6.5) | 46(100.0) |
| | Middle Age | 4 (33.3 ) | 7 (58.3 ) | 1 (8.3 ) | 12 (100.0) |
| | Old | 2 ( 50.0) | 2 ( 50.0) | | 4 (100.0) |
| | Total | 24( 38.7 ) | 34( 54.8 ) | 4(6.5 ) | 62 (100.0) |
| High | Age | Low | Moderate | High | Total |
| | Young | 14 ( 14.1) | 62 (62.6 ) | 23 ( 23.2) | 99 (100.0) |
| | Middle Age | 14 (23.7) | 41 (69.5 ) | 4 (6.8 ) | 59 (100.0) |
| | Old | 5 (8.2 ) | 53 ( 86.9) | 3 ( 4.9) | 61 (100.0) |
| | Total | 33(15.1 ) | 156( 71.2 ) | 30( 13.7 ) | 219(100.0 ) |

Analysis of data in Table 7.12 shows that the original bivariate association between 'age' and 'perceived sex discrimination' is affected by the third variable- 'wage disparities'. In other words there is no association between 'age' and 'perceived sex discrimination' when the effect of 'wage disparities' is controlled. The result shows that the original bivariate association is disappeared. That is the original association between the two variables- 'age' and 'perceived sex discrimination'- is completely accounted for by the third variable- 'wage disparities'. Thus it may be concluded that the bivariate association between 'age' and 'perceived sex discrimination' was ***spurious***. It may be inferred that there is no direct association between 'age' and 'perceived sex discrimination'. They are associated indirectly i.e. through 'wage disparities'. The results of the analysis can be diagrammatically shown in Figure 7.5.

**Figure 7.5 : Showing Spurious Association between Independent and Dependent Variable.**

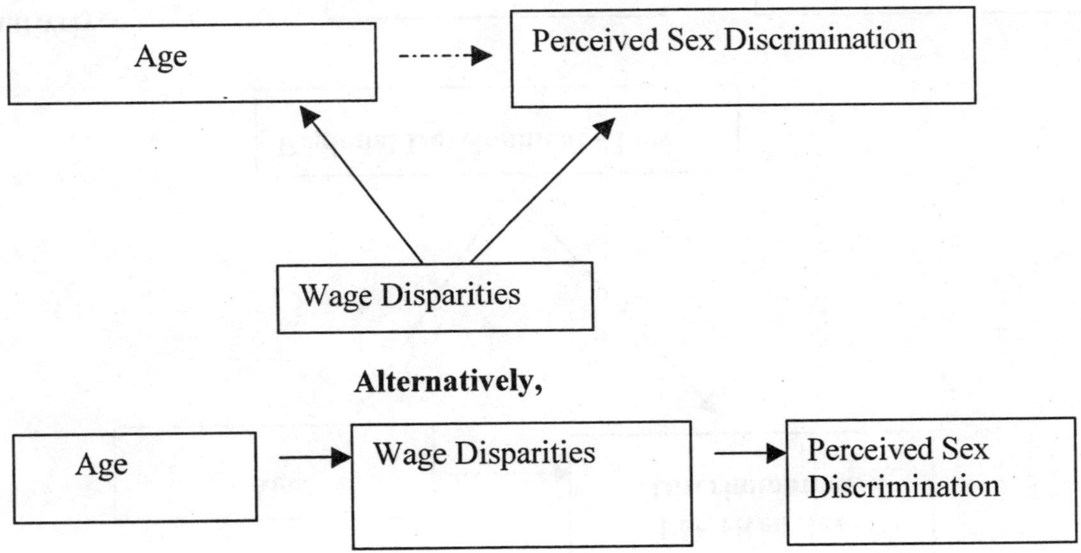

**Figure 5.2 : Showing Conditional Association between age and perceived sex discrimination when effect of regional development is controlled**

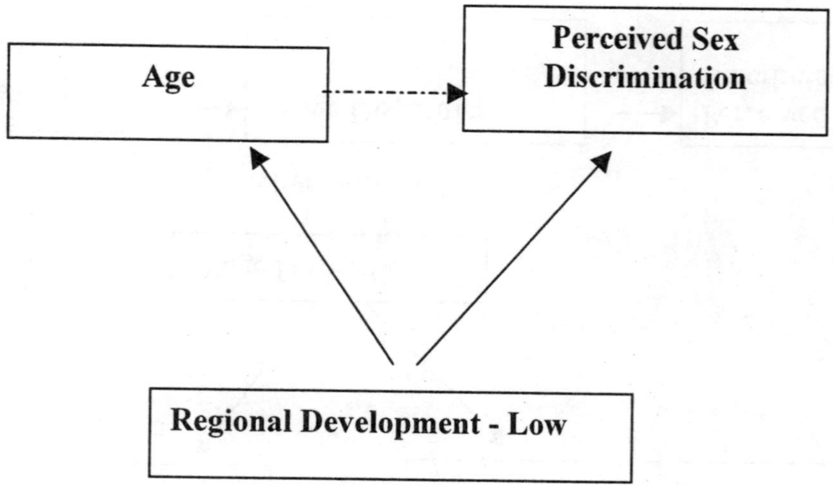


Alternatively,

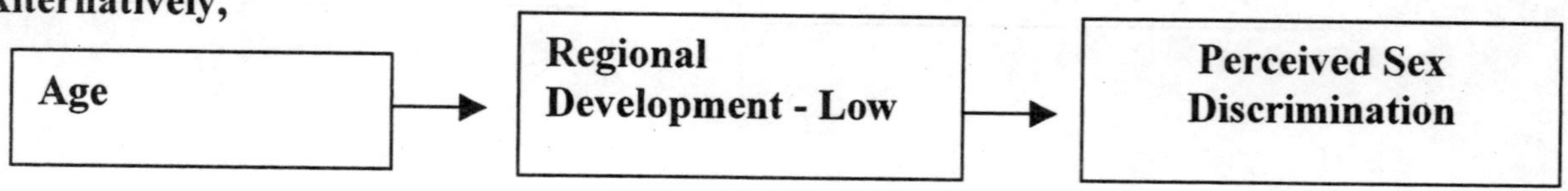

## TABLE 7.13
## AGE AND PERCEIVED SEX DISCRIMINATION (CONTROLLING FOR REGIONAL DEVELOPMENT)

| *Regional Development* | *Age* | *Perceived Sex Discrimination* | | | *Total* |
|---|---|---|---|---|---|
| | | *Low* | *Moderate* | *High* | |
| Low | Young | 66 (39.8 ) | 69 (41.6 ) | 31 (18.7) | 166 (100.0) |
| | Middle Age | 9 (24.3 ) | 23 ( 62.2) | 5 (13.5) | 37 (100.0) |
| | Old | 5 (16.7 ) | 25 (83.3 ) | | 30 (100.0) |
| | Total | 80 ( 34.3) | 117 ( 50.2) | 36 ( 15.5) | 233(100.0) |
| Moderate | Age | Low | Moderate | High | Total |
| | Young | 13 ( 34.2) | 21 (55.3 ) | 4 (10.5) | 38 (100.0) |
| | Middle Age | 17 (39.5 ) | 22 (51.2 ) | 4 (9.3) | 43 (100.0) |
| | Old | 3 ( 12.5) | 19 (79.2 ) | 2 (8.3) | 24 (100.0) |
| | Total | 33 ( 31.4 ) | 62 ( 59.0) | 10 (9.6 ) | 105(100.0) |
| High | Age | Low | Moderate | High | Total |
| | Young | 1 (5.6 ) | 16 (88.9 ) | 1 ( 5.6) | 18 (100.0) |
| | Middle Age | 7(41.2 ) | 9 ( 52.9) | 1 (5.9 ) | 17 (100.0) |
| | Old | 5 ( 18.5) | 19 (70.4 ) | 3 (11.1) | 27 (100.0) |
| | Total | 13(21.0) | 44 (71.0) | 5 (8.0) | 62(100.0) |

In Table 7.13 the bivariate association between age and perceived discrimination does not hold good for respondents having 'moderate' and 'high' wage disparities. The bivariate association remains unaffected only in case of respondents belonging to 'low wage disparities'. Thus, we can conclude that the bivariate association between age and perceived discrimination hold good only for respondents having 'low' wage disparities. This type of association is referred as 'Conditional Association'. Conditional association is diagrammatically is shown below :

While similar trend can be observed in Tables 7.14, 7.15, and 7.16 where as in Table 7.13 the bivariate association between age and perceived discrimination remains unaffected when effect of 'age' as third variable is controlled. Therefore, we can conclude that the bivariate association between age and perceived discrimination hold good for respondents when the effect of age is controlled. Alternatively, we can conclude that the bivariate association between age and perceived discrimination is '***non-spurious***' when the effect of age is controlled.

**TABLE 7.14**
**WAGE DISPARITIES AND PERCEIVED SEX DISCRIMINATION (CONTROLLING FOR AGE)**

| *Age* | *Wage Disparities* | *Perceived Sex Discrimination* | | | *Total* |
|---|---|---|---|---|---|
| | | *Low* | *Moderate* | *High* | |
| Young | Low | 48 ( 62.3 ) | 19 ( 24.7 ) | 10 ( 13.0 ) | 77 (100.0) |
| | Moderate | 18 ( 39.1 ) | 25 (54.3 ) | 3 ( 6.5 ) | 46 (100.0) |
| | High | 14 ( 14.1 ) | 62 ( 62.6 ) | 23 ( 23.2 ) | 99 (100.0) |
| | Total | 80 (36.00 ) | 106 (47.7 ) | 36 (16.3 ) | 222(100.0) |
| Middle Aged | Wage Disparities | Low | Moderate | High | Total |
| | Low | 15 ( 57.7 ) | 6 (23.1 ) | 5 ( 19.2 ) | 26 (100.0) |
| | Moderate | 4 ( 33.3 ) | 7 ( 58.3 ) | 1 (8.3 ) | 12 (100.0) |
| | High | 14 (23.7 ) | 41 ( 69.5 ) | 4 (6.8 ) | 59 (100.0) |
| | Total | 33 (34.0 ) | 54 ( 55.7) | 10 ( 10.3) | 97(100.0) |
| Old | Wage Disparities | Low | Moderate | High | Total |
| | Low | 6 ( 37.5 ) | 8 ( 50.0 ) | 2 (12.5 ) | 16 (100.0) |
| | Moderate | 2 ( 50.0 ) | 2 (50.0 ) | | 4 (100.0) |
| | High | 5 ( 8.2 ) | 53 (86.9 ) | 3 ( 4.9 ) | 61 (100.0) |
| | Total | 13(16.0 ) | 63 (77.8 ) | 5 (6.2 ) | 81(100.0) |

**TABLE 7.15**
**WAGE DISPARITIES AND PERCEIVED SEX DISCRIMINATION (CONTROLLING FOR REGIONAL DEVELOPMENT)**

| *Regional Development* | *Wage Disparities* | *Perceived Sex Discrimination* | | | *Total* |
|---|---|---|---|---|---|
| | | *Low* | *Moderate* | *High* | |
| Low | Low | 43 ( 67.2 ) | 13 ( 20.3 ) | 8 ( 12.5 ) | 64 (100.0) |
| | Moderate | 19 (45.2 ) | 20 ( 47.6 ) | 3 ( 7.1 ) | 42 (100.0) |
| | High | 18 ( 14.2 ) | 84 (66.1 ) | 25 ( 19.7 ) | 127 (100.0) |
| | Total | 80 (34.3 ) | 117 (50.2 ) | 36 (15.5 ) | 233(100.0) |
| Moderate | Wage Disparities | Low | Moderate | High | Total |
| | Low | 25 ( 56.8) | 13 ( 29.5 ) | 6 ( 13.6 ) | 44 (100.0) |
| | Moderate | 2 ( 16.7 ) | 9 ( 75.0 ) | 1 ( 8.3) | 12 (100.0) |
| | High | 6 ( 12.2 ) | 40 ( 81.6 ) | 3 (6.1 ) | 49 (100.0) |
| | Total | 33 (31.4 ) | 62 (59.0 ) | 10 (9.6 ) | 105(100.0) |
| High | Wage Disparities | Low | Moderate | High | Total |
| | Low | 1 ( 9.1 ) | 7 ( 63.6 ) | 3 ( 27.3 ) | 11 (100.0) |
| | Moderate | 3 ( 37.5 ) | 5 ( 62.5 ) | | 8 (100.0) |
| | High | 9 ( 20.9 ) | 32 (74.4 ) | 2 (4.7 ) | 43 (100.0) |
| | Total | 13 (21.0 ) | 44 ( 71.0) | 5 (8.0 ) | 62(100.0) |

**TABLE 7.16**
**REGIONAL DEVELOPMENT AND PERCEIVED SEX DISCRIMINATION (CONTROLLING FOR AGE)**

| *Age* | *Regional Development* | *Perceived Sex Discrimination* | | | *Total* |
|---|---|---|---|---|---|
| | | *Low* | *Moderate* | *High* | |
| Young | Low | 66 ( 39.8 ) | 69 ( 41.6 ) | 31 ( 18.7 ) | 166 (100.0) |
| | Moderate | 13 ( 34.2 ) | 21 ( 55.3 ) | 4 ( 10.5 ) | 38 (100.0) |
| | High | 1 (5.6 ) | 16 (88.9 ) | 1 ( 5.6 ) | 18 (100.0) |
| | Total | 80 (36.0 ) | 106 (47.7 ) | 36 (16.3 ) | 222(100.0) |
| Middle Aged | Regional Development | Low | Moderate | High | Total |
| | Low | 9 ( 24.3 ) | 23 ( 62.2 ) | 5 ( 13.5 ) | 37 (100.0) |
| | Moderate | 17 ( 39.5 ) | 22 ( 51.2 ) | 4 (9.3 ) | 43 (100.0) |
| | High | 7 ( 41.2 ) | 9 ( 52.9 ) | 1 ( 5.9 ) | 17 (100.0) |
| | Total | 33 (34.0 ) | 54 (55.7 ) | 10 (10.3 ) | 97 (100.0) |

*(Contd.)*

*(Contd.Table 7.16)*

| *Age* | *Regional Development* | *Perceived Sex Discrimination* | | | *Total* |
|---|---|---|---|---|---|
| | | *Low* | *Moderate* | *High* | |
| Old | Regional Development | Low | Moderate | High | Total |
| | Low | 5 ( 16.7 ) | 25 ( 83.3 ) | | 30 (100.0) |
| | Moderate | 3 (12.5 ) | 19 ( 79.2 ) | 2 ( 8.3 ) | 24 (100.0) |
| | High | 5 ( 18.5 ) | 19 (70.4 ) | 3 (11.1 ) | 27 (100.0) |
| | Total | 13 (16.0) | 63 (77.8 ) | 5 (6.2 ) | 81(100.0) |

## TABLE 7.17
## REGIONAL DEVELOPMENT AND PERCEIVED SEX DISCRIMINATION(CONTROLLING FOR WAGE DISPARITIES)

| *Wage Disparities* | *Regional development* | *Perceived Sex Discrimination* | | | *Total* |
|---|---|---|---|---|---|
| | | *Low* | *Moderate* | *High* | |
| Low | Low | 43 (67'2 ) | 13 ( 20.3 ) | 8 (12.3) | 64 (100.0) |
| | Moderate | 25 (56.8 ) | 13 ( 29.5) | 6 ( 13.6 ) | 44 (100.0) |
| | High | 1 ( 9.1 ) | 7 (63.6) | 3 ( 27.6) | 11 (100.0) |
| | Total | 69 (58.0 ) | 33 (27.7 ) | 17(14.3 ) | 119(100.0) |
| Moderate | Regional development | Low | Moderate | High | Total |
| | Low | 19 ( 45.2 ) | 20 ( 47.6 ) | 3 ( 7.1 ) | 42 (100.0) |
| | Moderate | 2 (16.7 ) | 9 ( 75.0 ) | 1 (8.3 ) | 12 (100.0) |
| | High | 3 ( 37.5 ) | 5 (62.5 ) | | 8 (100.0) |
| | Total | 24 (38.7 ) | 34( 54.8) | 4( 6.5) | 62(100.0) |
| High | Regional development | Low | Moderate | High | Total |
| | Low | 18 ( 14.2 ) | 84 ( 66.1 ) | 25 ( 19.7 ) | 127 (100.0) |
| | Moderate | 6 (12.2 ) | 40 (81.6 ) | 3 (6.1 ) | 49 (100.0) |
| | High | 9 ( 20.9 ) | 32 ( 74.4 ) | 2 (4.7 ) | 43 (100.0) |
| | Total | 33(15.0 ) | 156(71.2 ) | 30(13.6 ) | 219(100.0) |

## References

Baker, L. Therese (1988), *Doing Social Research,* McGraw Hill, New York.

Blalock, Hubert, M. (1972), *Social Statistics,* Mc Graw Hill, New York.

Brace. N. et.al. (2003). *SPSS for Psychologists.* New York : Pal grave Macmillan.

Buckingham, A and Saunders, (2004). P. *The Survey Methods Workbook.* Cambridge : Polity Press.

Craft, J.L. (1990). *Statistics and Data Analysis for Social Workers.* Illinois: F.E. Peacock Publishers

Kerlinger Fred R. (1964), *Foundations of Behavioural Research,* Surjeet Publications, Delhi.

Lal Das, D.K. (2000), *Practice of Social Research: A Social Work Perspective,* Rawat Publications, Jaipur.

Lal Das, D.K. (2005), *Designs of Social Research,* Jaipur: Rawat Publications.

Monete, Duane R. (et. al.) (1986), *Applied Social Research,* Tool For the Human Services, Holt, Chicago.

Nachmias, D and Nachmias, C. (1981), *Research Methods in the Social Sciences,* St. Martins Press, New York.

Nicola, B. et. al. (2003) SPSS for Psychologists: A Guide to Data Analysis using SPSS for Windows, New York : Palgrave Macmillan.

O'Leary Z. (2004).*The Essential Guide to Doing Research.* New Delhi : Vistaar Publications

# 8

# Selection and Application of Statistical Tests

## Introduction

In the previous chapter we discussed about the first step of data analysis that is formulation of univariate, bivariate and trivariate tables and application of descriptive statistics. The next step is to select and apply appropriate statistical measures.

Knowledge of statistics helps the social researchers in two ways. First, the knowledge allows the social researchers to be able to analyse the data as per their research objectives and draw inferences which in turn enable them to expand and improve the knowledge base of their profession. Second, as a consumer of research it enables them to understand the analysis of data, appreciate the statistical procedures used in research reports.

Statistical procedures are increasingly become a part of the social research support system. One of the significant reasons for this is availability of various statistical packages generally quite easy to perform. Consequently, in the recent years, there has been a sizable increase in the use of microcomputers by social researchers in analysing data.

In social research, we are not concerned with each individual respondent. The purposes of our research are to know about the group of individuals (the sample). A given respondent, for example, has extremely favourable attitudes toward banning child labour and that another respondent has moderately unfavorable attitudes towards the same issue. Our research is generally directed toward providing information about a particular 'population of respondents', a sample or the totality , which may be asked certain questions, related to the problem of our study. Let us suppose that we have asked a sample of 400 workers , a series of questions to gather information about their perception about sex discrimination at work. Our research would thus be directed toward providing information about the 'population' of workers out of which 400 cases is a sample.

As a necessary step to characterising this 'population', we would have to describe or summarize the information about sex discrimination-that we have obtained on the sample thereof tabulation is just a part of this step. In addition, we must estimate the reliability of generalisations to the 'population' from the obtained data. Statistical measures are useful in fulfilling both these functions.

Statistics, a branch of Applied Mathematics, is regarded as mathematics applied to observed data. Consequently, everything dealing with the collection, processing, analysis and interpretation of numerical data belongs to the domain of statistics. However, the term 'statistics' is used in several ways. It denotes a collection of data such as those found in the Labour Gazette or, say, Labour Statistics of the Labour Bureau published annually by the Government of India. A second meaning of the term statistics refers to the statistical principles and methods employed in the collection, processing, analysing and interpretation of any kind of data. In this sense it is a branch of applied mathematics and helps us to know the complex social phenomena better and lend precision to our ideas. It is this field of mathematics, which is the subject matter of this section of the chapter.

## Functions of Statistics

Statistics has two broad functions. The first of these functions is description, the summarising of information in such a manner as to make it more usable. The second function is induction, which involves either making generalisations about some population on the basis of a sample drawn from this population, or formulating general laws on the basis of repeated observations. The two functions of statistical methods can be easily understood by the following example.

As we have mentioned earlier that we would like to study the problem of sex discrimination at work —the first thing that is to be done is to analyse the various causes of discrimination and to study the impact of each one of these causes on the various categories of workers , namely, male workers and female workers. This kind of analysis will give us an insight into the problem, and we will be able to know from such analysis many things, for example, that the wages of male workers is much higher than the female workers and that the sex discrimination at work in developed region is much higher than in undeveloped region. Such an analysis leads us to the conclusion that backwardness of a region is responsible for sex discrimination at work. The former is the process of descriptive statistics whereas the latter is that of inductive statistics.

**The Place of Statistics in Social Research**

Knowledge of basic statistical concepts and techniques is necessary for an intelligent understanding of the problem. Out of the welter of single events, social researchers seek for general trends; out of the vast and confusing variety of individual characters, they continually search for underlying group characters.

There are essentially two reasons why social researchers using statistics and the need to study statistics have grown enormously in the field of social sciences. One reason is that the huge amount of data collected by researcher need simplification so as to render them capable of being commonly understood without much difficulty. The second and even more important reason is the dominance of quantitative approach currently being employed in social research.

In fact, statistical considerations enter only into the analysis stage of the research process, after the data have been collected, and at a point of time when the initial plans for analysis are made and a sample is to be drawn. But this does not mean that a social researcher can plan and carry out his entire research without any knowledge of statistics and then hand over the data to the statistician for analysis. If he/she did this the results of costly research project would probably be disappointing if not useless. Evidently, problems that will be encountered in analysis and interpretation have to be anticipated at every stage in the research process, and in this sense statistical measures may be involved throughout. This implies that statistics is useful tool for the social scientist. It is a much more useful tool for explanatory analyses than might possibly be imagined. Most social researches are based on highly tentative theoretical ideas. The variables that should be controlled in the analysis or even the priorities and sequence of analysis and steps that should be followed are neither precise nor predetermined. Researchers are generally surprised at the complexity of data-analysis as soon as one introduces a set of variables. It is in these instances especially, that knowledge of the statistical measures becomes an invaluable tool enabling the social researcher to disentangle highly complex interrelationships.

**Limitations of Statistics**

Some of the major limitations of statistics and the cautions that need to be practised while using statistical techniques in the course of a research exercise must be noted.

One of the obvious limitations of statistics is that it is readily applicable to problems that are amendable to quantitative expression and treatment. Although qualitative attributes may sometimes be subjected to statistical analysis, these, of necessity, have to be translated into quantitative indices by recourse to the operational definitions. But then, much would depend on the validity of the operational assumptions. Unfortunately, this is a pit many a researcher falls into, that is , qualitative data are often operationalised as numerical values without deeper concern regarding their validity, in which case, it is rather the poor data that stands to be blamed and not statistics. In as much as many problems of concern to social scientists are influenced greatly by subjective factors un-amenable to mathematical treatment, the statistical approach hardly helps us get a sound understanding of the problem.

It is understandable that the statistical laws are applicable to average of aggregates. These pathetically ignore the individual intricacies of solitary units. Such neglect may, in certain investigations, lead to merely superficial findings. The social sciences typically requisition a keen concern for the unique and the idiosyncratic aspects. Additionally, there is likelihood that statistics may be misused, so much so that the researcher may be in a position to twist them to suit his fond conclusions or hypotheses.

This is also equally applicable to the very sensitive tools that the statistical methods are. They are liable to be misused easily. This is where great caution needs to be exercised in using them. As we shall have an occasion to see later, the validity of certain statistical methods depends on, the nature of data, the levels of measurement, the knowledge of the pertinent aspects and lastly, the assumptions made vis-à-vis the sample from which the data are derived.

What is most important for us as potential users of statistical measures therefore is to bear in mind that statistics has powerful muscles that can only serve and not direct. Much would depend on the use we want to put it to and whether the situation justifies it. What is given out by statistical computations may not be the final truth, since it is basically an approximation of typicality and by nature probabilistic. It is left largely to our interpretative skills to bring out the message of truth underlying the statistical inferences and propositions.

Statistical measures can be classified into two groups; (a) Descriptive Statistical Measures, and (b) Inferential Statistical Measures. While descriptive statistical measures describe a set of data where as inferential statistical measures intend to estimate population characteristics based on sample statistics.

## Descriptive Statistical Measures

### Proportions, Percentages and Ratios

In order to make the data easily understandable and fit for analysis and interpretation, the size of the data is considerably reduced and a large number of figures are condensed. But even after these basic arithmetic operations, data might be fairly large and unwieldy and it may not be easy to draw inferences. However, this difficulty is removed by measures like proportions, percentages and ratios.

### Proportions

The proportions of cases in any given category are defined as the number in the category divided by the total number of cases. In calculation of proportions, it is presumed that the method of classification has been such that categories are mutually exhaustive and exclusive. That is, any given individual has been placed in one and only one category.

To illustrate, let us take a nominal scale consisting of four categories with $n_1$, $n_2$, $n_3$ and $n_4$ cases, respectively. Let the total number of cases be N. Therefore, proportion of individuals in the first, second, third and fourth categories are $n_1/N$, $n_2/N$, $n_3/N$ and $n_4/N$, respectively. The following illustration will clarify the point.

**TABLE 8.1**
**AGE OF THE RESPONDENTS**

| *Age (In years)* | *Frequencies* |
|---|---|
| Young (18-38) | 222 |
| Middle (39-58) | 97 |
| Old (59-78) | 81 |
| Total | 400 |

The proportion of young respondents in the sample is 222/ 400 or 0.555; the comparable figure for older respondents is 81/400 or 0.2025. Other proportions can be computed in a similar fashion and results summarised in tabular form in Table 8.2.

**TABLE 8.2**
PROPORTIONS OF RESPONDENTS IN DIFFERENT AGE GROUPS

| *S.No.* | *Age* | *Proportion* |
|---|---|---|
| 1 | Young | 0.555 |
| 2 | Middle | 0.242 |
| 3 | Old. | 0.202 |
| | Total | 1.00 |

The value of a proportion cannot be greater than one. Thus, if we add the proportions of cases in all categories, the result is one. This is an important property of proportions.

**Percentage**

The word per cent means per hundred. Hence percentages can be obtained from proportions by simply multiplying by 100. In other words, percentage is the rate per hundred.

The figures in Table 8.2 could just as well be expressed in terms of percentages.

**TABLE 8.3**
**PROPORTIONS AND PERCETAGE OF RESPONDENTS IN DIFFERENT AGE GROUPS**

| *S.No.* | *Age* | *Proportion* | *Percentage* |
|---|---|---|---|
| 1 | Young | 0.555 | 55.5 |
| 2 | Middle | 0.242 | 24.2 |
| 3 | Old. | 0.202 | 20.2 |
| | Total | 1.00 | 100.0 |

Conventionally, percentages are calculated up to the nearest decimal and adjustments are made in the last digits, so the totals are exactly 100.

## Ratios

The ratio of one number A to another number B is defined as the numerical quantity obtained by dividing A by B. Suppose that there are 800 male students and 300 female students in Master in Social Work classes then the ratio of male students to female students is 800/300. In calculating ratio the key term is the word 'to'. Whatever quantity precedes this word is placed in the numerator while the quantity following it becomes the denominator.

In practice, a ratio is either reduced to its simplest form by cancelling common factors or is expressed in terms of a denominator of one. Thus the ratio of male students to female students would be written as 8:3 or 2.66 to 1.

For use of proportions and percentages following rules of thumb are important.

(i) Total number of cases should be always reported along with proportions or Percentages,

(ii) Percentages must not be computed unless the number of cases on which the percentage is based is in the neighborhood of 50 or more, and

(iii) Percentages may be computed in either direction, and careful attention shouldbe given to each table to determine exactly how each percentage has been obtained.

### Measures of Central Tendency

In the preceding sections we discussed the various statistical derivatives like ratios, proportions and percentages. But these derivatives are not enough to make possible, the proper analysis and interpretation of data. It is often essential to represent a set of data by means of a single number which, in its way, is descriptive of the entire set. Obviously, the figure which is used to represent a whole series should neither have the lowest value in the series nor the highest value, but a value somewhere between these two limits, possibly in the centre. Such figures are called measures of typicality or central tendency or simply average.

### The Arithmetic Mean

The arithmetic mean is by far the most common of all the averages. It is relatively easy to calculate, simple to understand and is widely used in social work research. The arithmetic mean is defined as the sum of the values of all the items and dividing the total by the number of items. An example will help us learn how to calculate the arithmetic mean. Let us suppose that eight students receive 54, 58, 60, 62, 70, 72, 75 and 77 marks respectively, in an examination, the mean of marks will be:

$$\text{Mean} = \frac{54+58+60+62+70+72+75+77}{8} = \frac{528}{8} = 66$$

### The Median

The median is another simple measure of central tendency. We sometimes want to locate the position of the middle item when data have been arranged. Or we want to divide a group of students into quartiles by locating the individuals who have exactly 25 per cent of the class below them, exactly 75 per cent below them etc. These measures are known as positional averages. The median is perhaps the most important of such positional averages. We define the median as the size of the middle item when the items are arrayed in ascending or descending order of magnitude. This means that median divides the series in such a manner that there are as many items above or larger than the middle one as there are below or smaller than it.

**The Mode**

Another measure, which is sometimes used to describe the central tendency of a set of data, is the mode. It is defined as the value that is repeated most often in the data set. In the following series of values: 71, 73, 74, 75, 75, 75, 78, 78, 80 and 82, the mode is 75, because 75 occur more often than any other value (three times). In grouped data the mode is located in the class where the frequency is greatest. The mode is more useful when there are a larger number of cases and when data have been grouped.

In practice it is found that a set of grouped data often have more than one mode. Frequency distributions, which have one mode, are referred to as being unimodal. Those with two modes and three modes are described as bimodal and trimodal (more commonly multimodal).

The various measures of central tendency referred to above, not only make different assumptions about the nature of the data but provide also somewhat different kinds of information. The arithmetic mean may be thought of as the point on the scale around which the case balance, that is, one case at one extreme of the distribution, may be counter-balanced by one or more cases at the other extreme of the distribution. If cases are not symmetrically distributed around this point, the arithmetic mean may be very misleading in certain respects i.e., it may give out a distorted picture of the group in respect of given characteristics. This does not, however, mean that the knowledge of the mean (say, of the mean income of a group) is pointless information. Whether or not the knowledge of the mean is useful will depend on what one proposes to do with it.

The median also implies a concept of balance, but since it takes in to account only of the ordinal positions of scores rather than their absolute values, a person with a very high income may be counter-balanced by a pauper. But in the case of the arithmetic mean it takes a very large number of cases of low income to counter-balance one case of a person who has a very high income.

The use of the mode does away with the idea of a point of balance. In fact, it is possible to have more than one mode in a distribution. For example, we may find two equally large groups of students, one studying between one and two hours and another studying between three and four hours. In this distribution, there will thus be two modes, i.e., the distribution is bimodal. There may also be multi-modal distributions. In such cases, it is perhaps misleading to speak of central tendency. It is also possible for a distribution of scores to have no mode at all, i.e.; every score may be occurring about as frequently as every other. In this case too, it is misleading to speak of central tendency, a term suggesting that the cases tend to cluster around some point more or less in the middle of the distribution. In such instances, the arithmetic mean and the median might be useful in bringing out aspects of the distributions, which they describe.

**Measures of Dispersion**

In social research, we often wish to know the extent of homogeneity and heterogeneity among respondents with respect to a given characteristic. The set of social data is characterized by the heterogeneity of values. In fact, the extent to which they are heterogeneous or vary among themselves is of basic importance in statistics. Measures of central tendency describe one important characteristic of a set of data typically but they do not tell us anything about this other basic characteristic. Consequently, we need ways of measuring heterogeneity – the extent to which data are dispersed and the measures, which provide this description, are called measures of dispersion or variability.

**Range**

The range is defined as the difference between the highest and lowest values. Mathematically,

$$\text{R(Range)} = m_H - m_L$$

Where $m_H$ and $m_L$ stand for the highest and the lowest value. Thus, for the data set; 10, 22, 20, 14 and 14 the range would be the difference between 22 and 10, i.e., 12. In case of grouped data, we take the range as the difference between the midpoints of the extreme classes. Thus, if the midpoint of the lowest interval is 150 and that of the highest are 850 the range will be 700.

The only advantage of range, the measure which is seldom used, is that it can be easily calculated and readily understood. Despite this advantage, it is generally not a very useful measure of dispersion. Its main drawback is that it does not tell us anything about the dispersion of values, which are intermediate between the two extremes.

**Standard Deviation**

The most useful and frequently used measure of dispersion is standard deviation. The value of standard deviation indicates the dispersion of a distribution. The standard deviation is defined as the square root of the arithmetic mean of the squares of the deviations about the mean.

**Variance**

A measure of quantitative variation reflecting the average dispersion in the distribution. It is the squared standard deviation

**How to obtain Descriptive Statistics ? From the menu choose "Analyze" and click on it. You will get a drop down menu.**

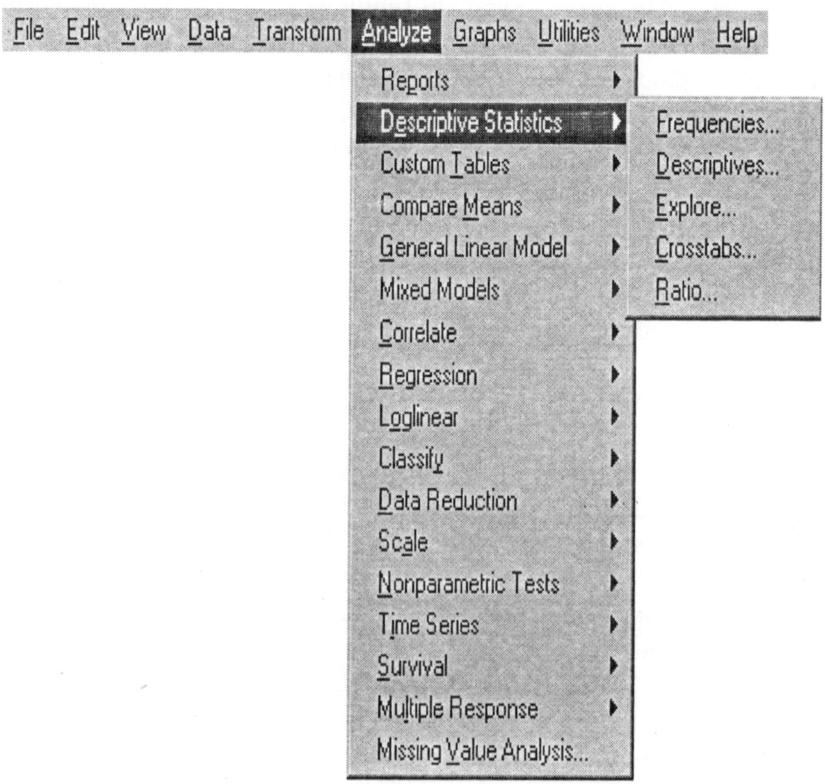

**From the drop down menu select "Descriptive Statistics" and click on it. Then select "Frequencies" and click it.**

You will get "Frequency Dialog Box" as shown below:

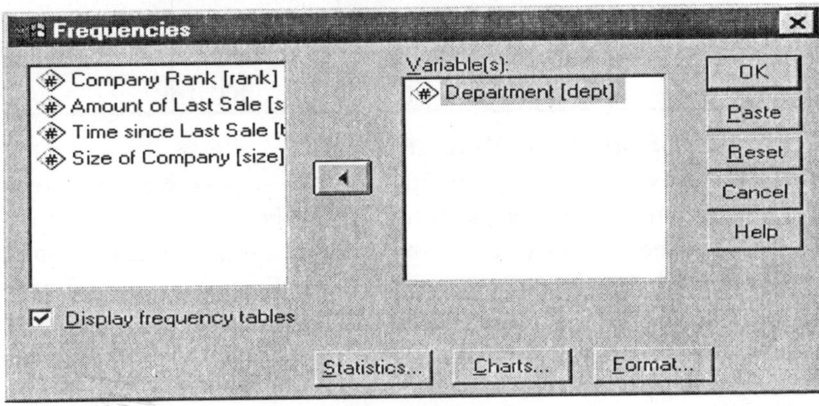


From the dialog box select Descriptive Statistics and Click the small blank boxes (on your click 'tick' mark ( √) will appear in the blank boxes.

Click 'Continue'.

Click 'OK'

A sample output of descriptive statistics is shown below:

**Frequencies**

**Statistics**

PERCEIVED DISCRIMINATION

| | | |
|---|---|---|
| N | Valid | 400 |
| | Missing | 0 |
| Mean | | 8.8125 |
| Std. Error of Mean | | .03195 |
| Median | | 9.0000 |
| Mode | | 9.00 |
| Std. Deviation | | .63903 |
| Variance | | .40836 |
| Range | | 2.00 |
| Minimum | | 8.00 |
| Maximum | | 10.00 |
| Sum | | 3525.00 |
| Percentiles | 25 | 8.0000 |
| | 50 | 9.0000 |
| | 75 | 9.0000 |

**PERCEIVED DISCRIMINATION**

| | | Frequency | Percent | Valid Percent | Cumulative Percent |
|---|---|---|---|---|---|
| Valid | Low | 126 | 31.5 | 31.5 | 31.5 |
| | Medium | 223 | 55.8 | 55.8 | 87.3 |
| | High | 51 | 12.8 | 12.8 | 100.0 |
| | Total | 400 | 100.0 | 100.0 | |

## Inferential Statistical Measures

We have discussed so far various statistical measures concerned with the description and analysis of a single variable. In social research, we often wish to know the association among different variables in the data with one another. You may wish to know, for instance, whether sex discrimination is somehow related to level of regional development , to wage disparities, to age etc. In other words, you are interested in ascertaining whether a change in one variable is associated with change in another variable. For example, whether the higher perceived sex discrimination is associated with higher level of regional development or contrariwise; whether the lower wage disparity is correlated with lower perceived sex discrimination.

Percentage difference, though , is very useful and simple way of assessing association has its own limitations. Assessment of association between variables by percentage difference just gives us an understanding of association likely to exist in sample. It does not tell us if the inference drawn will hold good to the population from which the sample is drawn. That means the inference may be just a chance. Therefore, to know that the inference is not by chance we need to compute some inferential statistical tests.

**Inferential** statistical measures can be classified into the following categories :

(a) Measures of Associations,

(b) Measures of Correlation,

(c) Measures of Difference , and

(d) Measures of Variance.

## Measures of Associations

### Chi square test

Chi-square ( $\chi^2$ ), pronounced as Ki-square, test, is a test of association and applied to null hypothesis of no association between attributes. The Chi-square test is perhaps the most commonly used in studies dealing with social – behavioural data. Hence a fuller exposition of the test is presented below.

The test provides us with a method to evaluate whether or not frequencies which have been empirically observed are associated significantly. It also measures if the two variables are independent of each other.

**How to obtain Chi square test value ?**
**To obtain crosstables:**
- **From menu, choose :**

**Analyse**
↓
**Descriptive Statistics** ⟶ **Frequencies**
**Descriptives**
**Crosstab**

**Click Crosstab.**
**You get Crosstab Dialog Box**

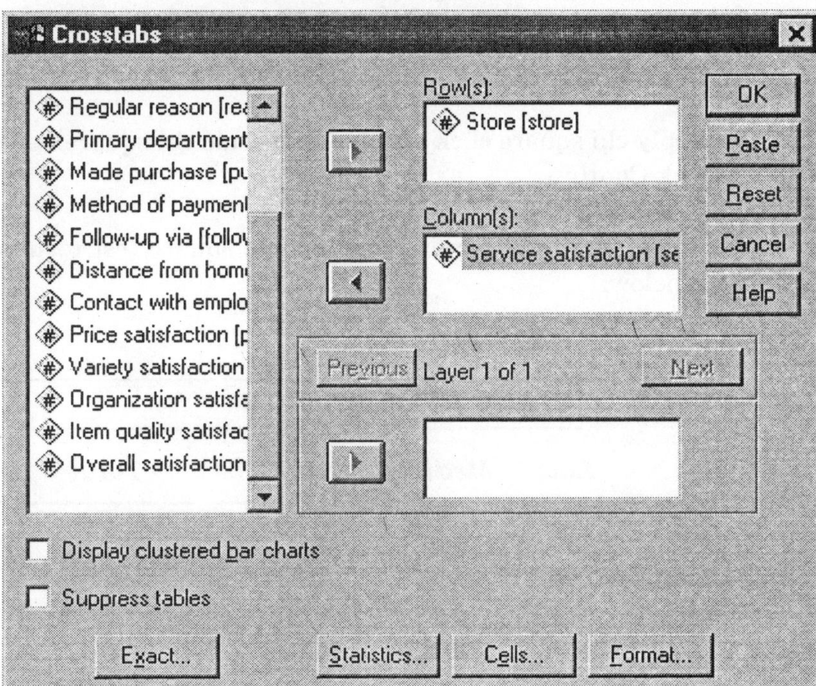

Highlight the variable (say 'regional development') and transfer it to the ROW Box.

Highlight another variable (say 'perceived sex discrimination') and transfer it to the COLUMN Box.

Select Statistics from the Dialog Box . Click Statistics button. You get Statistics Dialog Box :

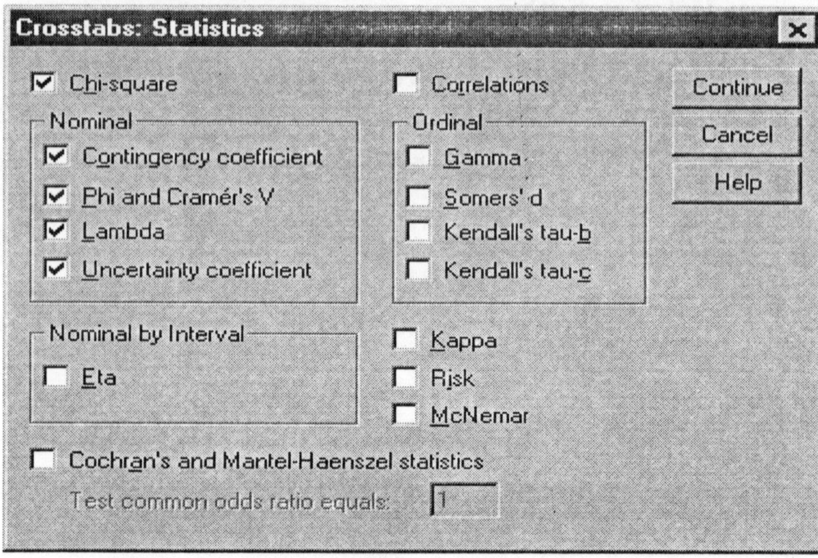


To apply chi square click in the box beside chi square.

- Click Continue.
- Click OK.

A sample output of a crosstable and chi square test results are shown below:

**Crosstabs**

| | *Perceived Discrimination* | | | |
|---|---|---|---|---|
| | *Low* | *Medium* | *High* | *Total* |
| Reg Dev Low | 80 | 106 | 36 | 222 |
| Medium | 33 | 54 | 10 | 97 |
| High | 13 | 63 | 5 | 81 |
| Total | 126 | 223 | 51 | 400 |

**Chi-Square Tests**

| | Value | df | Asymp. Sig. (2-sided) |
|---|---|---|---|
| Pearson Chi-Square | 22.678[a] | 4 | .000 |
| Likelihood Ratio | 23.837 | 4 | .000 |
| Linear-by-Linear Association | .884 | 1 | .347 |
| N of Valid Cases | 400 | | |

a. 0 cells (.0%) have expected count less than 5. The minimum expected count is 10.33.

**Symmetric**

| | | Value | Approx. |
|---|---|---|---|
| Nominal by | Contingency Coefficient | .232 | .000 |
| N of Valid | | 400 | |

a. Not assuming the null

b. Using the asymptotic standard error assuming the null

To include these SPSS outputs in your research report you need to modify the tables keeping in mind the conventions and format. A modified table with the hypothetical data is presented below:

**TABLE 8.4**
**REGIONAL DEVELOPMENT AND PERCEIVED SEX DISCRIMINATION**

| *Regional Development* | *Perceived Sex Discrimination* | | | *TOTAL* |
|---|---|---|---|---|
| | *High* | *Medium* | *Low* | |
| Low | 36(15.5) | 117(50.2) | 80(34.3) | 233(100.0) |
| Medium | 10(9.5) | 62(59.0) | 33(31.5) | 105(100.0) |
| High | 5(8.0) | 44(71.0) | 13(21.0) | 62(100.0) |
| Total | 51 | 223 | 126 | 400 |

$\chi^2 = 22.678$ df = 4 p = .000 C = .232

To interpret the statistical test results and draw inference first we have to understand two statistical concepts, namely, 'level of significance' and 'degree of freedom'.

## Level of Significance

Chi-square test is used to evaluate whether the association between the variables is due to the sampling fluctuations and as such insignificant or whether the association is due to some other reason and as such significant. Before drawing the inference, that the association is significant, researchers set up a hypothesis, often referred as a null hypothesis (symbolized as ($H_0$) as contrasted with the research hypothesis ($H_1$). Usually, although not always, the null hypothesis states that there is no association between the variables , whereas a research hypothesis may predict either a positive or a negative association. In other words, null hypcthesis assumes that there is absence of non-sampling errors and the association is due to chance alone. That means the null hypothesis in this case would be : There is no association between regional development and perceived discrimination. Then the probability of the occurrence of such an association is determined. The probability indicates the extent of reliance that we can place on the inferences drawn. These levels are called levels of significance.

## Degree of Freedom

To use the chi-square test, the next step is to calculate the degrees of freedom. Suppose we have a 2 x 2 contingency table as shown below :

| | Column 1 | Column 2 | |
|---|---|---|---|
| Row 1 | ✓ | X | $R_{t1}$ |
| Row 2 | X | X | $R_{t2}$ |
| | $ct_1$ | $Ct_2$ | |

Column totals

**Figure 8.1**

We know the row and the column total $r_{t1}$, $r_{t2}$ and $c_{t1}$ and $c_{t2}$. The number of degrees of freedom can be defined as the number of cell values that we can freely specify. In Figure 8.1, once we specify the one value of Row 1 (denoted by check in the figure) the second value in that row and the values of second row (denoted by X) are already determined; we are not free to specify these because we know the row totals and column totals. This shows that in a 2 x 2 contingency table we are free to specify one value only.

The following example would illustrate the concept:

| | **Affected**<br>**A** | **Non affected**<br>**α** | **Total** |
|---|---|---|---|
| **Inoculated**<br>**B** | AB<br>14<br>(20) | αB<br>26 | 40 |
| **Non inoculated**<br>**β** | Aβ<br>16 | αβ<br>4 | 20 |
| **Total** | 30 | 30 | 60 |

Let us suppose that the two attributes A and B are independent then the expected frequency of the cell AB would be

**40 x 30 / 60 = 20**

Consequently, the frequencies of remaining three cells are automatically fixed. Thus for cell ab expected frequency must be 40 – 20 = 20, similarly for the cell Ab it must be 30 – 20 = 10 and for ab it must be 10. This means that for 2 x 2 tables we have one choice of our own and in remaining three cells we have no freedom. Thus, degrees of freedom (*df*) can be calculated by the formula:

$df = (c - 1)(r - 1)$

Where *df* stands for the degrees of freedom, *c* for the number of columns and *r* for the number of rows.

Thus in 2 x 3 table (Table 14.8)

$df = (3 - 1)(2 - 1) = 2 \times 1 = 2$

## How to interpret Chi square test value?

The table values of chi-square are available at various probability levels (See Appendix F ). We can find out from the table the values of chi-square at certain levels of significance. Usually, (in social sciences problem) the value of chi-square at 0.05 or .01 levels of significance from the given degrees of freedom is seen from the table and is compared with observed value of Chi-square. From the sample table of chi square test results we have:

**$\chi^2$ (calculated value) =22.678**

Level of significance (P) = .05
Degree of freedom (df) = 4

**$\chi^2$ (table value) at (P= .05 and df=4) = 9.488**

**Decision Rules**

If the observed value of $\chi^2$ is more than the table value we reject the null hypothesis.

**How to report Chi square test value?**

Chi square test results show that the calculated ( obtained through SPSS) value is more than the table value /critical value , hence the null hypothesis "There is no association between 'regional development' and 'perceived sex discrimination' is rejected. That means research hypothesis is true and hence accepted. In other words we can say that the association between 'regional development' and 'perceived discrimination' is statistically significant.

Alternatively, since SPSS output provides exact significance, we can modify the decision rule as : "If the exact significance level is more than 0.05 we reject the null hypothesis". The test results show that the exact significance is .0000 which is less than .05 hence we reject the null hypothesis and accept the research hypothesis.

Since the association is statistically significant , now we can say that the inference drawn will hold good to the population from which the sample is drawn. Finally, we may infer that the association is due to some reasons and certainly it is not by chance.

While the chi-square measures indicate that there is a relationship between two variables, they do not indicate the strength of the relationship. As such, if you are interested in explaining the strength of association/relationship you have to find out Coefficient of Contingency(C). This measure indicates the strength and significance of the relationship between the row and column variables in a crosstable. The value of C has been found to be 0.232. We can say that the association is 'positive' and 'moderate'.

**Chi-square as a Test of Goodness of Fit**

By and large, we use chi-square as test of independence; that is whether to accept or reject a null hypothesis. The $\chi^2$ tests can also be used to decide whether there is a significant difference between an observed frequency distribution and a theoretical frequency distribution. In this manner, we can determine how good the fit is of the observed and expected frequencies.

That is the fit would be considered good if there is no significant divergence between observed and expected data when the curve of the observed frequencies is superimposed on the curve of expected frequencies.

We must remember, however, that even if proportions in the cells remain unchanged the chi-square value varies directly with the total number of cases (N). If we double the number of cases, the chi-square value gets doubled; if we triple them, we also triple chi-square and so on. The implications of this fact can be illustrated by an example given below:

**TABLE 8.5**
**MARITAL STATUS AND PERFORMANCE IN EXAMINATION**

| *Marital status* | *Performance in Examination* | | *Total* |
|---|---|---|---|
| | *Successful* | *Not successful* | |
| Married | 45 | 30 | 75 |
| Unmarried | 125 | 50 | 175 |
| Total | 170 | 80 | 250 |

In this example, the chi-square value is 3.15 and on this basis we would naturally infer that the relationship is not a significant one. Now, suppose data had been collected on 500 cases with the following results.

**TABLE 8.6**
**MARITAL STATUS AND PERFORMANCE IN EXAMINATION**

| *Marital status* | *Performance in Examination* | | *Total* |
|---|---|---|---|
| | *Successful* | *Not successful* | |
| Married | 90 | 60 | 150 |
| Unmarried | 250 | 100 | 350 |
| Total | 340 | 160 | 500 |

**Statistical Tests associated with Chi square**

Chi-square value as now computed from the figures, is 6.30, which is double than that of the value in the previous example. The value 6.30 is statistically significant. Had we expressed the results in terms of percentages there would not have been difference in interpretations. The above examples illustrate very important point, i.e.; chi-square is directly proportional to N. Thus we would need a measure which is not affected merely by a change in the number of cases. The measures Phi (ϕ) affected this facility i.e., the property we desire in our measure. This measure is simply a ratio between the chi-square value and the total value of cases studied.

**To Obtain Phi (ϕ) click in the box beside Phi and Cramer's V**

- Click Continue.
- Click OK.

**Using SPSS commands , now we can apply statistical measures to the remaining two bivariate tables and draw valid inferences.**

**TABLE 8.7**
**AGE AND PERCEIVED SEX DISCRIMINATION**

| *Age* | *Perceived Sex Discrimination* | | | *Total* |
|---|---|---|---|---|
| | *Low* | *Medium* | *High* | |
| Young (18-21) | 80 (36.0) | 106 (47.7) | 36 (16.2) | 222(100.0) |
| Middle (22-46) | 33(34.0) | 54( 55.7) | 10 ( 10.3) | 97(100.0) |
| Old (47-60) | 13 (16.0) | 63( 77.8) | 5 ( 6.2) | 81(100.0) |
| Total | 126 (31.5) | 223 (55.7) | 51 (12.8) | 400(100.0) |

**$\chi^2$ =74.77 df=4 Significance (p) =.000 C= .397**

To examine if the association is statically significant chi-Square test was applied. The chi-square test value was found to be 74.77, with 4 degrees of freedom. The value of level of significance

(p) was found to be 0.000. A low significance value (typically less than 0.05) indicates that there is an association between the two variables. Hence, we reject the null hypothesis : 'age' and 'perceived sex discrimination' are not associated and accept the research hypothesis ; 'age' and 'perceived sex discrimination' are associated.

TABLE 8.8

**WAGE DISPARITIES AND PERCEIVED SEX DISCRIMINATION**

| *Wage Disparities* | *Perceived Sex Discrimination* | | | *TOTAL* |
|---|---|---|---|---|
| | *High* | *Medium* | *Low* | |
| Low | 17(14.3) | 33(27.7) | 69(58.0) | 119(100.0) |
| Medium | 4(6.5) | 34(54.8) | 24(38.7) | 62(100.0) |
| High | 30(13.7) | 156(71.2) | 33(15.1) | 219(100.0) |
| Total | 51 | 223 | 126 | 400 |

**$\chi^2$ =10.096 df=4 Significance=.039 C=.157**

The test results show that the exact significance of chi square value is .0000 which is less than .05. Hence, we reject the null hypothesis : 'wage' and 'perceived sex discrimination' are not associated and accept the research hypothesis ; 'wage' and 'perceived sex discrimination' are associated.

**Use of Chi-square Test in Trivariate Analysis**

In the preceding chapter we discussed trivariate analysis of data by percentage difference and tried to understand if the variables are associated. We know that the assessment of association between variables by percentage difference gives us only an understanding of association likely to exist in sample. It does not tell us if the inference drawn will hold good to the population from which the sample is drawn. That means the inference may be just a chance. To rule out that the association is by chance and to infer that the interference will hold good to the population from which the sample is drawn, we will now compute chi square tests for the following trivariate tables and interpret the results :

(1) Age and Perceived Sex Discrimination-controlling the effect of Wage Disparities.

(2) Age and Perceived Sex Discrimination-controlling the effect of Regional Development.

(3) Wage Disparities and Perceived Sex Discrimination-controlling the effect of Age.

(4) Wage Disparities and Perceived Sex Discrimination-controlling the effect of Regional Development.

(5) Regional Development and Perceived Sex Discrimination-controlling the effect of Age.

(6) Regional Development and Perceived Sex Discrimination-controlling the effect of Wage Disparities.

To apply Chi square in Trivariate Tables :

From the menu choose 'Analyze' and click on it. You will get a drop down menu as shown below:

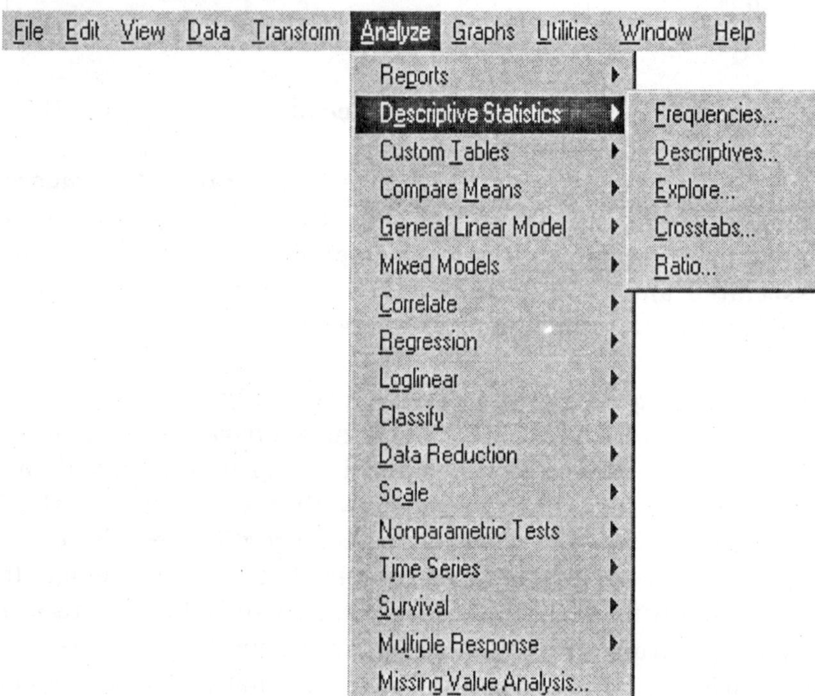

From sub menu select 'Crosstab' and click on it. You will get 'Crosstab' dialog box as shown below:

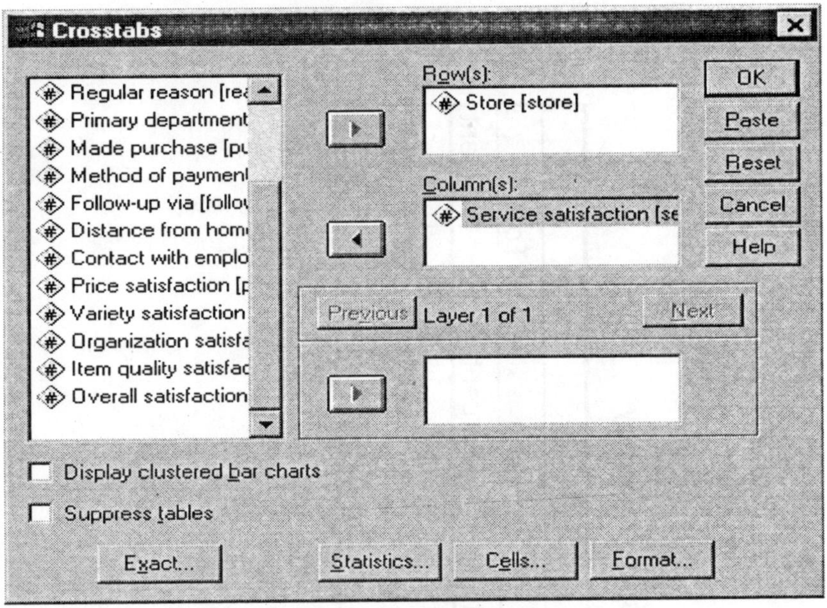


Select independent variable , say 'age' and transfer it to 'Row' box . Select dependent variable , say 'perceived sex discrimination' and transfer it to 'Column' box . Select the third variable (control variable) , say 'wage disparities' and transfer it to 'Layer 1 of 1' box . Click 'Statistics' button. You will get 'Crosstab : Statistics ' dialog box as shown below :

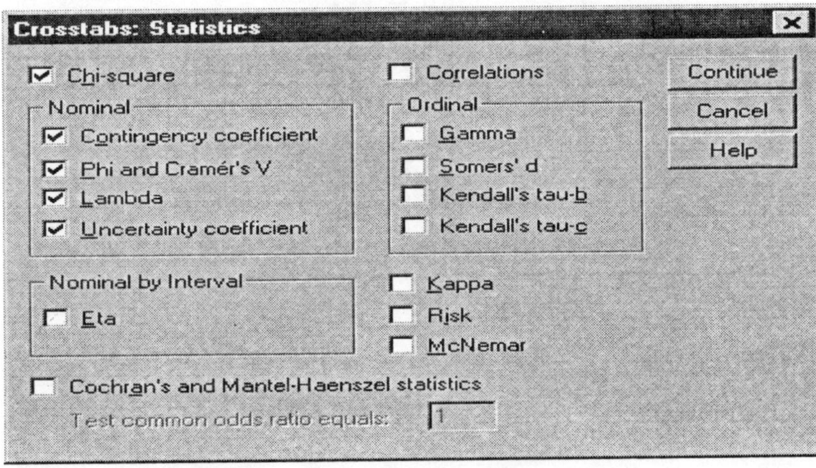

**Case Processing Summary**

| | Cases | | | | | |
|---|---|---|---|---|---|---|
| | Valid | | Missing | | Total | |
| | N | Percent | N | Percent | N | Percent |
| AGE * PERCEIVE DISCRIMINATION WAGE DISPARIT | 400 | 100.0% | 0 | .0% | 400 | 100.0% |

**AGE * PERCEIVED DISCRIMINATION * WAGE DISPARITIES Crosstabulation**

Count

| | | | PERCEIVED DISCRIMINATION | | | |
|---|---|---|---|---|---|---|
| WAGE DISPARITIES | | | Low | Medium | High | Total |
| Low | AGE | Low | 48 | 19 | 10 | 77 |
| | | Medium | 15 | 6 | 5 | 26 |
| | | High | 6 | 8 | 2 | 16 |
| | Total | | 69 | 33 | 17 | 119 |
| Medium | AGE | Low | 18 | 25 | 3 | 46 |
| | | Medium | 4 | 7 | 1 | 12 |
| | | High | 2 | 2 | | 4 |
| | Total | | 24 | 34 | 4 | 62 |
| High | AGE | Low | 14 | 62 | 23 | 99 |
| | | Medium | 14 | 41 | 4 | 59 |
| | | High | 5 | 53 | 3 | 61 |
| | Total | | 33 | 156 | 30 | 219 |

**Chi-Square Tests**

| WAGE DISPARITIES | | Value | df | Asymp. Sig. (2-sided) |
|---|---|---|---|---|
| Low | Pearson Chi-Square | 5.305 | 4 | .257 |
| | Likelihood Ratio | 4.893 | 4 | .298 |
| | Linear-by-Linear Association | 1.630 | 1 | .202 |
| | N of Valid Cases | 119 | | |
| Medium | Pearson Chi-Square | .594 | 4 | .964 |
| | Likelihood Ratio | .839 | 4 | .933 |
| | Linear-by-Linear Association | .040 | 1 | .842 |
| | N of Valid Cases | 62 | | |
| High | Pearson Chi-Square | 20.121 | 4 | .473 |
| | Likelihood Ratio | 20.432 | 4 | .000 |
| | Linear-by-Linear Association | 2.996 | 1 | .083 |
| | N of Valid Cases | 219 | | |

**Symmetric Measures**

| WAGE DISPARITIES | | | Value | Approx. Sig. |
|---|---|---|---|---|
| Low | Nominal by Nominal | Contingency Coefficient | .207 | .257 |
| | N of Valid Cases | | 119 | |
| Medium | Nominal by Nominal | Contingency Coefficient | .097 | .964 |
| | N of Valid Cases | | 62 | |
| High | Nominal by Nominal | Contingency Coefficient | .290 | .473 |
| | N of Valid Cases | | 219 | |

a. Not assuming the null hypothesis.

b. Using the asymptotic standard error assuming the null hypothesis.

Select 'Chi square' and 'Contingency coefficient' and click on them. Click 'Continue' and 'OK'.

This process can be repeated for the remaining trivariate tables.

The SPSS out puts are shown below :

## Crosstabs

**AGE * PERCEIVED DISCRIMINATION * REGIONAL DEVELOPMENT Crosstabulation**

Count

| REGIONAL DEVELOPMENT | | | PERCEIVED DISCRIMINATION | | | Total |
|---|---|---|---|---|---|---|
| | | | Low | Medium | High | |
| Low | AGE | Low | 66 | 69 | 31 | 166 |
| | | Medium | 9 | 23 | 5 | 37 |
| | | High | 5 | 25 | | 30 |
| | Total | | 80 | 117 | 36 | 233 |
| Medium | AGE | Low | 13 | 21 | 4 | 38 |
| | | Medium | 17 | 22 | 4 | 43 |
| | | High | 3 | 19 | 2 | 24 |
| | Total | | 33 | 62 | 10 | 105 |
| High | AGE | Low | 1 | 16 | 1 | 18 |
| | | Medium | 7 | 9 | 1 | 17 |
| | | High | 5 | 19 | 3 | 27 |
| | Total | | 13 | 44 | 5 | 62 |

**Chi-Square Tests**

| REGIONAL DEVELOPMENT | | Value | df | Asymp. Sig. (2-sided) |
|---|---|---|---|---|
| Low | Pearson Chi-Square | 21.149 | 4 | .000 |
| | Likelihood Ratio | 25.402 | 4 | .000 |
| | Linear-by-Linear Association | .344 | 1 | .557 |
| | N of Valid Cases | 233 | | |
| Medium | Pearson Chi-Square | 5.997 | 4 | .199 |
| | Likelihood Ratio | 6.607 | 4 | .158 |
| | Linear-by-Linear Association | 1.109 | 1 | .292 |
| | N of Valid Cases | 105 | | |
| High | Pearson Chi-Square | 7.574 | 4 | .109 |
| | Likelihood Ratio | 7.705 | 4 | .103 |
| | Linear-by-Linear Association | .058 | 1 | .810 |
| | N of Valid Cases | 62 | | |

**Symmetric Measures**

| REGIONAL DEVELOPMENT | | | Value | Approx. Sig. |
|---|---|---|---|---|
| Low | Nominal by Nominal | Contingency Coefficient | .288 | .000 |
| | N of Valid Cases | | 233 | |
| Medium | Nominal by Nominal | Contingency Coefficient | .232 | .199 |
| | N of Valid Cases | | 105 | |
| High | Nominal by Nominal | Contingency Coefficient | .330 | .109 |
| | N of Valid Cases | | 62 | |

(a) Not assuming the null hypothesis.
(b) Using the asymptotic standard error assuming the null hypothesis.

**Case Processing Summary**

| | Cases | | | | | |
|---|---|---|---|---|---|---|
| | Valid | | Missing | | Total | |
| | N | Percent | N | Percent | N | Percent |
| WAGE DISPARITIES * PERCEIVED DISCRIMINATION * REGIONAL DEVELOPMENT | 400 | 100.0% | 0 | .0% | 400 | 100.0% |

**WAGE DISPARITIES * PERCEIVED DISCRIMINATION * AGE Crosstabulation**

Count

| AGE | | | PERCEIVED DISCRIMINATION | | | Total |
|---|---|---|---|---|---|---|
| | | | Low | Medium | High | |
| Low | WAGE DISPARITIES | Low | 48 | 19 | 10 | 77 |
| | | Medium | 18 | 25 | 3 | 46 |
| | | High | 14 | 62 | 23 | 99 |
| | Total | | 80 | 106 | 36 | 222 |
| Medium | WAGE DISPARITIES | Low | 15 | 6 | 5 | 26 |
| | | Medium | 4 | 7 | 1 | 12 |
| | | High | 14 | 41 | 4 | 59 |
| | Total | | 33 | 54 | 10 | 97 |
| High | WAGE DISPARITIES | Low | 6 | 8 | 2 | 16 |
| | | Medium | 2 | 2 | | 4 |
| | | High | 5 | 53 | 3 | 61 |
| | Total | | 13 | 63 | 5 | 81 |

**Chi-Square Tests**

| AGE | | Value | df | Asymp. Sig. (2-sided) |
|---|---|---|---|---|
| Low | Pearson Chi-Square | 47.834 | 4 | .000 |
| | Likelihood Ratio | 51.043 | 4 | .000 |
| | Linear-by-Linear Association | 31.263 | 1 | .000 |
| | N of Valid Cases | 222 | | |
| Medium | Pearson Chi-Square | 15.888 | 4 | .003 |
| | Likelihood Ratio | 16.321 | 4 | .003 |
| | Linear-by-Linear Association | 2.122 | 1 | .145 |
| | N of Valid Cases | 97 | | |
| High | Pearson Chi-Square | 13.878 | 4 | .008 |
| | Likelihood Ratio | 12.370 | 4 | .015 |
| | Linear-by-Linear Association | 3.713 | 1 | .054 |
| | N of Valid Cases | 81 | | |

**Symmetric Measures**

| AGE | | | Value | Approx. Sig. |
|---|---|---|---|---|
| Low | Nominal by Nominal | Contingency Coefficient | .421 | .000 |
| | N of Valid Cases | | 222 | |
| Medium | Nominal by Nominal | Contingency Coefficient | .375 | .003 |
| | N of Valid Cases | | 97 | |
| High | Nominal by Nominal | Contingency Coefficient | .382 | .008 |
| | N of Valid Cases | | 81 | |

(a) Not assuming the null hypothesis.
(b) Using the asymptotic standard error assuming the null hypothesis.

**Case Processing Summary**

| | Cases | | | | | |
|---|---|---|---|---|---|---|
| | Valid | | Missing | | Total | |
| | N | Percent | N | Percent | N | Percent |
| REGIONAL DEVELOPMENT * PERCEIVED DISCRIMINATION * WAGE DISPARITIES | 400 | 100.0% | 0 | .0% | 400 | 100.0% |

**WAGE DISPARITIES * PERCEIVED DISCRIMINATION * REGIONAL DEVELOPMENT Cross**

Count

| REGIONAL DEVELOPMENT | | | PERCEIVED DISCRIMINATION | | | Total |
|---|---|---|---|---|---|---|
| | | | Low | Medium | High | |
| Low | WAGE DISPARITIES | Low | 43 | 13 | 8 | 64 |
| | | Medium | 19 | 20 | 3 | 42 |
| | | High | 18 | 84 | 25 | 127 |
| | Total | | 80 | 117 | 36 | 233 |
| Medium | WAGE DISPARITIES | Low | 25 | 13 | 6 | 44 |
| | | Medium | 2 | 9 | 1 | 12 |
| | | High | 6 | 40 | 3 | 49 |
| | Total | | 33 | 62 | 10 | 105 |
| High | WAGE DISPARITIES | Low | 1 | 7 | 3 | 11 |
| | | Medium | 3 | 5 | | 8 |
| | | High | 9 | 32 | 2 | 43 |
| | Total | | 13 | 44 | 5 | 62 |

**Chi-Square Tests**

| REGIONAL DEVELOPMENT | | Value | df | Asymp. Sig. (2-sided) |
|---|---|---|---|---|
| Low | Pearson Chi-Square | 58.187 | 4 | .000 |
| | Likelihood Ratio | 61.080 | 4 | .000 |
| | Linear-by-Linear Association | 35.973 | 1 | .000 |
| | N of Valid Cases | 233 | | |
| Medium | Pearson Chi-Square | 28.225 | 4 | .000 |
| | Likelihood Ratio | 29.360 | 4 | .000 |
| | Linear-by-Linear Association | 8.631 | 1 | .003 |
| | N of Valid Cases | 105 | | |
| High | Pearson Chi-Square | 8.318 | 4 | .081 |
| | Likelihood Ratio | 7.135 | 4 | .129 |
| | Linear-by-Linear Association | 2.276 | 1 | .131 |
| | N of Valid Cases | 62 | | |

**Symmetric Measures**

| REGIONAL DEVELOPMENT | | | Value | Approx. Sig. |
|---|---|---|---|---|
| Low | Nominal by Nominal | Contingency Coefficient | .447 | .000 |
| | N of Valid Cases | | 233 | |
| Medium | Nominal by Nominal | Contingency Coefficient | .460 | .000 |
| | N of Valid Cases | | 105 | |
| High | Nominal by Nominal | Contingency Coefficient | .344 | .081 |
| | N of Valid Cases | | 62 | |

(a) Not assuming the null hypothesis.
(b) Using the asymptotic standard error assuming the null hypothesis.

**Case Processing Summary**

| | Cases | | | | | |
|---|---|---|---|---|---|---|
| | Valid | | Missing | | Total | |
| | N | Percent | N | Percent | N | Percent |
| REGIONAL DEVELOPMENT * PERCEIVED DISCRIMINATION * WAGE DISPARITIES | 400 | 100.0% | 0 | .0% | 400 | 100.0% |

**REGIONAL DEVELOPMENT * PERCEIVED DISCRIMINATION * AGE Crosstabulation**

Count

| AGE | | | PERCEIVED DISCRIMINATION | | | Total |
|---|---|---|---|---|---|---|
| | | | Low | Medium | High | |
| Low | REGIONAL DEVELOPMENT | Low | 66 | 69 | 31 | 166 |
| | | Medium | 13 | 21 | 4 | 38 |
| | | High | 1 | 16 | 1 | 18 |
| | Total | | 80 | 106 | 36 | 222 |
| Medium | REGIONAL DEVELOPMENT | Low | 9 | 23 | 5 | 37 |
| | | Medium | 17 | 22 | 4 | 43 |
| | | High | 7 | 9 | 1 | 17 |
| | Total | | 33 | 54 | 10 | 97 |
| High | REGIONAL DEVELOPMENT | Low | 5 | 25 | | 30 |
| | | Medium | 3 | 19 | 2 | 24 |
| | | High | 5 | 19 | 3 | 27 |
| | Total | | 13 | 63 | 5 | 81 |

**Chi-Square Tests**

| AGE | | Value | df | Asymp. Sig. (2-sided) |
|---|---|---|---|---|
| Low | Pearson Chi-Square | 16.112 | 4 | .003 |
| | Likelihood Ratio | 17.932 | 4 | .001 |
| | Linear-by-Linear Association | .775 | 1 | .379 |
| | N of Valid Cases | 222 | | |
| Medium | Pearson Chi-Square | 2.856 | 4 | .582 |
| | Likelihood Ratio | 2.957 | 4 | .565 |
| | Linear-by-Linear Association | 2.330 | 1 | .127 |
| | N of Valid Cases | 97 | | |
| High | Pearson Chi-Square | 3.714 | 4 | .446 |
| | Likelihood Ratio | 5.355 | 4 | .253 |
| | Linear-by-Linear Association | .597 | 1 | .440 |
| | N of Valid Cases | 81 | | |

**Symmetric Measures**

| AGE | | | Value | Approx. Sig. |
|---|---|---|---|---|
| Low | Nominal by Nominal | Contingency Coefficient | .260 | .003 |
| | N of Valid Cases | | 222 | |
| Medium | Nominal by Nominal | Contingency Coefficient | .169 | .582 |
| | N of Valid Cases | | 97 | |
| High | Nominal by Nominal | Contingency Coefficient | .209 | .446 |
| | N of Valid Cases | | 81 | |

(a) Not assuming the null hypothesis.
(b) Using the asymptotic standard error assuming the null hypothesis.

**Case Processing Summary**

| | Cases | | | | | |
|---|---|---|---|---|---|---|
| | Valid | | Missing | | Total | |
| | N | Percent | N | Percent | N | Percent |
| REGIONAL DEVELOPMENT * PERCEIVED DISCRIMINATION * WAGE DISPARITIES | 400 | 100.0% | 0 | .0% | 400 | 100.0% |

**REGIONAL DEVELOPMENT * PERCEIVED DISCRIMINATION * WAGE DISPARITIES Crosstabulation**

Count

| | | | PERCEIVED DISCRIMINATION | | | |
|---|---|---|---|---|---|---|
| WAGE DISPARITIES | | | Low | Medium | High | Total |
| Low | REGIONAL DEVELOPMENT | Low | 43 | 13 | 8 | 64 |
| | | Medium | 25 | 13 | 6 | 44 |
| | | High | 1 | 7 | 3 | 11 |
| | Total | | 69 | 33 | 17 | 119 |
| Medium | REGIONAL DEVELOPMENT | Low | 19 | 20 | 3 | 42 |
| | | Medium | 2 | 9 | 1 | 12 |
| | | High | 3 | 5 | | 8 |
| | Total | | 24 | 34 | 4 | 62 |
| High | REGIONAL DEVELOPMENT | Low | 18 | 84 | 25 | 127 |
| | | Medium | 6 | 40 | 3 | 49 |
| | | High | 9 | 32 | 2 | 43 |
| | Total | | 33 | 156 | 30 | 219 |

**Chi-Square Tests**

| WAGE DISPARITIES | | Value | df | Asymp. Sig. (2-sided) |
|---|---|---|---|---|
| Low | Pearson Chi-Square | 13.371 | 4 | .010 |
| | Likelihood Ratio | 14.317 | 4 | .006 |
| | Linear-by-Linear Association | 6.950 | 1 | .008 |
| | N of Valid Cases | 119 | | |
| Medium | Pearson Chi-Square | 3.959 | 4 | .412 |
| | Likelihood Ratio | 4.780 | 4 | .311 |
| | Linear-by-Linear Association | .373 | 1 | .541 |
| | N of Valid Cases | 62 | | |
| High | Pearson Chi-Square | 10.520 | 4 | .033 |
| | Likelihood Ratio | 11.439 | 4 | .022 |
| | Linear-by-Linear Association | 5.769 | 1 | .016 |
| | N of Valid Cases | 219 | | |

**Symmetric Measures**

| WAGE DISPARITIES | | | Value | Approx. Sig. |
|---|---|---|---|---|
| Low | Nominal by Nominal | Contingency Coefficient | .318 | .010 |
| | N of Valid Cases | | 119 | |
| Medium | Nominal by Nominal | Contingency Coefficient | .245 | .412 |
| | N of Valid Cases | | 62 | |
| High | Nominal by Nominal | Contingency Coefficient | .214 | .033 |
| | N of Valid Cases | | 219 | |

(a) Not assuming the null hypothesis.

(b) Using the asymptotic standard error assuming the null hypothesis.

The SPSS out put can be modified and presented as shown below:

**TABLE 8.9**
**AGE AND PERCEIVED SEX DISCRIMINATION (CONTROLLING FOR WAGE DISPARITIES)**

| *Wage Disparities* | *Age* | *Perceived Sex Discrimination* | | | *Total* |
|---|---|---|---|---|---|
| | | *Low* | *Moderate* | *High* | |
| Low | Young | 48 | 19 | 10 | 77 |
| | Middle Age | 15 | 6 | 5 | 26 |
| | Old | 6 | 8 | 2 | 16 |
| | Total | 69 | 33 | 17 | 119 |
| Chi square =5.305 | | df=4 | | P = .257(N.S.) | C =.207 |
| Moderate | Age | Low | Moderate | High | Total |
| | Young | 18 | 25 | 3 | 46 |
| | Middle Age | 4 | 7 | 1 | 12 |
| | Old | 2 | 2 | | 4 |
| | Total | 24 | 34 | 4 | 62 |
| Chi square = .594 | | | df=4 | P = .964(N.S.) | C =.097 |
| High | Age | Low | Moderate | High | Total |
| | Young | 14 | 62 | 23 | 99 |
| | Middle Age | 14 | 41 | 4 | 59 |
| | Old | 5 | 53 | 3 | 61 |
| | Total | 33 | 156 | 30 | 219 |
| Chi square =2.201 | | | df= 4 | P =.473(N.S.) | C =.473 |

**S=Significant N.S.= Not Significant**

In Table 8.9 the bivariate association between 'age' and 'perceived sex discrimination does not hold good when the effect of 'wage disparities' (control variable) is controlled. The bivariate associations disappear in all the sub categories of 'wage disparities'. Thus, we can conclude that the bivariate association between 'age' and 'perceived sex discrimination' does not hold when the effect of 'wage disparities' is controlled. This type of association is referred as **'Spurious Association'**.

**TABLE 8.10**
**AGE AND PERCEIVED SEX DISCRIMINATION (CONTROLLING FOR REGIONAL DEVELOPMENT)**

| *Regional Development* | *Age* | *Perceived Sex Discrimination* | | | *Total* |
|---|---|---|---|---|---|
| | | *Low* | *Moderate* | *High* | |
| Low | Young | 66 | 69 | 31 | 166 |
| | Middle Age | 9 | 23 | 5 | 37 |
| | Old | 5 | 25 | | 30 |
| | Total | 80 | 117 | 36 | 233 |
| **Chi square =21.149** | | | **df=4** | **P =.000 ( S)** | **C =.288** |
| Moderate | Age | Low | Moderate | High | Total |
| | Young | 13 | 21 | 4 | 38 |
| | Middle Age | 17 | 22 | 4 | 43 |
| | Old | 3 | 19 | 2 | 24 |
| | Total | 33 | 62 | 10 | 105 |
| **Chi square = 5.997** | | | **df=4** | **P =.199 (N.S.)** | **C =.232** |
| High | Age | Low | Moderate | High | Total |
| | Young | 1 | 16 | 1 | 18 |
| | Middle Age | 7 | 9 | 1 | 17 |
| | Old | 5 | 19 | 3 | 27 |
| | Total | 13 | 44 | 5 | 62 |
| **Chi square = 7.574** | | | **df= 4** | **P =.109 (N.S.)** | **C =.330** |

In Table 8.10 the bivariate association between age and perceived discrimination does not hold good for respondents from 'moderate and high regional development'. The bivariate association remains unaffected only in case of respondents belonging to 'low regional development region'. Thus, we can conclude that the bivariate association between 'age' and 'perceived sex discrimination' hold good only for respondents belonging to 'low regional development' area. This type of association is referred as **'Conditional Association'**.

It is evident from Table 8.11 that the bivariate association between 'wage disparities' and 'perceived sex discrimination' remains unaffected when effect of 'age' as third variable is controlled. Therefore, we can conclude that the bivariate association between age and perceived discrimination hold good for respondents of all age groups. Alternatively, we can conclude that the bivariate association between 'wage disparities' and 'perceived sex discrimination' is '***non-spurious***' when the effect of age is controlled.

**TABLE 8.11**

**WAGE DISPARITIES AND PERCEIVED SEX DISCRIMINATION (CONTROLLING FOR AGE)**

| *Age* | *Wage Disparities* | *Perceived Sex Discrimination* | | | *Total* |
|---|---|---|---|---|---|
| | | *Low* | *Moderate* | *High* | |
| Young | Low | 48 | 19 | 10 | 77 |
| | Moderate | 18 | 25 | 3 | 46 |
| | High | 14 | 62 | 23 | 99 |
| | Total | 80 | 106 | 36 | 222 |
| **Chi square = 47.834** | **df=4** | **P =.000 (S)** | **C =.421** | | |
| Middle Aged | Wage Disparities | Low | Moderate | High | Total |
| | Low | 15 | 6 | 5 | 26 |
| | Moderate | 4 | 7 | 1 | 12 |
| | High | 14 | 41 | 4 | 59 |
| | Total | 33 | 54 | 10 | 97 |
| **Chi square =15.888** | **df=4** | **P =.003 (S)** | **C =.375** | | |
| Old | Wage Disparities | Low | Moderate | High | Total |
| | Low | 6 | 8 | 2 | 16 |
| | Moderate | 2 | 2 | | 4 |
| | High | 5 | 53 | 3 | 61 |
| | Total | 13 | 63 | 5 | 81 |
| **Chi square =13.878** | **df=4** | **P =.008 ( S)** | **C =.382** | | |

In Table 8.12 the bivariate association between 'wage disparities' and 'perceived sex discrimination' does not hold good for respondents from 'high regional development'. The bivariate association remains unaffected in cases of respondents belonging to 'low and moderate regional development region'. Thus, we can conclude that the bivariate association between 'wage disparities' and 'perceived sex discrimination' hold good only for respondents belonging to 'low and moderate regional development' areas. This type of association is referred as **'Conditional Association'**.

**TABLE 8.12**
**WAGE DISPARITIES AND PERCEIVED SEX DISCRIMINATION**
**(CONTROLLING FOR REGIONAL DEVELOPMENT)**

| *Regional Development* | *Wage Disparities* | *Perceived Sex Discrimination* | | | *Total* |
|---|---|---|---|---|---|
| | | *Low* | *Moderate* | *High* | |
| Low | Low | 43 | 13 | 8 | 64 |
| | Moderate | 19 | 20 | 3 | 42 |
| | High | 18 | 84 | 25 | 127 |
| | Total | 80 | 117 | 36 | 233 |
| **Chi square =58.187** | | | **df=4** | **P =.000 (S)** | **C =.447** |
| Moderate | Wage Disparities | Low | Moderate | High | Total |
| | Low | 25 | 13 | 6 | 44 |
| | Moderate | 2 | 9 | 1 | 12 |
| | High | 6 | 40 | 3 | 49 |
| | Total | 33 | 62 | 10 | 105 |
| **Chi square = 28.225** | | | **df=4** | **P =.000 (S)** | **C =.460** |
| High | Wage Disparities | Low | Moderate | High | Total |
| | Low | 1 | 7 | 3 | 11 |
| | Moderate | 3 | 5 | | 8 |
| | High | 9 | 32 | 2 | 43 |
| | Total | 13 | 44 | 5 | 62 |
| **Chi square = 8.318** | | | **df=4** | **P = .081(N.S.)** | **C =.344** |

In Table 8.13 the bivariate association between 'regional development' and 'perceived sex discrimination' does not hold good for 'middle aged' and 'old' respondents. The bivariate association remains unaffected only in case of 'young' respondents'. Thus, we can conclude that the bivariate association between 'regional development' and 'perceived sex discrimination' hold good only for 'young' respondents. The association is **'conditional '**.

**TABLE 8.13**
**REGIONAL DEVELOPMENT AND PERCEIVED SEX DISCRIMINATION (CONTROLLING FOR AGE)**

| *Age* | *Regional Development* | *Perceived Sex Discrimination* | | | *Total* |
|---|---|---|---|---|---|
| | | *Low* | *Moderate* | *High* | |
| Young | Low | 66 | 69 | 31 | 166 |
| | Moderate | 13 | 21 | 4 | 38 |
| | High | 1 | 16 | 1 | 18 |
| | Total | 80 | 106 | 36 | 222 |
| **Chi square =16.112** | **df=4** | **P =.003 (S)** | **C =.260** | | |
| Middle Aged | Regional Development | Low | Moderate | High | Total |
| | Low | 9 | 23 | 5 | 37 |
| | Moderate | 17 | 22 | 4 | 43 |
| | High | 7 | 9 | 1 | 17 |
| | Total | 33 | 54 | 10 | 97 |
| **Chi square = 2.856** | **df=4** | **P =.582 (N.S.)** | **C =.169** | | |
| Old | Regional Development | Low | Moderate | High | Total |
| | Low | 5 | 25 | | 30 |
| | Moderate | 3 | 19 | 2 | 24 |
| | High | 5 | 19 | 3 | 27 |
| | Total | 13 | 63 | 5 | 81 |
| **Chi square = 3.714** | **df=4** | **P =.446 (N.S.)** | **C =.209** | | |

## TABLE 8.14
## REGIONAL DEVELOPMENT AND PERCEIVED SEX DISCRIMINATION (CONTROLLING FOR WAGE DISPARITIES)

| *Wage Disparities* | *Regional development* | *Perceived Sex Discrimination* | | | *Total* |
|---|---|---|---|---|---|
| | | *Low* | *Moderate* | *High* | |
| Low | Low | 43 | 13 | 8 | 64 |
| | Moderate | 25 | 13 | 6 | 44 |
| | High | 1 | 7 | 3 | 11 |
| | Total | 69 | 33 | 17 | 119 |
| **Chi square = 13.371** | | **df= 4** | | **P =.010 ( S)** | **C =.318** |
| Moderate | Regional development | Low | Moderate | High | Total |
| | Low | 19 | 20 | 3 | 42 |
| | Moderate | 2 | 9 | 1 | 12 |
| | High | 3 | 5 | | 8 |
| | Total | 24 | 34 | 4 | 62 |
| **Chi square = 3.959** | | **df=4** | | **P =.412 (N.S.)** | **C =.245** |
| High | Regional development | Low | Moderate | High | Total |
| | Low | 18 | 84 | 25 | 127 |
| | Moderate | 6 | 40 | 3 | 49 |
| | High | 9 | 32 | 2 | 43 |
| | Total | 33 | 156 | 30 | 219 |
| **Chi square = 10.520** | | **df=4** | | **P = .033 (S)** | **C =.214** |

In Table 8.14 the bivariate association between 'regional development' and 'perceived sex discrimination' does not hold good for respondents having 'moderate wage disparities'. The bivariate association remains unaffected in cases of respondents having 'low and high wage disparities'. Thus, we can conclude that the bivariate association between 'regional development' and 'perceived sex discrimination' hold good for respondents having 'low and high wage disparities'. **The association is 'conditional ' because bivariate association exists only when wage disparities is either 'low' or 'high'.**

To sum up, we can say that trivariate analysis help us to draw clear and specific conclusions. It also establishes cause-effect relationships. From the above analysis we can conclude that 'wage disparities' is the most significant variable in causing 'perceived sex discrimination' of women working in unorganised sector.

**Pearson Coefficient of Correlation (r)**

Let us consider the hypothesis : Perceived sex discrimination and Wage disparities may be correlated. This hypothesis intends to examine 'correlation' between two variables, namely, perceived sex discrimination and wage disparities. The most frequently used measure of estimating correlation among variables is the coefficient of correlation (r).

**What is correlation ?**

In social research, we often wish to know the relation between variables. One may wish to know, for instance, whether the number of hours student devotes for studies is somehow related to their earlier academic performance, income, age etc. In other words, one may be interested in ascertaining whether a change in one variable is associated with change in another variable. For example, whether the higher income of parents is associated with high expectations of children in respect of salaries they will expect or contrariwise; whether the lower income of parents is correlated with lower expectation of children in regard to salaries they expect. The most frequently used measure of estimating correlations between variables is the coefficient of correlation (r).

The correlation coefficient (r) to be discussed here was introduced by Karl Pearson. Coefficient of correlation is calculated to identify the extent or degree of correlation between two variables. It does not mean that their relationship is functional or constant. In other words, correlation in two sets of data need not always be the result of mutual inter-dependence. Changes in one set of data may be the cause of changes in the other set (of data) and there may be a cause and effect relationship between these two sets. But it is also equally possible that the changes in the two sets of data are the effects of some third factors, which affects both sets of data. As such, the application of coefficient of correlation (r) particularly in social sciences is extremely limited.

**How to obtain Coefficient of Correlation ?**

**From the menu choose 'Analyze' and click on it. You will get a drop down menu as shown below:**

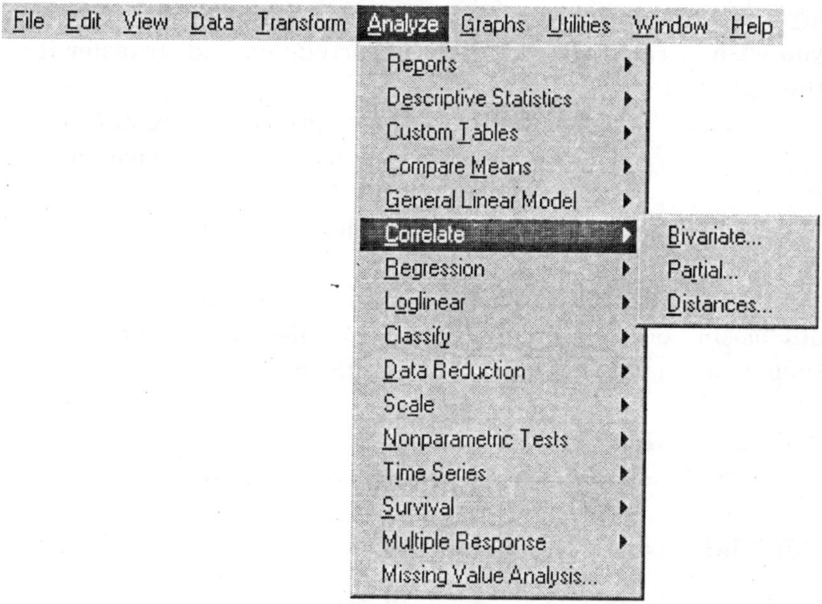


Select 'Correlate' and 'Bivariate' from the sub menu and click on it. The Bivariate Correlations dialog box shown below.

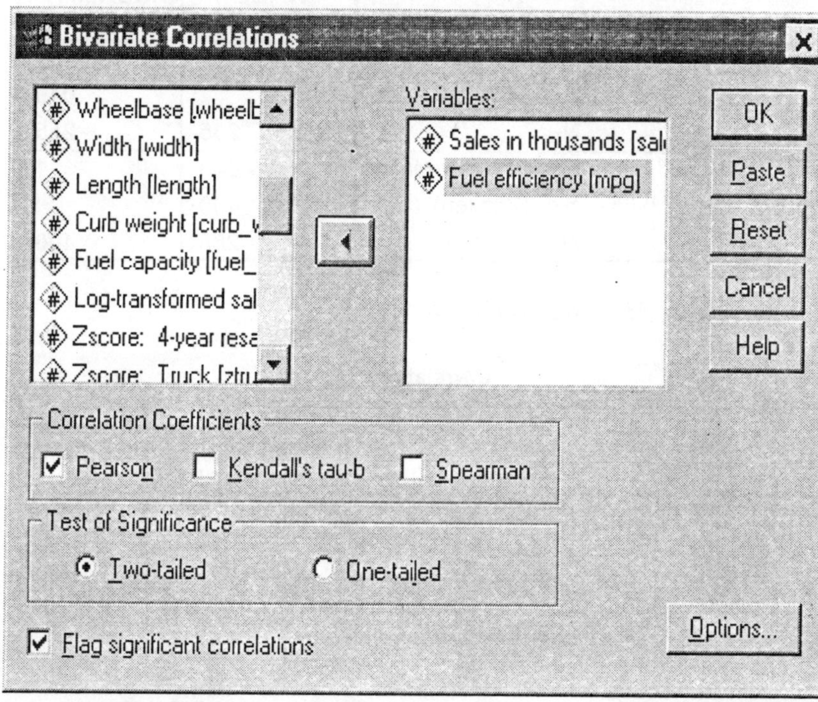

Now you need to select variables from the left box for which you wish to calculate coefficient of correlation and transfer it to the right box.

In the dialog box there are three options of correlations :

□ Pearson □ Kendall's tau-b □ Spearman

You can select the method you need to apply.

In the Bivariate Correlations dialog box , you have the option of choosing either a one-tailed or two tailed test, and SPSS will then give the value of *p* (level of significance).

Click **OK**.

The SPSS samples out put are shown below:

## Correlations

**Correlations**

| | | WAGE DISPARITIES | PERCEIVED DISCRIMINATION |
|---|---|---|---|
| WAGE DISPARITIE | Pearson Correlation | 1 | .434 |
| | Sig. (2-tailed) | . | .049 |
| | N | 255 | 255 |
| PERCEIVED DISCRIMINATION | Pearson Correlation | -.043 | 1 |
| | Sig. (2-tailed) | .490 | . |
| | N | 255 | 400 |

## Nonparametric Correlations

**Correlations**

| | | | WAGE DISPARITIES | PERCEIVED DISCRIMINATION |
|---|---|---|---|---|
| Spearman's rh | WAGE DISPARIT | Correlation Coeffici | 1.000 | .497 |
| | | Sig. (2-tailed) | . | .043 |
| | | N | 255 | 255 |
| | PERCEIVED DISCRIMINATION | Correlation Coeffici | -.050 | 1.000 |
| | | Sig. (2-tailed) | .430 | . |
| | | N | 255 | 400 |

### Coefficient of Correlation by Rank Differences (Spearman's Rho 'ρ' )

Where the direct qualitative measurement of the phenomenon under study is not possible, for example efficiency, intelligence etc., rank-difference method correlation is applied for finding out the degree of correlation. The formula for computing rank correlation is:

### Partial Correlation

Controlling the effect of a third variable on the bivariate relationship by cross-tabulation or partial table method is quite common in the empirical research. However, the method has a serious drawback that limits its use when the number of cases relatively small. The partial cross-tabulation involves subdivision of the sample into gradually smaller subgroups. This reduces the size of cell frequency, thus its reliability and validity is questionable.

An alternative to method of control is the partial correlation. This is a mathematical process of adjustment of the bivariate correlation, demand to nullify the effect of third variable (control variable) on the independent and dependent variables.

**To obtain Partial Correlation :**
**From the menu choose 'Analyze' and click on it. You will get a drop down menu as shown below:**

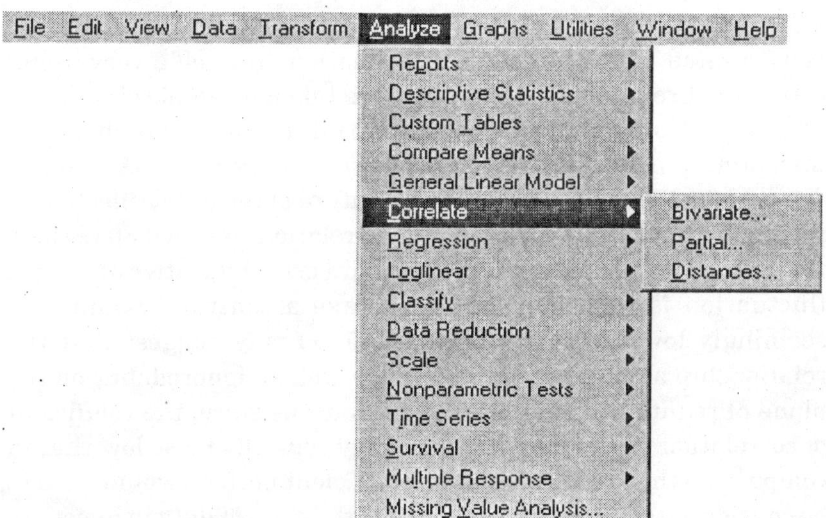

Select 'Correlate' and 'Partial' from the sub menu and click on it.

Click **OK**.

The SPSS samples out put are shown below:

**Partial Corr**

--- PARTIAL CORRELATION COEFFICIENT S ---

Controlling for.. V11

| | V9 | V58 |
|---|---|---|
| V9 | 1.0000 | -.0373 |
| | ( 0) | ( 251) |
| | P= . | P= .555 |
| V58 | -.0373 | 1.0000 |
| | ( 251) | ( 0) |
| | P= .555 | P= . |

(Coefficient / (D.F.) / 2-tailed Significance)

" . " is printed if a coefficient cannot be computed

A caution relating to the meaning of a coefficient of correlation is warranted. The coefficient of correlation, by itself a very useful estimate of relationship, should not be taken as an absolute proof of association among relevant variables in as much as its interpretation depends in a large measure on the size of the sample selected for the study as also on the nature of the data collected. A seemingly high value coefficient of correlation, say, of 0.80 (±) may really be quite misleading if the standard error indicative of sample fluctuation is relatively large. To take a contrary example, a seemingly low coefficient of say 0.45 (±) may suggest that the relationship among the variables may well be ignored, but on the plane of reality this may again be erroneous since, the coefficient of correlation for certain variables may typically be so low that in comparison the above correlation coefficient i.e. 0.45 would need to be considered relatively quite high for the class of data in question.

**Magnitude of Coefficient of Correlation ( r)**

Guilford (1950, p. 165) has offered the following descriptive scale in a partial attempt to answer the question of how 'large' a coefficient must be called 'big':

**TABLE 8.15**
**MAGNITUDE OF COEFFICIENT OF CORRELATION**

| *Absolute Magnitude of Coefficient* | *Degree of Relationship* |
|---|---|
| Less than .20 | Slight, almost negligible |
| .20-.40 | Low correlation, relationship definite but small |
| .40-.70 | Moderate correlation, substantial relationship |
| .70-.90 | High correlation, marked relationship |
| .90-1.00 | Very high correlation, very dependable relationship |

**Positive and Negative Correlation**

When one variable increases (or decreases) and the other changes is the same direction, the relation of the two series is positive; but if the changes in the two variables are in opposite directions, the correlation between the two series is negative. The coefficient of correlation (r) changes in value from positive one (+ 1.0) down through zero (0.0) to negative one or unity (- 1.0).

Usually there are two issues that have to be considered when we interpret the result-the coefficient of correlation. The first issue is concerned with probabilities, and the second issue concern with degree of relationship.

For a coefficient of correlation to be useful for ascertaining relationship it is necessary that coefficient of correlation to be great enough to infer that the coefficient is **not merely a** chance but actually reflects a 'real' association between the variables. SPSS out put for coefficient of correlation displays the probability (alpha).

It also needs to be stressed that a high correlation among two variables does not in itself constitute a proof that they are causally related. A significant correlation between variables; for example, between income and size of family or the size of an educational institution and the performance of the students is hardly any indication of a causal relationship. Suppose we were to find that higher income is inversely correlated with the number of issues i.e., higher the income of parents the lesser their number of issues (the coefficient of correlation is, say, - 0.8 which is statistically quite high), we shall be wrong and unjustified saying that higher income is the cause of lower fertility. It was pointed out earlier that an inference of causality is warranted only if three kinds of proof; concomitant variation, time order and elimination of any other variable as the determining condition of the hypothesised effect can be secured. In this case, following inferences may possibly be drawn in full consideration of the pronounced correlation evident among the variables of income and number of children; (a) one might be causing the other, (b) both the variables might be the effects of some other cause or causes, and (c) the association may be a mere chance occurrence. Casual inferences can obviously be very surely established in an experimental situation. In social sciences, it is very difficult to set up experiments, so most of the studies are non-experimental ones. Analytical procedures have, however, been devised to draw inferences about causal relationship in non-experimental studies. We shall consider these procedures later in this chapter.

**Multivariate Analysis**

So far, we have discussed the relation between two variables where one independent variable is to determine the dependent variable question. In rarity particularly in social sciences however, there is hardly any situation where one independent variable determines the dependent variable. Often we have situations where a set of independent variable is associated with dependent variable. In other words, more often several independent variables contribute to the prediction of the dependent variable. Multiple Regressions is commonly used to estimate the effect of multiple independent variables.

**To obtain Regression**

**From the menu choose 'Analyze' and click on it. You will get a drop down menu as shown below:**

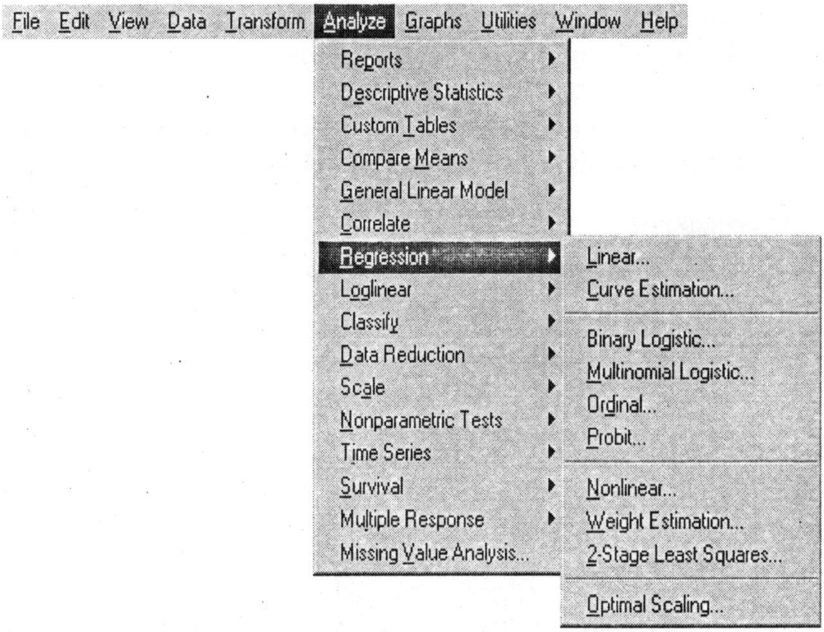


Select 'Regression' and 'Linear' from the sub menu and click on it. You will get Linear Regression Dialog Box as shown below:

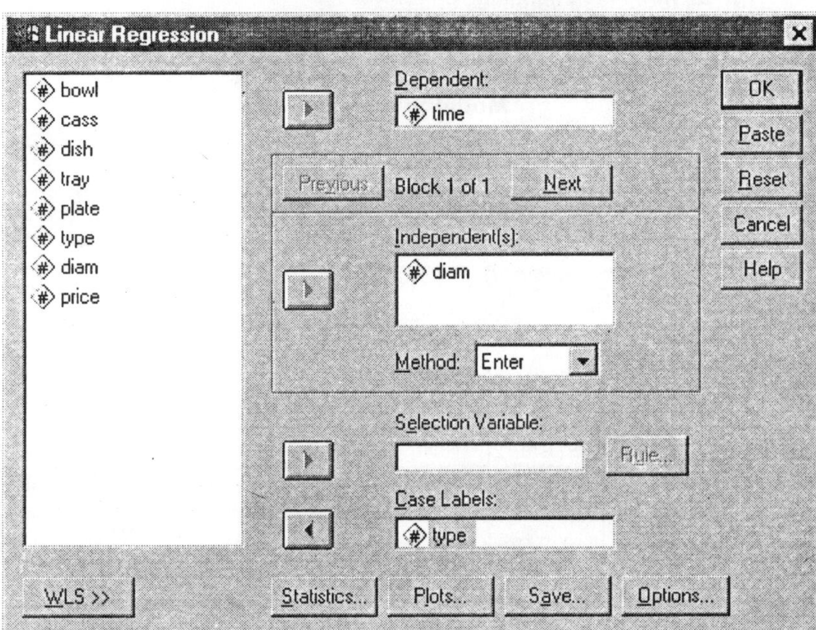

**Select dependent variable from the left box and transfer it to Dependent Variable Box.**

**Select independent variables from the left box and transfer it to Independent Variable Box.**

Click **OK**.

The SPSS samples out put are shown below:

## Regression

**Variables Entered/Removed[b]**

| Model | Variables Entered | Variables Removed | Method |
|---|---|---|---|
| 1 | REGIONAL DEVELOPMENT, WAGE DISPARITIES[a] | . | Enter |

(a) All requested variables entered.
(b) Dependent Variables : PERCIEVED DISCRIMINATION

**Model Summary**

| Model | R | R Square | Adjusted R Square | Std. Error of the Estimate |
|---|---|---|---|---|
| 1 | .043[a] | .002 | -.006 | .66892 |

(a) Predictors : (Constant), REGIONAL DEVELOPMENT, WAGE DISPARITIES

**ANOVA [b]**

| Mode | | Sum Square | df | Mean | F | Sig. |
|---|---|---|---|---|---|---|
| 1 | Regressio | .208 | 2 | .104 | .233 | .793[a] |
| | Residua | 112.31 | 251 | .447 | | |
| | Total | 112.52 | 253 | | | |

(a) Predictors : (Constant), REGIONAL DEVELOPMENT, WAGE DISPARITIES
(b) Dependent Variable : PERCEIVED DISCRIMINATION

**Interpretation of Regression Analysis**

In all, four variables were included in the regression analysis. The regression co-efficient, given in the above Table explains the relative importance of each variable. The negative co-efficient of the variables indicate that increase in the value of these variables is likely to reduce the score measuring the dependent variable. Say, for example, the increase in 'regional development' by one unit, is likely to decrease perceived discrimination by seven units of the score.

'Regional development' was found to be the most important correlate that affected the 'perceived discrimination'. In addition to this, 'wage disparities' and 'age' were also found to be important correlates.

**Tests of Difference**

In the preceding sections we dealt with some tests of associations. The following sections deal with some tests of difference. Parametric tests are based on the assumption that the population is normally distributed. In addition these tests use higher measurement levels, intervals and ratio.

**T- Tests**

There are two types of t –tests; one is called paired t-test, the other one is called t –test for independent samples. The first test is used for the two sets of scores of one group and it is assumed that there are logical relationships between the scores that have been obtained for the group. The other one is used for the scores of one group and is independent of the scores of the other group. That means there are no logical relationships between the scores that have been obtained for one group when compared with other group. However, both the tests are used to assess significance of difference.

**The Paired t – test**

Let us consider the following research hypothesis :

**"There is likely to be a significant difference between wage disparities and perceived sex discrimination".**

We establish a null hypothesis that there is no difference between wage disparities and perceived sex discrimination.

**To obtain t-test value:**

**From menu, choose 'Analyze' and click on it. You will get a drop down menu as shown below :**

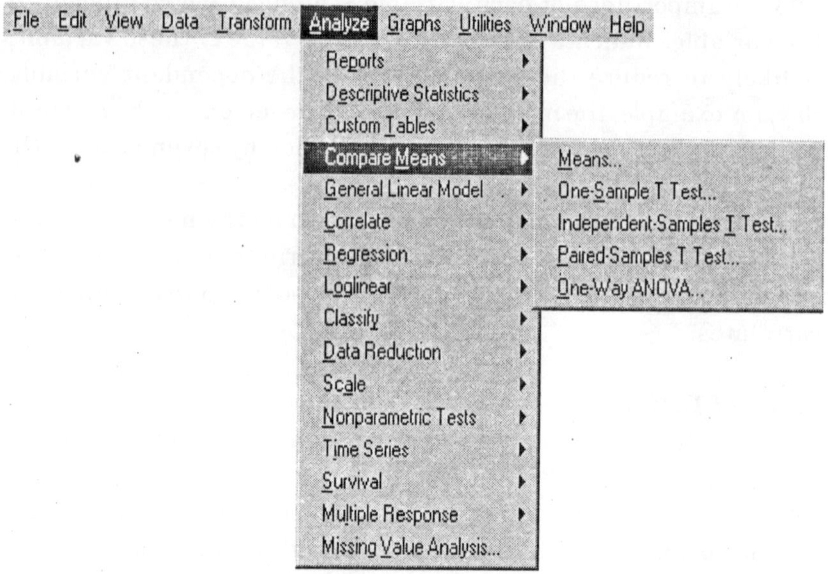


**From the drop down menu choose 'Compare Means' and select 'Paired –Samples T Test...' from the sub menu and click on it . You will get the Paired–Samples Tests dialog box:**

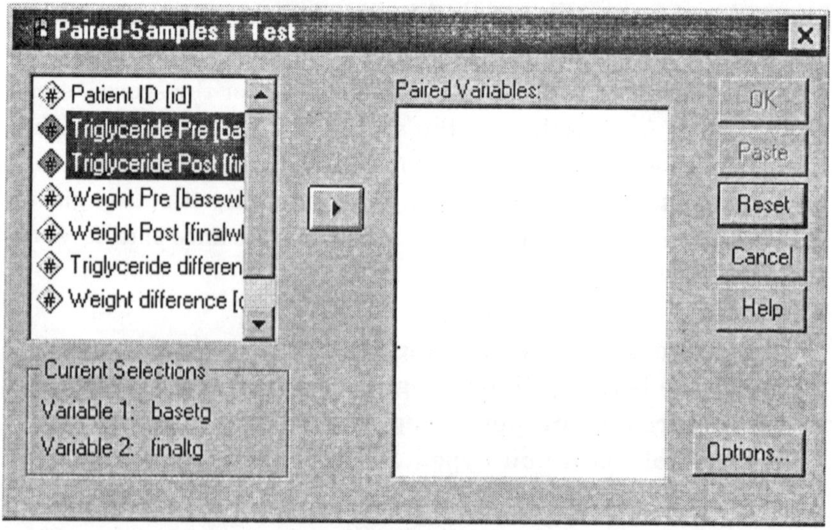

**Select the pair of variables from left box on which you wish to apply t-test and transfer it to the right box.**

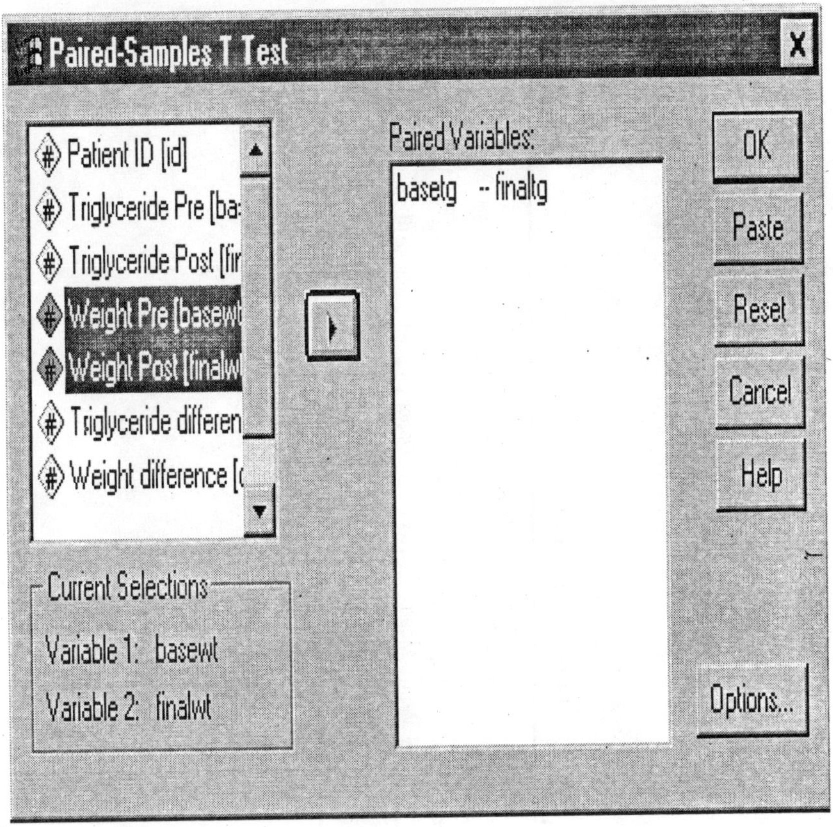


**Click OK.**

**SPSS sample out put**

**T-Test**

**Paired Samples Statistics**

| | | Mean | N | Std. Deviation | Std. Error Mean |
|---|---|---|---|---|---|
| Pair 1 | WAGE DISPARI | 3.25 | 255 | 1.530 | .096 |
| | PERCEIVED DISCRIMINATIC | 8.7882 | 255 | .66571 | .04169 |

**Paired Samples Test**

| | | Paired Differences | | | | | t | df | Sig. (2-tailed) |
|---|---|---|---|---|---|---|---|---|---|
| | | | | | 95% Confidence Interval of the Difference | | | | |
| | | Mean | Std. Deviation | Std. Error Mean | Lower | Upper | | | |
| Pair 1 | WAGE DISPARITIE - PERCEIVED DISCRIMINATION | -5.5333 | 1.69467 | .10612 | -5.7423 | -5.3243 | -52.140 | 254 | .000 |

**Paired Samples Correlations**

| | | N | Correlation | Sig. |
|---|---|---|---|---|
| Pair 1 | WAGE DISPARITIES & PERCEIVED DISCRIMINATION | 255 | -.043 | .490 |

### Interpretation of Paired Samples T Test Results

The test results show that the exact significance is .0000 which is less than .05 hence we reject the null hypothesis and accept the research hypothesis and it can be inferred that there is statistically significant difference in 'wage disparities' and 'perceived sex discrimination' of respondents.

### Independent –Sample T-Test

The t – test for two independent samples examines the difference between their means to see how close or apart they are.

Suppose you are interested in studying whether there is significant difference among male and female respondents with regard to their perception of sex discrimination.

### To obtain t-test value:

From menu, choose 'Analyse' and click on it. You will get a drop down menu as shown below :

Compare Means ——► Independent –Sample T-Test

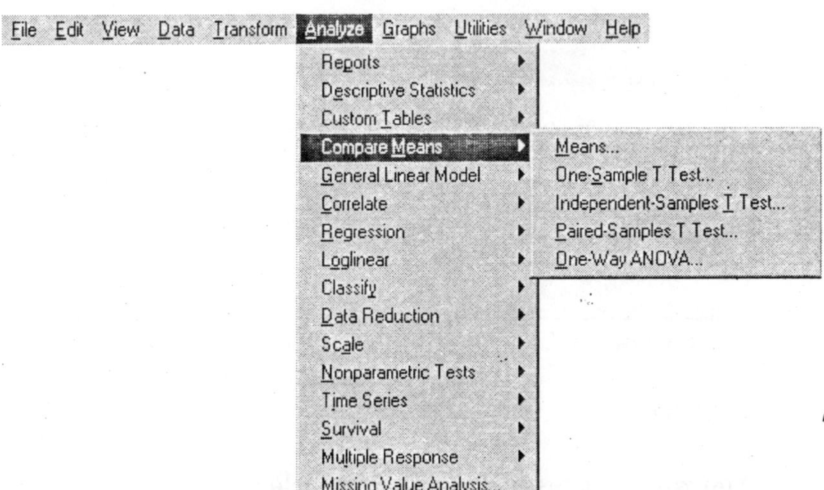

**Click** Independent –Sample T-Test.

You will get Independent-Sample T-Test Dialog Box:

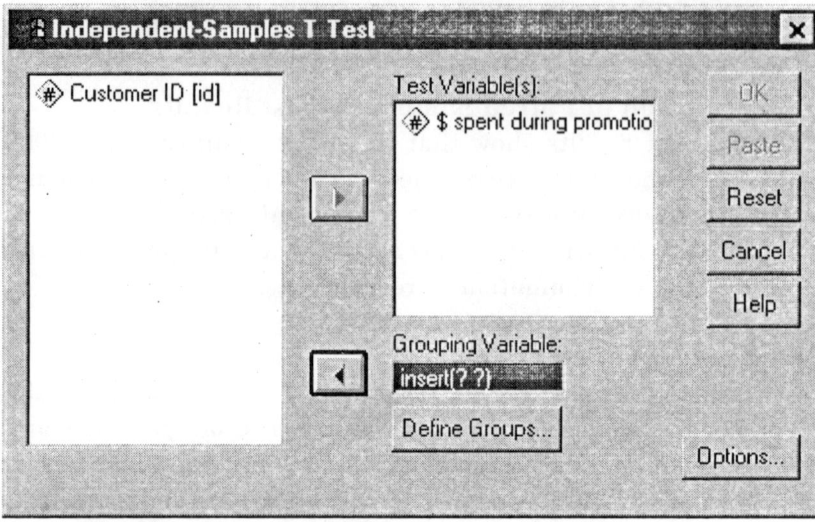


Highlight "Perceived Discrimination" and transfer it to 'Test Variable Box".

Highlight 'Gender' and transfer it to 'Grouping Variable' box.

Click 'Define Variable' button.

Enter 1 (Male) in group 1 and enter 2 (Female) in group 2.

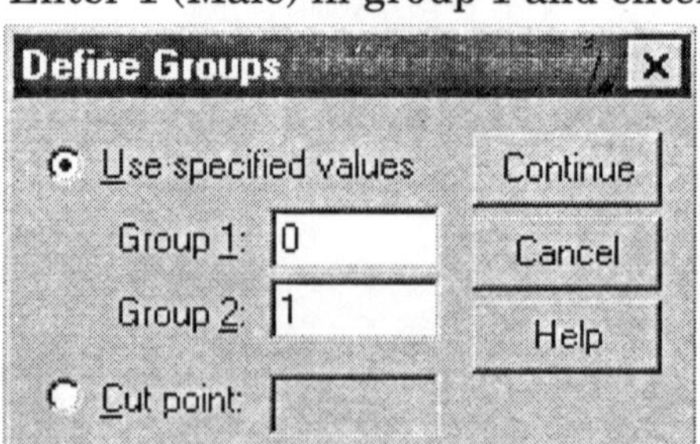


Click 'Continue'.

Click 'O.K.'.

You will get t-test value as shown below:

| | | Paired Differences | | | | | t | df | Sig. (2-tailed) |
|---|---|---|---|---|---|---|---|---|---|
| | | Mean | Std. Deviation | Std. Error Mean | 95% Confidence Interval of the Difference: Lower | 95% Confidence Interval of the Difference: Upper | | | |
| Pair 1 | Triglyceride Pre - Triglyceride Post | 15.56 | 51.794 | 12.949 | -12.04 | 43.16 | 1.202 | 15 | .248 |
| Pair 2 | Weight Pre - Weight Post | 6.81 | 2.257 | .564 | 5.61 | 8.02 | 12.071 | 15 | .000 |

**Interpretation of Independent samples T-Test Results**

Say, for example, we have applied the t-test and the value of the test was found to be 1.202, with 15 degrees of freedom. The value of level of significance (P) was found to be 0.248. A high significance value (typically more than 0.05) indicates that there is no difference between the two variables. Hence, we reject the hypothesis and we can infer that perceived discrimination does not differ by gender.

**The One-Way Analysis of Variance ( F-Test )**

The analysis of variance (some times obtained as ANOVA or F – test) determines whether there is a statistically significant difference between more than two groups on the basis of their means.

There are two variances that are calculated in F – test procedure. The first variance is obtained from between the groups and the second variance is obtained from the values within each of the groups. Suppose, the proposed hypotheses of our research study are reformulated as shown below:

**"Wage disparities may vary by levels of regional development."**

To test this hypothesis we have to examine if wage disparities vary by regional development (three sub- groups-high , medium and low) we have to apply ANOVA. F-test is another test of difference especially designed for examining difference between three sub-groups. F-test procedure compares means for three sub - groups of cases to assess significant difference in means.

**To obtain ANOVA (F-test value):**

From menu, choose 'Analyse' and click on it. You will get a drop down menu as shown below **:**

From the drop down menu, choose "Compare Means" and select "One-Way ANOVA" you will get the following dialog box :

Highlight "Wage Disparities" and transfer it to 'Dependent List Box".

Highlight "Regional Development" and transfer it to 'Factor' box.

Click OK.

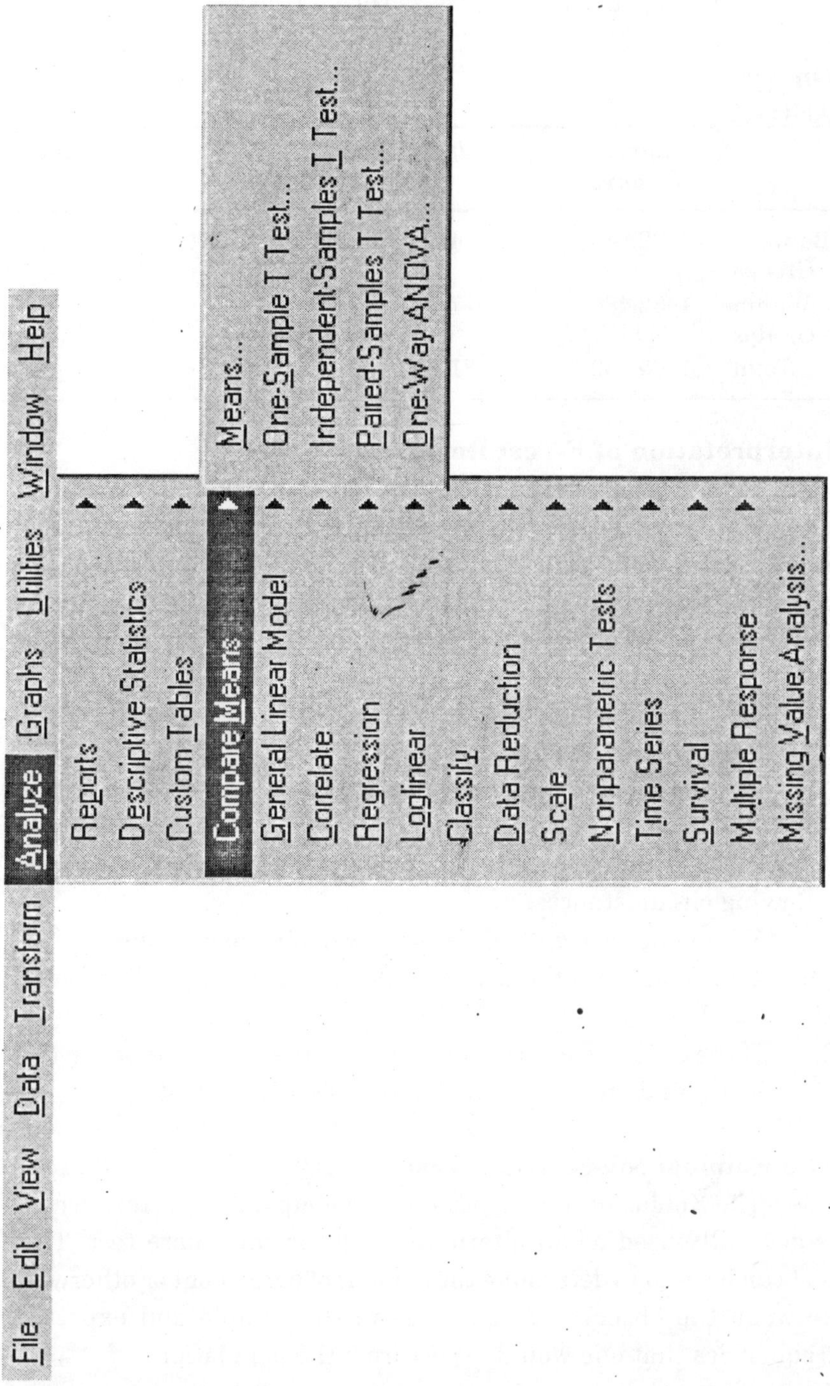
File
Edit
View
Data
Transform
Analyze
Graphs
Utilities
Window
Help
Reports
Descriptive Statistics
Custom Tables
Compare Means
General Linear Model
Correlate
Regression
Loglinear
Classify
Data Reduction
Scale
Nonparametric Tests
Time Series
Survival
Multiple Response
Missing Value Analysis...
Means...
One-Sample T Test...
Independent-Samples T Test...
Paired-Samples T Test...
One-Way ANOVA...

You will get F-Test values as shown below :

**Oneway**
**ANOVA**

| | *Sum of Squares* | *df* | *Mean Square* | *F* | *Sig.* |
|---|---|---|---|---|---|
| Between Groups | 72.845 | 4 | 18.211 | 4.793 | .001 |
| Within Groups | 1432.488 | 377 | 3.800 | | |
| Total | 1505.332 | 381 | | | |

## Interpretation of F-Test Results

Analysis of variance (F-Test) shows, say for example, F=4.793. The value of level of significance (P) was found to be 0.001. A low significance value (typically less than 0.05) indicates that the variance in wage disparities is statistically significant. Hence, we accept the hypothesis and we can infer that wage disparities vary by regional development.

## Non-Parametric Statistical Tests

Nonparametric statistical tests require either no, or very few, assumptions about the population distribution. These tests should be used in preference to the equivalent parametric tests under following circumstances:

1. When data are only of ordinal level of measurement;
2. If the data are interval or ratio, but are abnormally distributed ; and
3. If the data are interval or ratio, but the variances of the two samples do not meet an equality of variance test.

## The Kolmogorov-Smirnov Test

The Kolmogorov-Smirnov test is a nonparametric test, which is generally used as an alternative test for chi-square test. This test can be used to determine the amount of agreement or otherwise between the observed frequencies in the sample and expected frequencies that one would expect from the population.

Let us use the Kolmogorov-Smirnov test for the analysis of this data pertaining to 'regional development' and 'perceived sex discrimination' presuming that they are abnormally distributed.

**To obtain Kolmogorov-Smirnov Test (Non-parametric Chi square Test):**

From menu, choose 'Analyse' and click on it. You will get a drop down menu as shown below :

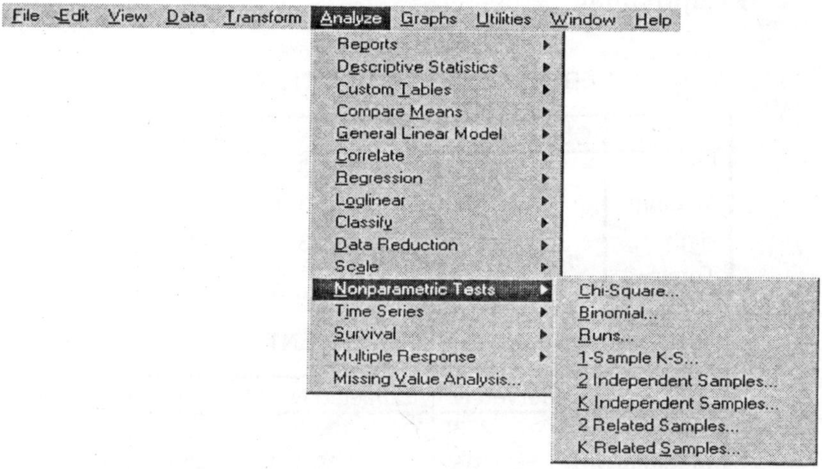


From the drop down menu, choose "Nonparametric Tests". Select "Chi-Square" you will get the following dialog box :

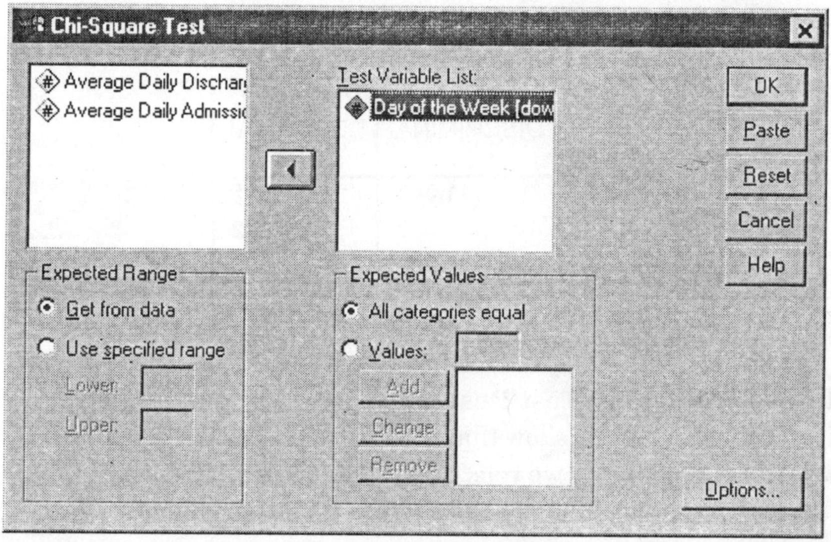

Highlight "Wage Disparities" and "Regional Development" and transfer it to 'Test variable List' box.

**Click OK.**

You will get Chi-square Test values as shown below :

**NPar Tests**

**Chi-Square Test**

**Frequencies**

**PERCEIVED DISCRIMINATION**

| | Observed N | Expected N | Residual |
|---|---|---|---|
| Low | 126 | 133.3 | -7.3 |
| Medium | 223 | 133.3 | 89.7 |
| High | 51 | 133.3 | -82.3 |
| Total | 400 | | |

**REGIONAL DEVELOPMENT**

| | Observed N | Expected N | Residual |
|---|---|---|---|
| Low | 233 | 133.3 | 99.7 |
| Medium | 105 | 133.3 | -28.3 |
| High | 62 | 133.3 | -71.3 |
| Total | 400 | | |

**Test Statistics**

| | PERCEIVED DISCRIMINATION | REGIONAL DEVELOPMENT |
|---|---|---|
| Chi-Square[a] | 111.545 | 118.685 |
| df | 2 | 2 |
| Asymp. Sig. | .000 | .000 |

(a) 0 Cells (.0%) have expected frequencies less than 5. The minimum expected cell frequency is 133.3.

## Interpretation of Test Results

The test results show that the exact significance is .000 which is less than .05 hence we reject the null hypothesis and accept the research hypothesis and it can be inferred that there is statistically significant association between 'regional development' and 'perceived sex discrimination' of respondents.

**To obtain Non-parametric Two independent Sample t-test**

**Choose 'Analyse' from the menu and click on it. You will get a drop down menu as shown below:**

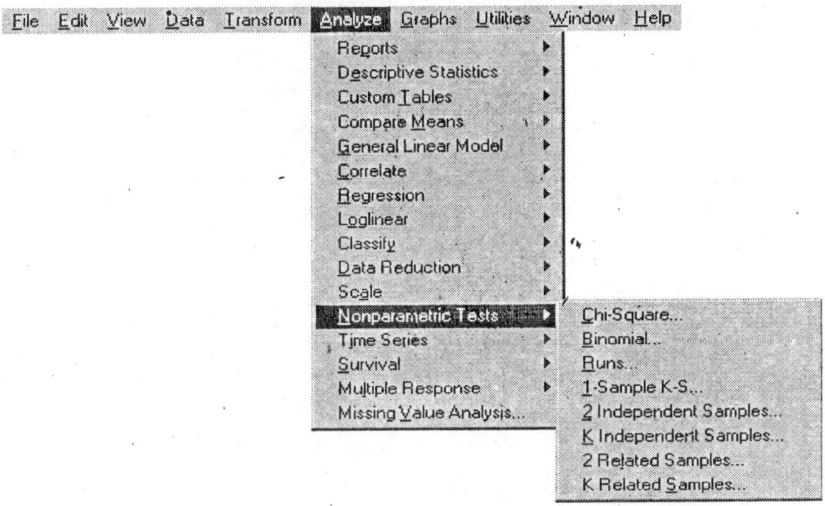


From the drop down menu choose 'Non-parametric Tests' and from the sub menu select '2 Independent-Sample' and click on it. You will get '2 Independent-Sample Tests' dialog box.

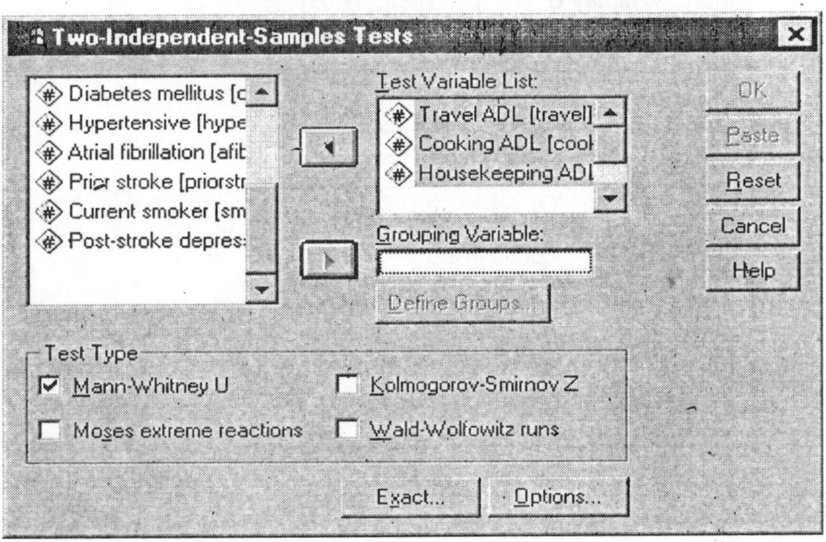

Select the variable, say 'perceived discrimination' from the right box and send it to 'Test Variable List' box . Select Grouping Variable, 'gender' and transfer it to 'grouping variable' box. Define groups; say for Group '1' type '0' (male) and for Group '2' type '1' (female) as shown below :

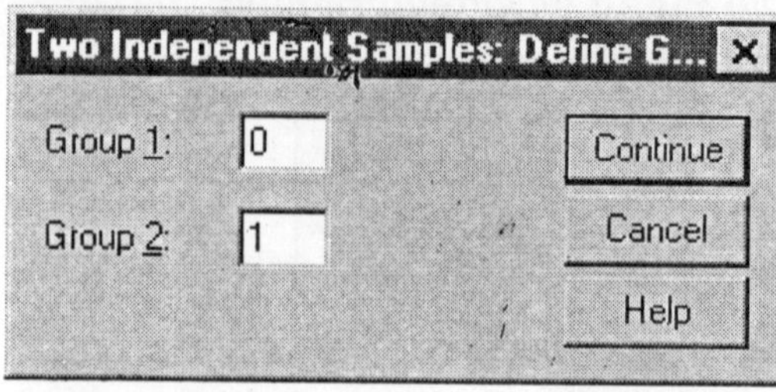


**Click 'Continue'.**
**Click 'OK'.**

**SPSS Sample out put**
**NPar Tests**
**Mann-Whitney Test**

**Test Statistics**[a]

| | PERCEIVED DISCRIMINATION |
|---|---|
| Mann-Whitney U | 10542.000 |
| Wilcoxon W | 15295.000 |
| Z | -.327 |
| Asymp. Sig. (2-tailed) | .744 |

**Ranks**

| | AGE | N | Mean Rank | Sum of Ranks |
|---|---|---|---|---|
| PERCEIVED DISCRIMINATION | YOUNG | 222 | 161.01 | 35745.00 |
| | MIDDLE AGED | 97 | 157.68 | 15295.00 |
| | Total | 319 | | |

(a) Grouping Variable : AGE

## Interpretation of Test Results

The test results show that the exact significance is .744 which is more than .05 hence we accept the null hypothesis and reject the research hypothesis and it can be inferred that there is no association between 'age' and 'perceived sex discrimination' of respondents.

**To obtain Non-parametric Two Related Sample t-test :**

**Choose 'Analyse' from the menu and click on it . You will get a drop down menu as shown below:**

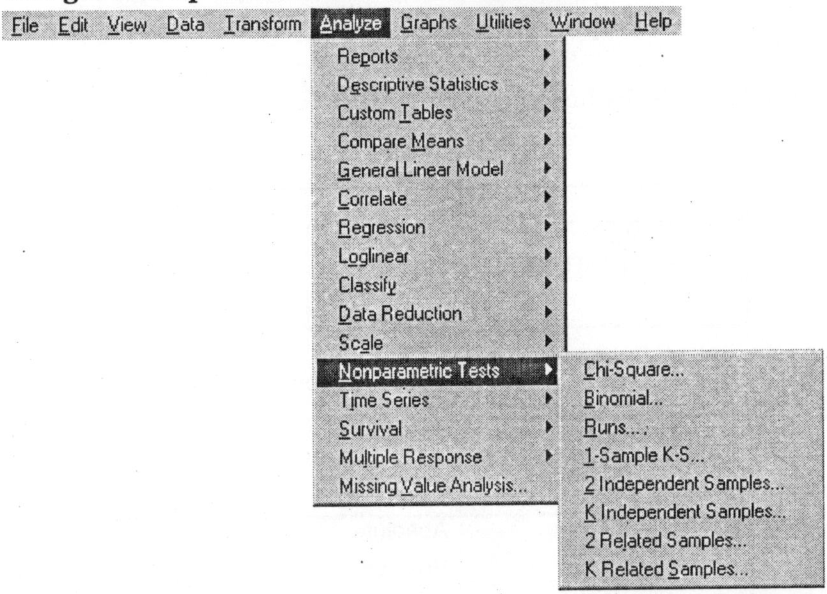


From the drop down menu choose 'Non-parametric Tests' and from the sub menu select '2 Related Sample' and click on it. You will get '2 Related Sample Tests' dialog box.

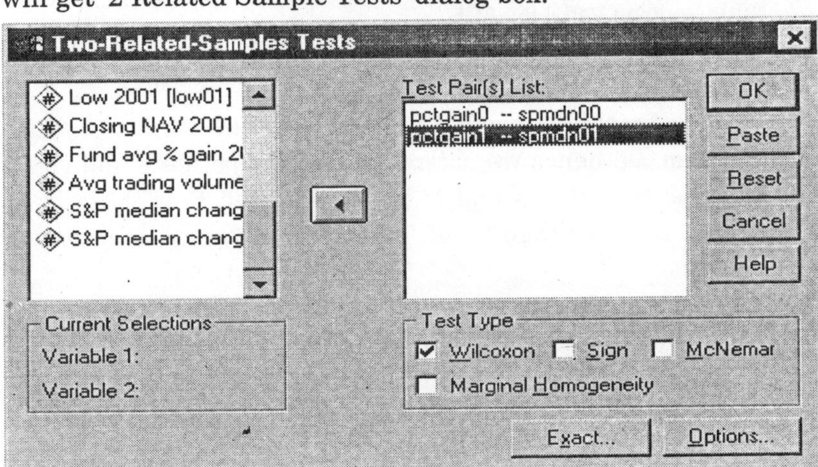

Select the variables, say 'age' and 'perceived discrimination' from the right box and send it to 'Test Pairs List' box . Click 'Wilcoxon'.

**Click 'Continue'.**

**Click 'OK'.**

**SPSS Sample out put**

**Two-Sample Kolmogorov-Smirnov Test**

**Frequencies**

| | AGE | N |
|---|---|---|
| PERCEIVED DISCRIMINATION | YOUNG | 222 |
| | MIDDLE AGED | 97 |
| | Total | 319 |

**Test Statistics[a]**

| | | PERCEIVED DISCRIMINATION |
|---|---|---|
| Most Extreme Differences | Absolute | .059 |
| | Positive | .020 |
| | Negative | -.059 |
| Kolmogorov-Smirnov Z | | .485 |
| Asymp. Sig. (2-tailed) | | .973 |

(a) Grouping Variable : AGE

## Interpretation of Test Results

The test results show that the exact significance is .973 which is more than .05 hence we accept the null hypothesis and reject the research hypothesis and it can be inferred that there is no association between 'age ' and 'perceived sex discrimination' of respondents.

## Selection of Statistical Procedures

Selection of statistical tests primarily, depends upon the nature of hypothesis. For example, let us take the following hypotheses :

1. There may be a direct *association* between regional development and perceived sex discrimination.

2. Perceived sex discrimination and Wage disparities may be *correlated*.

3. Perceived sex discrimination against women at work is likely to *differ* by personal characteristics, say, gender.

4. Wage disparities may *vary* by levels of regional development.

First hypothesis intends to examine 'association' between two variables, namely, regional development and perceived sex discrimination, second is about testing the extent of 'correlation' between two variables, the third one intends to find out if perceived sex discrimination 'differ' by gender. The last hypothesis aims at assessing the extent of 'variance' in wage disparities by regional development. Accordingly, the statistical tests can be categorised into the following categories:

The statisticians have devised scores of statistical tests to measure of association, correlations, difference and variance. We will discuss selection and application of some of the important and commonly used statistical tests.

To select a statistical test we also need to see the level of measurement of data and method of sampling. In Chapter V we have discussed in detail the four levels of measurement, namely; nominal, ordinal, interval and ratio. Various statistical tests have been designed keeping in view the levels of measurement and sampling methods. There are some tests which have been designed considering the structure of table in addition to levels of measurement and sampling methods.

The above discussion about application of statistical tests can be summarized in a tabular form as shown below:

**TABLE 8.16**
**APPLICATION OF STATISTICAL PROCEDURES**

| *Measurement Level of Independent Variable* | *Single Variable Procedures* | *Two-variable (bivariate) Procedures* | | | |
|---|---|---|---|---|---|
| | | *Measurement Level of Dependent variable* | | | |
| | | *Dichotomy* | *Nominal (e categories)* | *Ordinal* | *Interval and Ratio* |
| Dichotomy | Proportions, Percentages, Ratios | Difference of Proportions, Chi square | | | |
| Nominal (e categories) | Proportions, Percentages, Ratios | Chi square | Chi square | | |
| Ordinal | Medians, Quartiles | Mann-Whitney, Smirnov | Analysis of Variance with Ranks | Spearman's Rho (Rank order Correlation | |
| Interval and Ratio | Means, Medians, Standard Deviations | Difference of Means (t-tests ) | Analysis of Variance | | Correlation and Regression |

## References

Abram, M. (1950), *Social Surveys and Social Action,* London : Heinemann.

Ackoff, R.L. (1953) *The Design of Social Research,* Chicago: University of Chicago Press.

Bailey, Kenneth D. (1978). *Methods of Social Research*, London: The Free Press.

Baker, L. Therese. (1988). *Doing Social Research,* New York: McGraw Hill.

Black, James A. and Champion, (1976) .Dean J. *Methods and Issues in Social Research* New York: John Wiley.

Blalock, H.M. (1988) . *Social Statistics*, New Delhi : McGraw –Hill Book Company.

Brace, Nicola. et. al.(2003 ). *SPSS for Psychologists*, New York : Palgrave McMillan.

Buckingham, A and Saunders, (2004). P. *The Survey Methods Workbook.* Cambridge :Polity Press.

Craft, John. (1990). *Statistics and Data Analysis for Social Workers,* Illinois: Peacock Publishers.

Festinger. L. and Katz. D. (eds.). (1953). *Research Methods in the Behavioral Sciences,*New York: The Dryden Press.

Goode. W.J. and Hat. P.K. (1952). *Methods in Social Research,* New York: McGraw Hill.

Guilford, J. P. (1950). *Fundamental Statistics in Psychology and Education.* 2nd ed. New York : McGraw Hill.

Kerlinger. Fred R. (1964). *Foundations of Behavioral Research* , Delhi : Surjeet Publications.

Kidder, Louise H. (1981). *Research Methods in Social Relations,* New York: Holt.

Lal Das, D.K. (2000), *Practice of Social Research : A Social Work Perspective,* Rawat Publications, Jaipur.

Lal Das, D.K. (2005), *Designs of Social Research,* Jaipur: Rawat Publications.

Miller. D.C. .(1964). *Handbook of Research Design and Social Measurement* New York : David Mckey Co.

Monette, Duane R. et. al. (1986). *Applied Social Research: Tool for the Human Services* Chicago: Holt.

Moser. C.A. and Kalton. *Survey Methods in Social Investigation* London : Heinemann Educational Books, 1975.

Nachmias D and Nachmias C. (1981). *Research Methods in the Social Sciences*, New York: St. Martins press.

Rubin, Allen & Babbie E. (1989). *Research Methodology for Social Work*, Belmof, California, Wadsworth.

Sellitz. G. et. al. (1973). *Research Methods in Social Relations.* New York: Holt. Rinehart and Winston (3rd edition.

Stouffer. S.A. *Social Research to Test ideas* New York: Free Press of Glencoe, 1962.

Suchman, E.A. (1953).*The Principles of Research Design*. In John T Dobyet. al., An Introduction to Social Research, New York : The Stackpole.

Wilkinson, T.S. and Bhandarkar, P.L. *Methodology and Techniques of Social Research*: Bombay: Himalayan, 1977.

# 9

# Writing of Research Report

## Introduction

Every research study is concluded by presenting the major findings, conclusions and discussions. The reporting of a research study depends on the purpose with which it was undertaken. One might have conducted a study to present a dissertation for a Post-graduate degree or a Doctoral Degree. It could also be a personal research for preparing a research article to be sent to a research journal for publication. Yet another research study might have been undertaken as an institutional project funded by an outside agency.

Research studies, are scientific studies, hence, it follow certain standard patterns, conventions, styles and formats for maintaining parity in reporting and for easy grasp by others who are concerned with those studies. This chapter is devoted to "Writing of research report". It starts with the purposes of writing a research report, followed by the components of the report itself (the beginning, the main body, and the end).

Once you complete your research project, you are expected to write the report. A research report is a precise presentation of the work done by a researcher while investigating a particular problem.

In the following sections we shall discuss the main components of a research report. The entire research report is mainly divided into three major divisions as shown below:

| *The Beginning* | *The Main Body* | *The End* |
|---|---|---|
| · Title Page<br>· Second Cover<br>· Acknowledgements<br>· Contents.<br>· List of Tables<br>· List of Figures<br>· Glossary | · Introduction<br>· Review of Literature<br>· Designs of Research<br>· Analysis and Interpretation of Data<br>· Major Findings and Conclusions | · Bibliography /References<br>· Appendices |

**The Beginning**

The beginning of a report is crucial to the entire reporting. The beginning or the preliminary section of the research report contains the following items, more or less in the order given below:

- Title Page
- Acknowledgements
- Contents
- List of Tables
- List of Figures and Illustrations
- Glossary

**Title page**

The title page is the beginning of the report, though different universities and sponsoring institutions prescribe their own format for the title page of their project report thesis, generally, it indicates

- Title of the topic,
- Relationship of the report to a degree, course, or organisational requirement,
- Name of the researcher,
- Name of the supervisor,
- Name of the institution where the report is to be submitted, and
- The date of submission.

The title page should carry a concise title of the research study. The title should briefly convey what the study is about. Researchers tend to make errors in giving the title by using too many redundant and unimportant words.

The title should be written in upper case (capital letters) and be placed in the central portion of the top of the cover page. Here, we have reproduced the cover page of a research report in Box 8.1.

**Box 8.1 Sample Title Page of a Research Report**

**LIFE SATISFACTION AMONG OLDER ADULTS**
**: A study in Hyderabad and Secunderabad**

A Thesis Submitted to Osmania University for the Award of the Degree of Doctor of Philosophy in Social Work

**Mrs.T.Saraswati**
**Research Scholar**

**Dr. D.K. Lal Das**
**Research Supervisor**

**Faculty of Social Sciences,**
**Osmania University Hyderabad**

**April 2005**
College of Social Work (ICSW)
Red Hills, Hyderabad - 500004
March, 2002

### Acknowledgements

Acknowledgements should include a short statement of the problem followed by list of people who had extended help in conducting the study. As far as possible it should be simple and specific.

### Contents

A table of contents indicates the logical division of the report into various sections, subsections and chapters. It should also indicate the page reference for each chapter or section and sub-section on the right hand side of the table. Sample table of contents is given below:

Box 8.2 : Table of Contents

## CONTENTS

**Box 8.3 Sample List of Tables**

## LIST OF TABLES



**List of Tables**

The table of contents page is followed by the page containing a list of tables. The list contains the exact title of each table, table number and the page number on which the table has appeared. We provide you in Box 8.3 an example of a list of tables.

**List of Figures and Illustrations**

The page' List of Figures' comes immediately after the 'List of Tables' page. You will observe in the following example that the list of figures is written in the same way as the list of tables.

Box 8.4 Sample List of Figures and Illustrations

LIST OF FIGURES AND ILLUSTRATIONS



**Glossary**

A glossary is a short dictionary, explaining the technical terms and phrases which are used with special connotation by the author. Entries of the technical termed are made in alphabetical order. A glossary may appear in the introductory pages although it usually comes after the bibliography. An exemplar glossary is given below.

**Box 8.5 Sample of Glossary**

**GLOSSARY**

| | | |
|---|---|---|
| Attributes | : | Characteristics of persons or things. |
| Coding | : | The process whereby raw data are transformed into standardized form suitable for computer processing and analysis. |
| Dichotomous Variable | : | A variable having only two categories. |
| Respondent | : | A person who provides data for analysis. |

### Abbreviations

To avoid repeating long names again and again, a researcher uses abbreviations. Since abbreviations are not universal, it is necessary to provide the full form of the abbreviations in the beginning. List of abbreviation is given below.

**BOX 8.6 Sample of Abbreviations**

**ABBREVIATIONS**

| | |
|---|---|
| ANOVA | Analysis of Variance |
| DF | Degree of Freedom |
| M.S.W. | Master of Social Work |
| Ph.D. | Doctor of Philosophy |
| SD | Standard Deviation |
| SRS | Simple Random Sampling |

### The Main Body

The main body of the report presents the research study conducted by a researcher. It tells us about the research study from the problem formulation to conclusions and suggestions. By and large, the main body of a research report contains the following :

- Introduction of the Research Problem
- Review of Literature
- Design of the Study
- Analysis and Interpretation of Data
- Major Findings
- Conclusions and Discussions

### Introduction

The first chapter of a research report is 'Introduction'. It introduces the topic or research under investigation and its importance. The introductory chapter gives the background to the specific area of investigation. This is followed by a brief statement of the problem under study. It is also necessary to explain the significance of the present problem.

In this chapter, researcher is expected to describe precisely and clearly the objective(s) of the research study. This is followed by the statement of the proposed hypotheses of the study that would be tested through statistical procedures. All the concepts, constructs and variables to be used in data analysis are stated precisely in this chapter. Finally, the researcher explains the scope and limitations of the investigations.

Although the order of the contents of the introductory chapter explained above are common, it is not necessary to follow the order strictly; there may be variation in the order of the contents. Sometimes the review of literature related to the problem under investigation is also presented in the first chapter and is placed immediately after providing the background to the problem. Many researchers prefer review of literature to be included in this chapter only and argue that it is essential for identification of objectives and formulation of the hypotheses.

**Review of Literature**

The review of literature is the first task for a researcher in order to decide on a specific problem for study. This chapter of a research report usually contains the review of the relevant literature. This includes a critical analysis of earlier research studies. As such, while reviewing literature, you have to keep in mind that literature has to be critically analysed in terms of agreements and disagreements among the researchers in order to justify the necessity for conducting your investigation.

Review of literature is one of the important stages of research. Some important functions of review of literature are :

(1) Firstly, it helps researchers to select a research problem/topic of study, identify objectives, formulate hypotheses and formulate the theoretical framework for the entire study.
(2) Secondly, such a review indicates the understanding of the researcher in relation to the area of study under investigation, and thus his/her competency to carry out the study.
(3) Thirdly, the review helps reader who wishes to know more about the study by referring to the books mentioned in the review of literature

**Design of Study**

The design of a study is usually described in the third chapter of the report. Broadly speaking, this chapter provides a detailed overview of "how" the study was conducted. The various sub-sections include:

(i) description of the research design of the study,
(ii) variables: the independent, dependent and control variables with their operational definitions;
(iii) sampling procedures : defining the population, and drawing of sample for the present study;
(iv) listing and describing methods and tools of data collection used in the study, like questionnaires, attitude scales, etc., their reliability, validity and administration etc.;
(v) describing the statistical procedures used in the analysis of data including the rationale of the use and method of data analysis.

**Analysis and Interpretation of Data**

This is fourth chapter of the research report. It is the heart of the whole report, for it includes the outcome of the research. The collected data are presented in tabular form and analysed with the help of statistical procedures –parametric and non-parametric. The tables are interpreted and if necessary, the findings are also presented graphically. The figures do not necessarily, repeat the tables, but present data visually for easy understanding and easy comparisons. Data may be presented in parts under relevant sections. The analysis of the data not only includes the actual calculations but also the final results. It is essential that at each stage of analysis the objective(s) and hypotheses of the study taken care of. This chapter also presents the details about the testing of each hypothesis and the conclusions arrived at.

**Major Findings and Conclusions**

This is usually the fifth chapter in a research report. The major findings of the study analysed and interpreted in the preceding chapter are precisely and objectively stated in this chapter. The fourth chapter contains such presentations as only a trained researcher can understand because of the complexities involved; but in the fifth chapter the major findings are presented in a non-technical language so that even non-trained researchers such as a planner or an administrator in the field can make sense out of them.

The major findings are followed by a discussion of the findings. The major findings are compared with the findings of other related research studies which have already been reviewed in the second chapter of the report. Accordingly, the hypotheses formulated in the first chapter are either accepted or rejected. In case the null-hypotheses are rejected, alternative hypotheses are accepted. If the findings do have any discrepancy in comparison with those of other researches, or if the findings do not explain sufficiently the situation or problem under study, or if they are inadequate for generalisations, explanations with proper justification and explanation have to be provided.

The implications should suggest activities for and provide some direction to the practitioners in the field. Unless these implications are clearly and categorically noted, it becomes difficult for the practitioners to implement them on the one hand, and on the other research findings do not get utilised at all even if they have been recorded in a report.

**Writing Style**

The style of writing a research report is different from other writings. The report should be very concise, unambiguous, and creatively presented. The presentation should be simple, direct and in short sentences. Special care should be taken to see that it is not dull and demotivating.

Statements made should be as precise as possible – they should be objective and there should be no room on for subjectivity, personal bias and persuasion. Similarly, over generalisation must by avoided. There is no place for hackneyed, slang and flippant phrases and folk expressions. The writing style should be such that the sentences describe and explain the data, but do not try to convince or persuade the reader. Since the report describes what has already been completed, the writing should be in the past tense.

In the case of citations, only the last name of the author is used, and in all cases academic and allied titles like, Dr., Prof., Mr., Mrs., etc. should the avoided. Some authors recommend that the use of personal pronouns like "I", "We" etc., should be avoided. Similarly, a large number of research reports use passive voice which is strongly discouraged by the linguists.

Special care should be taken while using quantitative terms in a report, such as *few* for number, *less* for quantity etc. No sentence should begin with numerical like "40 students"; instead it should start as "Forty students". Commas should be used when numbers exceed three digits –2,66,556 or 5,23,489, etc.

Language, grammar and usage are very important in a research report, the *Roget's Thesaurus Handbook of Style* by Campbell and Ballon (1974), and a good dictionary would be of much help. MS-Word software provides good support to :

— Spelling and Grammar
— Thesaurus
— Auto Correct
— Auto Summarise

A researcher is advised to use these features on the MS-Word to make the report error free. It is always advisable to show the report to learned friends or language experts for correction before it is finally typed. Revision is an important feature of good report writing – even experienced researchers with much publication revise their reports many times before giving them for final typing.

**References**

Articles, papers, books, monographs, etc. quoted inside the text should always accompany relevant references, i.e., the author and the year of publication e.g., (Das, 2000). If three or more lines are quoted from a source, the page number too should be noted e.g., (Lal Das, 2000 : 120-124). Besides, full reference should be placed in the Reference section of the report.

**Tables and Figures**

**Tables:**

Preparation and appropriate placement of tables in the text are equally important. They need careful attention from the researcher. Tables help the readers to get a quick view of the data and comprehend vast data at one go. However, tables should be presented only when they are necessary. As such you need to be selective in presenting tables in the report. All the tables should be numbered serially in the text, so that they may be quoted or referred to with the help of those numbers conveniently. The title of the table should be brief but self-explanatory.

**Figures:**

Figures are necessary when the data is to be presented in the graphic form. They include charts, maps, photographs, drawings, graphs, diagrams, etc. The important function of a figure is to represent the data in a visual form for clear and easy understanding. Textual materials should not be repeated through figures unless very necessary.

Figures should be as simple as possible and the title of each figure should precisely explain the data that has been presented. Usually, a figure is accompanied by a table of numerical data. Again, figures are presented only after textual discussion and not the other way round. The title design of figures should be followed consistently throughout the report. Every first letter of a word of the title should be in capitals, and figures should be numbered in Indian numerals like 1, 2, 3 etc. And the title, unlike for tables, is presented below the figure.

**The End**

The end of the research report consists of references/ bibliography and appendices. The last section labeled as references/ bibliography appears at the top of a new sheet of paper. The reference section is a list of the works that have been cited in the report/thesis. All references quoted in the text are listed alphabetically according to the last name of the authors. The works of the same author should be listed according to the date of publication with the earliest appearing first.

**Bibliography and References**

Research reports present both bibliographies and references. Although many researchers use these terms interchangeably, the two terms have definite and distinct meanings. A bibliography is a list of books, research reports, articles, etc. that may or may not have been referred to in the text of the research report. References include only such studies, books or papers that have been actually referred to in the text of the research report. Whereas research reports should present references, books meant for larger circulation may be listed in bibliographies that should include all such titles as have been referred to.

There are mainly two style manuals detailing general format and style for research reports. These are:

- American Psychological Association, *Publication Manual,* 3rd ed. Washington, DC: American Psychological Association, 1983.

- *The Chicago Manual of Style, 13th* rev.ed., Chicago University of Chicago Press, 1982.

Style of Referencing

References/bibliographies are arranged in alphabetical order starting with name of the author (in reverse order) and year of publication of the work, title of the book/articles, place of publication and name of the publisher. Place of publication of a book precedes the name of the publisher separated by a ':'(colon).

For example, entries in a reference section may look like the following:

In the case of single author books are referred as:

Lal Das, D.K. (2000), Practice of Social Research, Jaipur : Rawat Publications.

To indicate two authors, 'and' is used between the first and the second author :

Black, James A. and Champion, Dean J. (1976), *Methods and Issues in Social Research,* New York : John Wiley.

In case of more than two authors, only the name of the first author is mentioned followed by *et al.* :

Monette, Duane R. et. al. (1986), *Applied Social Research: Tool For the Human Services,* Chicago : Holt.

In the case of edited Book we need to mention 'ed' as shown below:

Mukhopadhyay, M. (ed.) (1990), *Educational Technology: Challenging Issues*, New Delhi : Sterling Publishers.

In the case of an article in a Journal names of journals are followed by the volume and issue numbers usually in the form 10(3) – Volume 10, Number 2 and page numbers.

Lal Das, D.K. "Correlates of Wage Differential", *Indian Journal of Social Work, 45.3*

In the case of unpublished thesis or dissertation titles are not highlighted and the word 'unpublished' is mentioned.

Saraswati, T. (2005), Life Satisfaction among Older Adults : A Study in Hyderabad and Secunderabad, Unpublished Doctoral Dissertation, Osmania University, Hyderabad.

In references/bibliography all studies are arranged in alphabetical order as shown below :

Black, James A. and Champion, Dean J. (1976), *Methods and Issues in Social Research,* New York : John Wiley.

Lal Das, D.K.(2000), Practice of Social Research, Jaipur : Rawat Publications.

Monette, Duane R. et. al. (1986), *Applied Social Research: Tool For the Human Services* , Chicago : Holt.

Mukhopadhyay, M. (ed.) (1990), *Educational Technology: Challenging Issues*, New Delhi : Sterling Publishers.

**Referring Web Based Documents**

Internet is a rich academic resource. World Wide Web (WWW) is the easiest and most popularly used browsing mechanism on the Internet. Here we will very briefly explain as how to write the references when we quote from any Web Site. When you access the entire Web site (not a specific document on the site), you just give the address of the site in the text. It is not necessary to enter in the reference section.

For examples :

http://www.ignou.ac.in

http://www.webct.com/

Citation of specific document on a web site has a similar format to that for print. Here, we give few examples of how to cite documents. The Web information is given at the end of the reference section. The date of retrieval of the site should be given because documents on the Web can change in content or they may be removed from a site.

Examples :

Duchier, D. (1996), Hypertext, New York: Intelligent Software Group.

[Online] http://www.isg.sfu.ca/duchier/misc/hypertext - review/ chapter4.htm ]Accessed on 25/1/99].

Flinn, S. (1996), Exploiting information structure to guide visual browsing and exploratory search in distributed information systems [Online] http://www.cs.ubc.ca/reading-room/ [Accessed June 1998]

**Appendices**

Usually, the appendix presents the true copy of the tools of data collection used in the study.

In order to demonstrate research report writing, a research article published in a research journal is presented below:

**Box 8.7 Sample of a Research Article Published in a Research Journal**

## SOME SOCIO-ECONOMIC CORRELATES OF MALE-FEMALE WAGE DIFFERENTIAL

**D.K. LAL DAS**

The principle of "Equal Pay for Equal Work" has been accepted all over the world. The Indian Constitution categorically asserts equal pay for equal work, and the Indian Government reinforces this commitment with a legislative measure that provides for the payment of equal remuneration to men and women workers. Nonetheless, the study reveals that the wage differential on the ground of sex exists in some areas of employment. Wage differentials were found to be significantly related to the level of awareness, work experience and education of the employees.

### Introduction

It has been accepted all over the world that women workers should be provided with some special protection and facilities. This opinion at the world level has crystallised in the form of Conventions of the International Labour Organisation1* and the United Nations' Declaration on the Elimination of Discrimination against Women2. **

In India, the Constitution promises equality to all citizens and provides special protection for the realisation of equality for women. Article 39(d), specifically, envisages that the State shall see that there is equal pay for equal work, for both men and women. This principle of "equal pay for equal work" was translated into practice by the enactment of the Equal Remuneration Act, 1976 (here after referred to as 'the Act'). The Act aims to provide for the payment of equal remuneration for the same work or work of similar nature, to men and women workers and for the prevention of discrimination on the ground of sex against women, in the matter of employment.

In spite of all these legal enactments disparities still persist between the wages of male and female employees working on the same job or job of a similar nature, and discrimination on the basis of sex in the matter of employment also exists. It is rather disappointing to find that the effectiveness of this well-intentioned legislation has been extremely limited.

What causes the observed wage differentials, on the basis of sex is controversial. However, the following are a few propositions, often quoted by research scholars as causes for discrimination against women at work place:

(a) Young women are too likely to withdraw from the labour force for marriage and child bearing.

(b) Men have a greater responsibility than women do for supporting a family, and so have a greater right to a job.

(c) Women, who re-enter the labour force later in life, lack the sustained work experience that most men have.

(d) Women always earn, not to support the family, but to supplement the family income and, as such, women could be available for work even below 'the cost of living'.

(e) Women avoid confrontation for the fear of losing their jobs and suffer silently.

Thus, the areas that call for investigation are:

(a) The role of labour administration (law enforcement machinery) with regard to implementation of the Act could be one of the important areas of study, in the sense that it is the authority that can translate the provisions of the Act into actual practice.

(b) Non-compliance of the statutory provisions by the employers, which may account for much of the wage differential, requires proper investigation. There may be cases, where provisions of the Act may not be observed in their true sense. This may result in a wide gap between what the law provides for and the actual practice.

(c) Often, due to inappropriate social circumstances, state of economic development, their ignorance and the fear of losing their jobs, women accept whatever terms and conditions of employment are offered to them. As such, the existing wage disparities and discrimination could be attributed to the socio-economic characteristics of female employees (here after referred to as SECE).

This paper deals only with data relating to the third interface.

The aim of the present study was to investigate the disparities in wages/salary of male and female employees for work of similar nature, and to identify the important SECE correlates of wage differential. Specifically, the following objectives were sought to be achieved through a multivariate analysis of data:

(a) What is the relationship between the observed wage differential and SECE variables?

(b) Which SECE correlate or set of SECE correlates is most critical in explaining variation in observed wage differential?

(c) What is the individual contribution of each correlate in influencing observed wage differential?

**Some Research Findings**

There have been quite a few micro-studies (Gambhir, 1979; Khanna and Mathew, 1979; Patel, 1982), that show that the disparities in wages/salary of male and female employees for work of similar nature, is part of the general discrimination against women at the work place. Particularly, in unorganised sector, women are invariably paid much less than the males.

According to the studies conducted by Pais (1980), Labour Bureau (1979), Occupational Wages Surveys (1963), with respect of select industries as well as employment, the adoption of the principle of "equal pay for equal work" has discouraged employers from employing women workers profitably. Most probably, one of the reasons for employing women workers was that it was cheaper.

What is the relationship between wage differential and regional development? This aspect was studied by the Prgoramme Evaluation Organisation of the Planning Commission (1961). The results show that inter-state variations are quite significant.

**Research Methodology .**

**Estimation of Wage Differential (Dependent Variable)**

Observed wage differential is defined operationally as the difference between the total monthly incomes (before deductions) of a male and a female employee, working on the same job or job of a similar nature.

**Study Area and Sampling**

The study was confined to the three regions of the State of Andhra Pradesh: Coastal Andhra (developed). Telangana (developing) and Rayalseema (underdeveloped). The sampling frame included all the 52 employments specified in the list of employment under the Act.

A major portion of the 52 employments specified under the Act includes industrial establishments. Therefore, a large portion of the sample covers industrial workers. Apart from industries, the other establishments included in the sample are hospitals, educational institutions, welfare services, air transport, and sanitary services, banks, hotels, agriculture and construction work.

In order to be included in the sample, an employee had to satisfy the following conditions:

(i) Male and female employees doing the same work or work of a similar nature.
(ii) Male and female employees having same designation; and
(iii) Both working in the same organisation.

Pairs of respondents (male and female), who satisfied these conditions, were selected from the different areas of employment.

Of the 139 pairs of employees that qualified, 17 respondents (both male and female) could not be contacted. Thus, the study involves interviews with 122 pairs of respondents. The size of sample selected for the study is 244.

**Tools and Methods of Data Collection**

Data on wages/salary and personal characteristics were collected from payroll records and employment application forms. For other SECE variables, data were collected by using a pretested interview schedule.

**Results and Discussion**

Table 1 presents the inequality of income between male and female employees.

The mean of the total monthly income for female employees was Rs. 496.87 (SD=234.19; n=122); for the male employees this mean was Rs. 706.16 (SD=379.67; n=122). These data indicate the extent of wage differential between male and female employees. The wage differential is found to be significantly different (t=93.32; p<0.001).

The differentials are large in economic terms. For example, the Rs. 118.54 differential in monthly wages/salary, between male and female employees, implies an annual male-female wage differential of Rs. 1422.48.

**TABLE 1**
**INEQUALITY OF INCOME BETWEEN MALE AND FEMALE EMPLOYEES (OBSERVED)**

| *Workers* | *Average Monthly Income* | *S.D.* | *CV* | *t* | *Average Male – Female wage differential* | *S.D.* |
|---|---|---|---|---|---|---|
| Male | 706.16 | 379.67 | 33.765 | 93.321* | 118.54 | 455.79 |
| Female | 496.87 | 234.19 | 47.133 | | | |

Observed wage differential is defined operationally, as the difference between the total monthly income of a male and a female employee working on the same job. Ideally, the sample of female employees should have been matched with male employees for their work experience, level of education, level of skills, age, and for year of appointment (and many other variables), to determine the true wage differential. This was clearly impossible, given the occupational heterogeneity of the sample. Instead, under the assumption that sex discrimination was not operative for men, multiple regression were obtained for the male sample to determine the optimal weighing of selected variables in predicting wages. The results of these multiple regression are presented in Table 3.

**TABLE 2**
**BETA WEIGHTS OF SELECTED VARIABLES OBTAINED FROM THE SAMPLE OF MALE EMPLOYEES**

| *S.No.* | *Variables* | *Beta Weights* |
|---|---|---|
| 1. | COLL | 336.224 |
| 2. | DEVING | 203.700 |
| 3. | TOEXP | 17.651 |
| 4. | ILL | 121.574 |
| 5. | UNDEV | 59.772 |
| 6. | AGE | 1.494 |

Multiple $R^2$ = 0.3647
Multiple R = 0.60398
Percentage variation Explained = 36.47914
Constant = 136.14583

**TABLE 4**
**RATIOS OF WAGE DIFFERENTIAL TO EXPECTED AND OBSERVED VALUES**

| *Mean* | *Standard Deviation* | *t-value* | *Wage Differential (= Observed expected)* | *Ratio of Discrepancy to Expected Value** | *Ratio of discrepancy to Observed Value** | |
|---|---|---|---|---|---|---|
| Observed Value | 496.8653 | 234.1930 | 40.784 | *** -89.7658 | *** -15.30191 | -18.06642 |
| **Expected Value** | **586.6311** | **353.6689** | | **(SD=503.5495)** | | |

$* = \dfrac{\text{Observed Value - expected Value}}{\text{expected value}} \times 100$

$** = \dfrac{\text{Observed Value - expected Value}}{\text{expected value}} \times 100$

*** Negative sign affixed to the value indicates that the female worker received fewer wages than would be expected/observed.

On the basis of the weights provided by the multiple regression computed on the sample of male employees, expected wages/salary were computed for the sample of female employees. Ratios of wage differential to expected and observed values were then computed. The results are presented in Table 4.

The mean wage differential (wage differential = observed ware-expected wage) for female employees was Rs. 89.77 (SD=Rs. 503.55; n=122); for male employees this mean was Rs. 285.00 (SD=Rs. 303.85; n=122). Sex differences in wage differentials, for female and male employees, indicate the extent to which the principle of wage fixation was differentially applied to female employees and to male employees. The differentials between the wages/salary of female employees 'should' have received, based on the multiple regression equation, and the wages/salary they 'in fact' received, was significantly different from the comparable differentials for the male employees ($t=75.890$; $p<0.001$).

By dividing the mean wage differential (female) by their mean expected wages/salary, it was possible to calculate the percentage of a male employee's estimated wage/salary that an equally qualified female employee would receive. According to this estimate, an equally qualified female employee would receive 15.30 per cent less than a comparable male employee's income.

Similarly, by dividing the mean wage differential (female) by their mean observed wages/salary it was possible to calculate the percentage of her present wages/salary that each female employee 'lost' by virtue of being a woman. The average figure that resulted was 18.07 per cent. In other words, the average female employee should have received 18.07 per cent more than her current wages/salary, to make her wages/salary equivalent to a man with the same scores on the selected variables.

In order to study the correlates of wage differentials, a set of 10 variables were considered. Table 5 presents the intercorrelation matrix for the variables.

It may be inferred from Table 5, that three independent variables are not significantly correlated to each other, which means that the effect of these independent variables on the wage differential (dependent variable) is likely to be its individual effect and is not influenced by other independent variables. However, seven independent variables (marked with asterisk) have been found to be significantly correlated with the dependent variable.

## TABLE 5

## INTERCORRELATION MATRIX FOR THE SELECTED VARIABLES

| *Variable No.* | *X1* | *X2* | *X3* | *X4* | *X5* | *X6* | *X7* | *X8* | *X9* | *X10* | *X11* |
|---|---|---|---|---|---|---|---|---|---|---|---|
| X1 | 1.000 | 0.523 | 0.260 | -0.270 | -0.033 | -0.298 | -0.059 | -0.034 | -0.317 | 0.024 | 0.025 |
| X2 | 0.523 | 1.000 | -0.031 | -0.133 | 0.070 | 0.092 | -0.195 | 0.227 | -0.012 | 0.262-0.28** | |
| X3 | 0.260 | 0.031 | 1.000 | -0.666 | 0.196 | -0.318 | -0.070 | 0.105 | -0.357 | -0.040 | 0.3** |
| X4 | -0.270 | -0.133 | -0.666 | 1.000 | -0.162 | 0.212 | 0.027 | -0.138 | 0.319 | 0.036 | -0.3** |
| X5 | -0.033 | 0.070 | 0.196 | -0.162 | 1.000 | -0.121 | 0.060 | -0.147 | -0.232 | -0.036 | -0.046 |
| X6 | -0.298 | 0.092 | -0.318 | 0.212 | -0.121 | 1.000 | -0.134 | 0.324 | 0.848 | 0.148 | -0.2** |
| X7 | -0.059 | -0.195 | -0.070 | 0.027 | 0.060 | -0.134 | 1.000 | -0.455 | -0.153 | -0.473 | 0.18* |
| X8 | -0.034 | 0.227 | 0.105 | -0.138 | -0.147 | 0.324 | -0.455 | 1.000 | 0.198 | 0.530 | -0.142 |
| X9 | -0.317 | -0.012 | -0.357 | 0.819 | -0.232 | 0.848 | -0.153 | 0.198 | 1.000 | 0.210 | -0.3** |
| X10 | 0.051 | 0.262 | -0.040 | 0.036 | -0.036 | 0.148 | -0.473 | 0.530 | 0.210 | 1.000 | -0.2** |
| X11 | 0.025 | -0.283 | 0.320 | -0.330 | -0.046 | -0.260 | 0.186 | -0.142 | -0.337 | -0.258 | 1.000 |

'R' Significant at 0.05 = 0.17613

R Significant at 0.01 – 0.22892

* Significant at 0.05 level

** significant at 0.01 level

**TABLE 6**
**REGRESSION ANALYSIS OF INDEPENDENT VARIABLES**

Dependent Variable : Wage Differential (Observed)
Mean : 188.54
Standard Deviation : 455.79

| *Variable No.* | *Explanatory Variables* | *Standardised Beta Co-efficient (B)* | *Regression Co-efficient (b)* | *Standard Error* | *t-Values* |
|---|---|---|---|---|---|
| X9 | AWAR | -0.43969 | -485.12908 | 184.85340 | 2.62440* |
| X2 | TOEXP | -0.29998 | -30.89918 | 10.53238 | 2.93373* |
| X4 | COLL | -0.22218 | -240.82327 | 117.08562 | 2.05681* |
| X5 | MARR | -0.17932 | -185.80535 | 89.29196 | 2.08087* |
| X10 | OBS | -0.04076 | -20.22793 | 51.18891 | 0.39516 |
| X6 | ATUNEQ | 0.26494 | 357.73318 | 228.88216 | 1.56296 |
| X3 | ILL | 015119 | 140.57127 | 103.37046 | 1.35988 |
| X8 | UNDEV | -0.16709 | -154.85873 | 124.48085 | 1.24404 |
| X1 | AGE | 0.01892 | 1.14754 | 6.36663 | 0.18024 |

Multiple $R^2$ = 0.33033
Multiple R = 0.57474
Percentage Variation
Explained = 33.03299
Constant = 2143.81995
*significant at .05 level.

The correlation is negative in nature, except in the case of 'illiterate'. Since there are only zero-order correlation, it is difficult to determine the exact contribution of each correlate in explaining variations in wage differential. To quantify the contribution of the independent variables, the technique of regression analysis was applied.

In all, ten variables were included in the regression analysis. One variable did not have any additional impact on the dependent variable beyond that which the first nine variables had. In other words, one variable turned out to be insignificant as far as wage differential is concerned. The regression co-efficient, given in Table 6, explains the relative importance of each variable. The negative co-efficient of the six variables indicate that increase in the value of these variables is likely to reduce the score measuring the dependent variable. Say, for example, the increase of the level of awareness of the Act by one unit, is likely to subtract 0.44 units in the score determining the wage differential.

The level of awareness about the Act, was found to be the most important correlate that affected the wage differential. In addition to this, work experience and level of education were also found to be important correlates. The combination of these three correlates was identified as the 'best equation' on the basis of the following criteria:

(a) The combination should explain maximum variation in the wage differential.

(b) The contribution of each correlate in the equation should be negative.

(c) The contribution of each correlate should be statistically significant at the 5 per cent level.

The 'best equation' can be expressed in the following regression form **3

**Y = Const. +b1 X1 +b2 X2 + b3 X3**

**Where Y is wage differential, b1, b2 and b3 are regression co-efficients and X1, X2 and X3 are correlates.**

The equation can be evaluated by using the regression co-efficients of correlates:

Wage Differential = 2143.820 – 485.129 (AWAR) – 30.899 TOEXP – 2440.823 COLL.

**TABLE 7**
**INDIVIDUAL CONTRIBUTION OF EACH CORRELATE**

| *Variable No.* | *Name of the Correlate* | *Zero-Order Correlation with Wage differential Yxy* | *1st –Order Partial Correlation with Wage Differential* | *Regression Co-efficient (b)* | *Standardised Beta Co-efficient (B)* | *Individual Contribution B.Yxy* |
|---|---|---|---|---|---|---|
| X13 | AWAR | -0.337** | -0.242** | -485.129** | -0.440** | 0.148 |
| X2 | TOEXP | -0.283** | -0.268** | -30.899** | -0.300** | 0.085 |
| X5 | COLL | -0.330** | -0.192** | -240.823 | -0.222** | 0.073 |
| | | | | | Total | 0.306 |

*p<.05 **p< 01

**TABLE 8**
**CORRELATES OF WAGE DIFFERENTIAL**

| *SECE* | | *Wage Differential* | | | *Total* | $X^2$ | *Degree* | *Probability of freedom* |
|---|---|---|---|---|---|---|---|---|
| | | *Low* | *Med.* | *High* | | | | |
| 1. Aware of the Act | Yes | 4(50) | 3(37.5) | 1(12.5) | 8(100) | 4.463 | 2 | P 0.02 |
| | No | 33(20.2) | 47(41.2) | 44(38.6) | 114(100) | | | |
| | Total | 27 | 50 | 45 | 122 | | | |
| 2. Total Work Experience in years | | | | | | | | |
| 1 - 4 | | 11(25.6) | 17(39.5) | 15(34.9) | | 43(100) | | |
| 5 - 6 | | 10(19.6) | 18(35.3) | 23(45.1) | | 51(100) | 3.943 | 4 P 0.05 |
| 10 - 22 | | 6(21.4) | 15(53.6) | 7(25.0) | | 28(1000 | | |
| | Total | 27 | 50 | 45 | | 122 | | |

*(Contd.)*

*(Contd. Table-8)*

| SECE | Wage Differential Low | Med. | High | Total | $X^2$ | Degree of freedom | Probability |
|---|---|---|---|---|---|---|---|
| 3. Level of Education | | | | | | | |
| Illiterate | 8(9.4) | 39(45.9) | 38(44.7) | 85(100) | | | |
| Upto Matric | 5(50.0) | 3(30.0) | 2(20.0) | 10(100) | 26.793 | 4 | P 0.001 |
| Above Matric | 14(51.8) | 8(29.6) | 5(18.5) | 27(100) | | | |
| Total | 27 | 50 | 45 | 122 | | | |

'Awareness' , 'total experience' , and 'college education' , the three correlates included in the best equation, were found to be the most critical correlates of wage differentials. Together, these three correlates account for 31 per cent variations in the wage differential. The break-up of this explanatory power, in terms of individual contribution of each correlate, is shown in Table 7.

A look at Table 8 will show that nearly 93 per cent of the respondents are not even aware of the existence of the Act. This clearly indicates that the basic *sine qua non* of a law, i.e. strong communication network, is missing in the present implementation of the scheme and, therefore, needs to be carefully articulated. Surprisingly, even till date, no suitable method has been evolved to communicate the enacted law to the people whom they concern. It is, perhaps, one of the reasons why the disparities on the ground of sex still persist, and discrimination on the basis of sex in the matter of employment exists.

**TABLE 9**

**MEAN VALUES FOR INDICATOR OF "INTERMITTENCY"**

| *Sex* | *Mean Value of Variable* | |
|---|---|---|
| | *Previous Jobs held* | *Gap between Jobs in years* |
| Male | 1.35 | 2.15 |
| Female | 2.45 | 3.00 |

As can be seen from Table 8 and 9, the women in our sample differ from the men with respect to work experience, number of jobs held prior to the present job, and the gap between jobs. First, they are, on an average, less experienced than men. Second, women have held fewer jobs than have men, despite their greater intermittency. It could be attributed to the withdrawal of women employees from the labour force for marriage and child-bearing. This analysis, therefore, reinforces the significance of work experience as a correlate of wage differential. Though the literacy and the education of women have been of special concern to Indian planners and social reformers, the literacy among females (24.88

per cent, according to 1981 census) lags far behind literacy among males (46.74 per cent). These data for female and male employees (respondents), under the study, are 45.6 per cent and 71.9 per cent (Table 8), respectively. Thus, it appears that women have to go a long way, in order to achieve an equal position to men, with respect to literacy. This could be another reason, why women employees continue to be oppressed and exploited at their place of work. How will they benefit from legislation, if they do not know how to make use of it? An examination of Table 8 reveals that wage differentials are significantly low (X**2 = 26.793, d.f. = 4, p<0.001) for respondents having a higher level of education.

**Conclusion**

Considering the three SECE correlates together, it may be conclusively said that strategies for reducing wage differentials, by merely enacting laws, will not work very well. Such strategies seldom involve direct efforts at making the employees aware of their rights and responsibilities. Thus, direct efforts to reduce the wage differential, would have to be focused on the education of the employees about the provisions of the Act, because education is essential for increasing their awareness of their rights and responsibilities.

**Notes**

1. The ILO has evolved two such conventions on the subject: (a) Equal Remuneration, 1951, (Convention-100) prescribes equal remuneration for men and women for work of equal value; and (b) Discrimination Convention (Employment and Occupation), 1958, (Convention-111), refers to any distinction, exclusion or preference made on the basis of race, colour, sex, religion or social origin which has the effect to nullifying or impairing equality of opportunity or treatment in employment or occupation.
2. In 1967, the General Assembly of the United Nations unanimously adopted a "Declaration on the Elimination of Discrimination Against Women" which guarantees a broad range of rights to equality in education, work and marriage.
3. Justification for the use of linear probability model can be found in Ladd (1966) and Maddala (1983).

## References

Gambhir, G.D. (1979) "Labour in Small Scale Indistries", Nagpur University: Dissertation.

Khanna, K.P. & Mathew, M. (1979) "Women Workers in Unorganised Sector of Coir Industries in India", I.C.S.S.R. Research Abstract.

Labour Bureau. (1979). *A Study of Working and Living Condition in Industry*, New Delhi: Ministry of Labour.

Ladd, G. (1966). "Linear Probability Functions and Discriminant Functions", Econometrics Vol. 34. 873-85.

Maddaka, G.S.(1983).*Limited Dependent and Qualitative Variables in Econometrics,* Cambridge: Cambridge university Press.

Pais, H. (1980 ) "Employment of Women in India", Indian Labour Journal, April.

Patel, Vibhuti, (1982 ) "Women and Work". (Mimeographed) SNDT Women's University.

Planning Commission, (1961 ) *"Report of the Planning Commission*, New Delhi.

Ministry of Labour (1980) : Report on 1st and 2nd Occupational Wage Surveys, New Delhi.

## For Further Readings

Anderson, J. et. al. (1970). *Thesis and Assignment Writing.* New Delhi : Wiley Eastern Limited.

Baker, L., Therese (1988), *Doing Social Research,* McGraw Hill, New York.

Kidder, Louise H. (1981), *Research Methods in Social Relations,* Holt, New York.

Lal Das, D.K. (2000), *Practice of Social Research : A Social Work Perspective,* Rawat Publications, Jaipur.

Lal Das, D.K. (2005), *Designs of Social Research,* Jaipur: Rawat Publications.

Monette, Duane R. et. al. (1986), *Applied Social Research: Tool For the Human Services,* Holt, Chicago.

Nachmias D and Nachmias C. (1981), *Research Methods in the Social Sciences*, St. Martins Press, New York.

O'Leary Z. (2004). *The Essential Guide to Doing Research*. New Delhi: Vistaar Publications.

Ramachandran, P. (2000). *Research and Statistics for Social Work.* Secnderabad : Andhra Pradesh Social Service Society.

Rubin, Allen & Babbie E. (1989), *Research Methodology for Social Work*, Belmont, Wadsworth, California.

# Appendix A

## COMPUTATION OF STATISTICAL MEASURES

### Calculation of Arithmetic Mean

### Discrete Series

In this method the deviation of each item value from the assumed mean is found and is multiplied by its corresponding frequency. The algebraic sum of the product is divided by obtaining the total frequency (N) and added to the assumed mean.

**Symbolically:**

$$\overline{X} = a + \frac{\Sigma f.dx}{N}$$

Where 'a' stands for the assumed mean, $\Sigma f.dx$ for the sum of deviations from the assumed mean; and N for the total number of frequencies.

| *Gain in Kg. (X)* | *No. of children (f)* | *Deviation from assumed mean (5) dx* | *'f.dx* |
|---|---|---|---|
| 1 | 3 | -4 | -12 |
| 2 | 4 | -3 | -12 |
| 3 | 6 | -2 | -12 |
| 4 | 9 | -1 | -9 |
| 5 | 12 | 0 | 0 |
| 6 | 11 | +1 | +11 |
| 7 | 9 | +2 | +18 |
| 8 | 7 | +3 | +21 |
| 9 | 4 | +4 | +16 |
| | N = 65 | | Σf.dx= 21 |

**Calculation:**

$$\overline{X} = a + \frac{\Sigma f.dx}{N} = 5 + \frac{21}{65}$$

$$= 5 + 0.32 = 5.32 \text{ (approximately)}$$

Mean weight = 5.32 kg. (approximately)

**Continuous Series**

In calculating arithmetic mean of a continuous series, we take the mid-value of each class as representative of that class (and it is presumed that the frequencies of that class are concentrated on mid-point), multiply the various mid-values by their corresponding frequencies and sum of the products is divided by sum of the frequencies.

The following illustration will explain the method:

**DISTRIBUTION OF RAG PICKERS BY THEIR DAILY INCOME**

| *Daily Income (in Rs.)* | *Mid-values (m)* | *Number of Rag -Pickers(f)* | *m x f* |
|---|---|---|---|
| 110-130 | 120* | 15 | 1800 |
| 130-150 | 140 | 30 | 4200 |
| 150-170 | 160 | 60 | 9600 |
| 170-190 | 180 | 95 | 17100 |
| 190-210 | 200 | 82 | 16400 |
| 210-230 | 220 | 75 | 16500 |
| 230-250 | 240 | 23 | 5520 |
| | | Σf = N = 380 | Σmf = 71120 |

**Calculation:**

$$\text{* Mid-value} = \frac{\text{Lower limit + Upper limit}}{2} = \frac{110 + 130}{2}$$

$$= \frac{240}{2} = 120$$

$$\overline{X} = \frac{\Sigma m f}{\Sigma f} = \frac{\Sigma m f}{N}$$

= 71120/380 = 187.16

Arithmetic Mean = Rs.187.16 (approximately)

**Solution: Short-cut method**

**Table 12.17**

| *Monthly wages (in Rs.)* | *Mid-values (m)* | *No. of workers (f)* | *Deviation from assumed mean. 180 (dx)* | *Step deviation (d)* | *Total deviation (fd)* |
|---|---|---|---|---|---|
| 110-130 | 120 | 15 | -60 | -3 | -45 |
| 130-150 | 140 | 30 | -40 | -2 | -60 |
| 150-170 | 160 | 60 | -20 | -1 | -60 |
| 170-190 | 180 | 95 | 0 | 0 | 0 |
| 190-210 | 200 | 82 | +20 | +1 | +82 |
| 210-230 | 220 | 75 | +40 | +2 | +150 |
| 230-250 | 240 | 23 | +60 | +3 | +69 |
| | | N = 380 | | | Σfd = 136 |

$$\text{Arithmetic Mean } (\overline{X}) = a + \frac{\Sigma fd}{N} \times i$$

Where 'a' stands for the assumed mean, $\Sigma fd$ for the sum of total deviations, N for total number of frequencies and 'i' for class interval. Now substituting the values in the formula from the table we get :

$$= 180 + \frac{136}{380} \times 20$$

= 180 + 7.16

Arithmetic Mean = Rs.187.16 (approximately)

## Calculation of Median

### Discrete Series

In a discrete series the frequencies are cumulated and then the value of the middle item is located. The following example will illustrate the steps:

| *Gain in kg.* | *No. of children (f)* | *Cumulative frequency (CF)* |
|---|---|---|
| 1 | 3 | 3 |
| 2 | 4 | 7 |
| 3 | 6 | 13 |
| 4 | 9 | 22 |
| 5 | 12 | 34 |
| 6 | 11 | 45 |
| 7 | 9 | 54 |
| 8 | 7 | 61 |
| 9 | 4 | 65 |
| | N = 65 | |

**Solution:**

**X = Gain in weight of N/2 th item**

= Gain in weight of 65/2th item
= Gain in weight of 32.5$^{th}$ item
Median (X) = 5 kg.

(It is clear from the above table that the value of items from 23$^{rd}$ to 34$^{th}$ items is 5. Thus, the value of 32.5$^{th}$ item is also 5).

### Continuous Series

In continuous series we do not know every observation. Instead, we have record of the frequencies with which the observations appear in each of the class-intervals as in the following Table. Nevertheless, we can compute the median by determining which class-interval contains the median.

In the case of data given in Table 12.23 the median value is that value on either side of which N/2 or 380/2 or 190$^{th}$ items lie. Now the problem is to find the class interval containing the 190$^{th}$ item. The cumulative frequency for the first three classes is only 105. But when we move to the fourth class interval 95 items are added to 105 for total of 200. Therefore, the 190th item must be located in this fourth class-interval (the interval from Rs.170 – Rs.190.

**TABLE 12.23**
**DAILY INCOME OF RAG-PICKERS**

| *Daily Income in Rs.* | *Number of Rag-Pickers (f)* | *Cumulative frequencies (CF)* |
|---|---|---|
| 110 – 130 | 15 | 15 |
| 130 – 150 | 30 | 45 |
| 150 –170 | 60 | 105 |
| 170 – 190 | 95 | 200 |
| 190 – 210 | 82 | 282 |
| 210 – 230 | 75 | 357 |
| 230 – 250 | 23 | 380 |
| | N = 380 | |

The median class (Rs.170 – Rs.190) for the series contains 95 items. For the purpose of determining the point, which has 190 items on each side, we assume that these 95 items are evenly spaced over the entire class interval 170-190. Therefore, we can interpolate and find the values for 190th item. First, we determine that the 190th item is the 95th item in the median class:

$$190 - 105 = 85$$

Then we can calculate the width of the 95 equal steps from Rs.170 to Rs.190 as follows:

$$\frac{190 - 170}{95} = 0.21053 \text{ (approximately)}$$

The value of 85th item is 0.2105 x 85 = 17.89. If this (17.89) is added to the lower limit of the median class, we get 170 + 17.89 = 187.89. This is the median of the series.

This can be put in the form of formula:

$$X = L + \frac{N/2 - C}{f} \times i$$

Where X = median,

L = lower limit of the class in which median lies

N = total number of items

C = cumulative frequency of the class prior to the median class.

*f* = frequency of the median class

i = class interval of the median class.

**Calculation of Median by Formula:**

**DAILY INCOME OF RAG-PICKERS**

| *Daily Income in Rs.* | *Number of Rag-Pickers (f)* | *Cumulative frequencies (CF)* |
|---|---|---|
| 110 – 130 | 15 | 15 |
| 130 – 150 | 30 | 45 |
| 150 –170 | 60 | 105 = C |
| L = 170 – 190 | 95 = f | 200 |
| 190 – 210 | 82 | 282 |
| 210 – 230 | 75 | 357 |
| 230 – 250 | 23 | 380 |
| | N = 380 | |

$$X = L + \frac{N/2 - C}{f} \times i$$

$$= 170 + \frac{380/2 - 105}{95} \times (190 - 170)$$

$$= 170 + \frac{190 - 105}{95} \times (190 - 170)$$

$$= 170 + \frac{85}{95} \times (190 - 170)$$

$$= 170 + (0.8947 \times 20)$$

= 187.89 (approximately)

Median Income= Rs.187.89 (approximately)

**Location of Median in Discrete Series**

In a discrete series the frequencies are cumulated and then the value of the middle item is located. The following example will illustrate the steps:

TABLE 12.21
**GAIN IN WEIGHT (KG)**

| *Gain in kg.* | *No. of children* |
|---|---|
| 1 | 3 |
| 2 | 4 |
| 3 | 6 |
| 4 | 9 |
| 5 | 12 |
| 6 | 11 |
| 7 | 9 |
| 8 | 7 |
| 9 | 4 |
| | N = 65 |

TABLE 12.22
ITEMS ARRANGED IN ORDER OF MAGNITUDE

| *Gain in kg.* | *No. of children (f)* | *Cumulative frequency (CF)* |
|---|---|---|
| 1 | 3 | 3 |
| 2 | 4 | 7 |
| 3 | 6 | 13 |
| 4 | 9 | 22 |
| 5 | 12 | 34 |
| 6 | 11 | 45 |
| 7 | 9 | 54 |
| 8 | 7 | 61 |
| 9 | 4 | 65 |
| | N = 65 | |

*Solution:* X = **Gain in weight of N/2th item**

= Gain in weight of 65/2th item
= Gain in weight of $32.5^{th}$ item

Median (X) = 5 kg.

(It is clear from the above table that the value of items from 23rd to 34th items is 5. Thus, the value of 32.5th item is also 5).

**Determination of Median in a Continuous Series**

In continuous series we do not know every observation. Instead, we have record of the frequencies with which the observations appear in each of the class-intervals as in the following Table. Nevertheless, we can compute the median by determining which class-interval contains the median.

**TABLE 12.23**
**DAILY INCOME OF RAG-PICKERS**

| *Daily Income in Rs.* | *Number of Rag-Pickers (f)* | *Cumulative frequencies (CF)* |
|---|---|---|
| 110 – 130 | 15 | 15 |
| 130 – 150 | 30 | 45 |
| 150 –170 | 60 | 105 |
| 170 – 190 | 95 | 200 |
| 190 – 210 | 82 | 282 |
| 210 – 230 | 75 | 357 |
| 230 – 250 | 23 | 380 |
| | N = 380 | |

In the case of data given in Table 12.23 the median value is that value on either side of which N/2 or 380/2 or 190th items lie. Now the problem is to find the class interval containing the 190th item. The cumulative frequency for the first three classes is only 105. But when we move to the fourth class interval 95 items are added to 105 for total of 200. Therefore, the 190th item must be located in this fourth class-interval (the interval from Rs.170 – Rs.190.

The median class (Rs.170 – Rs.190) for the series contains 95 items. For the purpose of determining the point, which has 190 items on each side, we assume that these 95 items are evenly spaced over the entire class interval 170-190. Therefore, we can interpolate and find the values for 190th item. First, we determine that the 190th item is the 95th item in the median class:

$$190 - 105 = 85$$

Then we can calculate the width of the 95 equal steps from Rs.170 to Rs.190 as follows:

$$\frac{190 - 170}{95} = 0.21053 \text{ (approximately)}$$

The value of $85^{th}$ item is 0.2105 x 85 = 17.89. If this (17.89) is added to the lower limit of the median class, we get 170 + 17.89 = 187.89. This is the median of the series.

This can be put in the form of formula:

**Calculation of Median by Formula:**

$$\dot{X} = L + \frac{N/2 - C}{f} \times i$$

Where $\dot{X}$ = median,

L = lower limit of the class in which median lies
N = total number of items
C = cumulative frequency of the class prior to the median class.
'f = frequency of the median class
i = class interval of the median class.

**TABLE 12.24**
**DAILY INCOME OF RAG-PICKERS**

| *Daily Income in Rs.* | *Number of Rag-Pickers (f)* | *Cumulative frequencies (CF)* |
|---|---|---|
| 110 – 130 | 15 | 15 |
| 130 – 150 | 30 | 45 |
| 150 –170 | 60 | 105 = C |
| L = 170 – 190 | 95 = f | 200 |
| 190 – 210 | 82 | 282 |
| 210 – 230 | 75 | 357 |
| 230 – 250 | 23 | 380 |
| | N = 380 | |

$$\dot{X} = L + \frac{N/2 - C}{f} \times i$$

$$= 170 + \frac{380/2 - 105}{95} \times (190 - 170)$$

$$= 170 + \frac{190 - 105}{95} \times (190 - 170)$$

$$= 170 + \frac{85}{95} \times (190 - 170)$$

$$= 170 + (0.8947 \times 20)$$

$$= 187.89 \text{ (approximately)}$$

Median Income= Rs.187.89 (approximately)

***Calculation of Mode in Discrete Series***

In a discrete series the value against which the frequency is the largest would be the modal value. If we look at Table 12.22 we will find that 12 is the largest frequency. Thus, 5, being the value against which the frequency is the largest, is the mode of this series. If, however, there is more than one value around which figures concentrate, it becomes difficult to determine the value of mode. In such cases attempts are made to find the point of maximum concentration with the help of grouping method. The procedure is as follows:

(i) First the frequencies are added in two's in two ways: (a) by adding frequencies of item numbers 1 and 2; 3 and 4; 5 and 6 and so on, and (b) by adding frequencies of item numbers 2 and 3; 4 and 5; 6 and 7 and so on.

(ii) Then the frequencies are added in three's. This can be done in three ways: (a) by adding frequencies of item numbers 1, 2 and 3; 4,5 and 6; 7,8 and 9; and so on. (b) by adding frequencies of item numbers 2,3 and 4; 5, 6 and 7; 8,9 and 10; and so on and (c) by adding frequencies of item numbers 3,4 and 5; 6,7 and 8; 9,10 and 11 and so on.

If necessary grouping of frequencies can be done in four's and five's also. After grouping, the size of items containing maximum frequencies is circled. The item value, which will contain the maximum frequency the largest number of times, is the mode of the series. This is shown in Tables 12.25 and 12.26.

**TABLE 12.25**

**GAIN IN WEIGHT FOR 65 CHILDREN DURING A SPECIFIED PERIOD.**

| Gain in Kg. | No. of children (1) | (2) | (3) | (4) | (5) | (6) |
|---|---|---|---|---|---|---|
| 1 | 3 | 7 | | 13 | | |
| 2 | 4 | | 10 | | 19 | |
| 3 | 6 | 15 | | | | |
| 4 | 9 | | 21 | | | |
| 5 | (12) | 23 | | | | 27 |
| 6 | 11 | | 20 | 32 | | |
| 7 | 9 | 16 | | | 32 | |
| 8 | 7 | | 11 | 20 | | 27 |
| 9 | 4 | | | | | |
| | N = 65 | | | | | |

To find out the point of maximum concentration the data can be arranged in the shape of table as follows:

| COLUMN NO. | SIZE OF ITEM CONTAINING MAXIMUM FREQUENCY | | | | | | | | |
|---|---|---|---|---|---|---|---|---|---|
| | *1 Kg.* | *2 Kg.* | *3 Kg.* | *4 Kg.* | *5 Kg.* | *6 Kg.* | *7 Kg.* | *8 Kg.* | *9 Kg.* |
| 1 | | | | | 1 | | | | |
| 2 | | | | | 1 | 1 | | | |
| 3 | | | | 1 | 1 | | | | |
| 4 | | | | 1 | 1 | 1 | | | |
| 5 | | | | | 1 | 1 | 1 | | |
| 6 | | | | | | 1 | 1 | 1 | |
| No. of times a size occurs | | | | 2 | (5) | 4 | 2 | 1 | |

Since size 5 kg occurs the largest number of times it is the modal size. Thus the mode of this series is 5 kg.

### *Determination of Mode in a Continuous Series*

In the case of continuous series the determination of mode involves two steps. First, the process of grouping locates the class of maximum concentration. After this the value of mode is interpolated by the use of the following formula.

$$X = L + \frac{f_1 - f_0}{2f_1 - f_0 - f_2} \times i$$

Where X stands for the mode, L is the lower limit of the modal class, $f_0$ stands for the frequencies of the preceding class, $f_1$ stands for the frequencies of the modal class, $f_2$ for the frequencies of the succeeding class and *i* stand for the class interval of the modal class.

Illustration: Determine mode of the following distribution.

**TABLE 12.27**
**WEEKLY FAMILY INCOMES (IN RS.)**

| *Weekly Income* | *Number of families* |
|---|---|
| 100 – 200 | 5 |
| 200 – 300 | 6 = $f_0$ |

(*Contd.*)

*(Contd.)*

| *Weekly Income* | *Number of families* |
|---|---|
| L - 300 – 400 | 15 = $f_1$ |
| 400 – 500 | 10 = $f_2$, |
| 500 – 600 | 5 |
| 600 – 700 | 4 |
| 700 – 800 | 3 |
| 800 – 900 | 2 |
| Total | N = 50 |

**TABLE 12.28**

**LOCATION OF MODAL CLASS BY GROUPING**

| *Weekly Income* | *F(1)* | *(2)* | *(3)* | *(4)* | *(5)* | *(6)* |
|---|---|---|---|---|---|---|
| 100 – 200 | 5 | 11 | | 26 | | |
| 200 – 300 | 6 | | 21 | | 31 | |
| 300 – 400 | 15 | 25 | | | | 30 |
| 400 – 500 | 10 | | 15 | 19 | | |
| 500 – 600 | 5 | 9 | | | 12 | |
| 600 –700 | 4 | | 7 | | | 9 |
| 700 –800 | 3 | 5 | | | | |
| 800 –900 | 2 | | | | | |

Therefore 330-400 group is the modal group. Using the formula of interpolation, viz.,

$$X = L + \frac{f_1 - f_0}{2f_1 - f_0 - f_2} \times i$$

$$\overline{X} = 300 + \frac{15 - 6}{2x15 - 6 - 10} \times 100$$

= 300 + 9/14 x 100

= 300 + 900/14

= 300 + 64.29

= 364.29 (approximately)

## TABLE 12.29
## ANALYSIS TABLE

| COLUMN | CLASS CONTAINING MAXIMUM FREQUENCY | | | | | | | |
|---|---|---|---|---|---|---|---|---|
| | 100-200 | 200-300 | 300-400 | 400-500 | 500-600 | 600-700 | 700-800 | 800-900 |
| 1 | | | 1 | | | | | |
| 2 | | | 1 | 1 | | | | |
| 3 | | 1 | 1 | | | | | |
| 4 | 1 | 1 | 1 | | | | | |
| 5 | | 1 | 1 | 1 | | | | |
| 6 | | | 1 | 1 | 1 | | | |
| No. of times a class occurs | 1 | 3 | (6) | 3 | 1 | | | |

**Range**

The range is defined as the difference between the highest and lowest values. Mathematically,

R(Range) = $m_H$ - $m_L$

Where $m_H$ and $m_L$ stand for the highest and the lowest value. Thus, for the data set; 10, 22, 20, 14 and 14 the range would be the difference between 22 and 10, i.e., 12. In case of grouped data, we take the range as the difference between the midpoints of the extreme classes. Thus, if the midpoint of the lowest interval is 150 and that of the highest are 850 the range will be 700.

**Calculation of Standard Deviation in Discrete Series**

In a discrete series the deviations from an assumed mean are first computed and multiplied by the respective frequencies of items. The deviations are squared and multiplied by the respective frequencies of the items. These products are totaled and divided by the total of the frequencies. The standard deviation is calculated with the help of following formula.

$$\sigma = \sqrt{\frac{\Sigma fd^2}{N} - \left(\frac{\Sigma fd}{N}\right)^2}$$

*The following illustration would explain the formula:*

**TABLE 13.12**
**GAIN IN WEIGHT FOR 65 CHILDREN DURING A SPECIFIED PERIOD**

| *Gain in kg* | *No. of children* |
|---|---|
| 1 | 3 |
| 2 | 4 |
| 3 | 6 |
| 4 | 9 |
| 5 | 12 |
| 6 | 11 |
| 7 | 9 |
| 8 | 7 |
| 9 | 4 |
| | N = 65 |

**Table 13.13**

| *Gain in kg* | *No. of children (f)* | *Deviation from the assumed mean (d)* | *Total Deviations (f x d)* | *Deviations squared (d2)* | *f.d²* |
|---|---|---|---|---|---|
| 1 | 3 | -4 | -12 | 16 | 48 |
| 2 | 4 | -3 | -12 | 9 | 36 |
| 3 | 6 | -2 | -12 | 4 | 24 |
| 4 | 9 | -1 | -9 | 1 | 9 |
| 5 | 12 | 0 | 0 | 0 | 0 |
| 6 | 11 | +1 | 11 | 1 | 11 |
| 7 | 9 | +2 | 18 | 4 | 36 |
| 8 | 7 | +3 | 21 | 9 | 63 |
| 9 | 4 | +4 | 16 | 16 | 64 |
| | N = 65 | | Σfd = 21 | | Σ fd² = 291 |

$$\sigma = \sqrt{\frac{\sum fd^2}{N} - \left(\frac{\sum fd}{N}\right)^2}$$

$$\sigma = \sqrt{\frac{291}{65} - \left(\frac{21}{65}\right)^2}$$

$$= \sqrt{4.4769 - 0.1044}$$

$$= \sqrt{4.3725}$$

= 2.09 (approximately)

***Calculation of Standard Deviation in Continuous Series***

In a continuous series the class intervals are represented by their midpoints. However, usually the class-intervals are of equal size and thus, the deviations from the assumed average is expressed in class interval units. Alternatively, step deviation is found out by dividing the deviations by the magnitude of the class interval. Thus, the formula for computing standard deviation is written as follows;

$$\sigma = \sqrt{\frac{\Sigma fd^2}{N} - \left(\frac{\Sigma fd}{N}\right)^2} \times i$$

Where 'i' stands for the common factor or the magnitude of the class-interval. The following example would illustrate this formula;

**Table 13.14 Weekly Family Income (In Rs.)**

| *S.No.* | *Monthly Income* | *Number of families (f)* |
|---|---|---|
| 1 | 100 – 200 | 5 |
| 2 | 200 – 300 | 6 |
| 3 | 300 – 400 | 15 |
| 4 | 400 –500 | 10 |
| 5 | 500 –600 | 5 |
| 6 | 600 –700 | 4 |
| 7 | 700 –800 | 3 |
| 8 | 800 - 900 | 2 |
| | | N = 50 |

$$\sigma = \sqrt{\frac{\Sigma fd^2}{N} - \frac{\Sigma fd}{N}^2} \times i$$

$$\sigma = \frac{164}{50} - \frac{-12}{50}^2 \times 100$$

$$= 3.28 - 0.0576 \quad \times 100$$

**Table 13.15**

| S.No. | Weekly Income | Mid values (m) | Number of families (f) | Step deviation from ass. Ave (450) (d) | fd | $d^2$ | $fd_2$ |
|---|---|---|---|---|---|---|---|
| 1 | 100 – 200 | 150 | 5 | -3 | -15 | 9 | 45 |
| 2 | 200 – 300 | 250 | 6 | -2 | -12 | 4 | 24 |
| 3 | 300 – 400 | 350 | 15 | -1 | -15 | 1 | 15 |
| 4 | 400 –500 | 450 | 10 | 0 | 0 | 0 | 0 |
| 5 | 500 –600 | 550 | 5 | +1 | 5 | 1 | 5 |
| 6 | 600 –700 | 650 | 4 | +2 | 8 | 4 | 16 |
| 7 | 700 –800 | 750 | 3 | +3 | 9 | 9 | 27 |
| 8 | 800 - 900 | 850 | 2 | +4 | 8 | 16 | 32 |
| | | | N = 50 | | $\Sigma fd = -12$ | $\Sigma fd^2 = 164$ | |

$$\sigma = \sqrt{\frac{\sum fd^2}{N} - \frac{\sum fd}{N}^{2}} \times i$$

$$\sigma = \frac{164}{50} - \left(\frac{-12}{50}\right)^{2} \times 100$$

$$= 3.28 - 0.0576 \quad \times 100$$

**Karl Pearson's Coefficient of Correlation (Individual Observation)**

The formula to compute the degree and direction of correlation of Karl Pearson's is as under;

$$\text{'}r = \frac{\sum dx\, dy - N\left(\frac{\sum dx}{N}\right)\left(\frac{\sum dy}{N}\right)}{N\sqrt{\frac{\sum dx^2}{N} - \left(\frac{\sum dx}{N}\right)^2}\sqrt{\frac{\sum dy^2}{N} - \left(\frac{\sum dy}{N}\right)^2}}$$

Where *dx* is the deviation of various items of the first variable from assumed average and *dy* the corresponding deviations of the second variable from assumed average and N stands for the number of pairs of items.

**TABLE 14.1**

**MARKS OBTAINED BY 10 MSW STUDENTS IN SOCIAL WORK RESEARCH (THEORY) AND RESEARCH PROJECT (PRACTICAL)**

| *S.No.* | *Marks obtained in Social Work Research (Theory)* | *Marks obtained in Research Project (Practical)* |
|---|---|---|
| 1 | 40 | 42 |
| 2 | 26 | 29 |
| 3 | 70 | 66 |
| 4 | 32 | 24 |
| 5 | 52 | 58 |
| 6 | 30 | 28 |
| 7 | 48 | 46 |
| 8 | 48 | 50 |
| 9 | 42 | 44 |
| 10 | 62 | 66 |

## TABLE 14.2
## CALCULATION OF KARL PEARSON'S COEFFICIENT OF CORRELATION

| *S.No.* | *Marks obtained in social work research* | *Deviations from ass. Ave. (48) (dx)* | *$dx^2$* | *Marks obtained in Research Project* | *Deviations from ass. Ave. (46) (dy)* | *$dy^2$* | *dx.dy* |
|---|---|---|---|---|---|---|---|
| 1 | 40 | -8 | 64 | 42 | -4 | 16 | +32 |
| 2 | 26 | -22 | 484 | 29 | -17 | 289 | +374 |
| 3 | 70 | +22 | 484 | 66 | +20 | 400 | +440 |
| 4 | 32 | -16 | 256 | 24 | -22 | 484 | +352 |
| 5 | 52 | +4 | 16 | 58 | +12 | 144 | +48 |
| 6 | 30 | -18 | 324 | 28 | -18 | 324 | +324 |
| 7 | 48 | 0 | 0 | 46 | 0 | 0 | 0 |
| 8 | 48 | 0 | 0 | 50 | +4 | 16 | 0 |
| 9 | 42 | -6 | 36 | 44 | -2 | 4 | +12 |
| 10 | 62 | +14 | 196 | 66 | +20 | 400 | +280 |
| N =10 | $\bar{X} = 45$ | $\Sigma dx = -30$ | $\Sigma dx^2 = 1860$ | $\bar{Y} = 45.3$ | $\Sigma dy = -7$ | $\Sigma dy^2 = 2077$ | $\Sigma dxdy = 1862$ |

We explain the application of the formula in the following example.

6. Compute coefficient of correlation by the formula as explained below.

$$r = \frac{\Sigma dx\,dy - N\left(\frac{\Sigma dx}{N}\right)\left(\frac{\Sigma dy}{N}\right)}{N\sqrt{\frac{\Sigma dx^2}{N} - \left(\frac{\Sigma dx}{N}\right)^2}\sqrt{\frac{\Sigma dy^2}{N} - \left(\frac{\Sigma dy}{N}\right)^2}}$$

$$r = \frac{1862 - 10\left(\frac{-30}{10}\right)\left(\frac{-7}{10}\right)}{10\sqrt{\frac{1860}{10} - \left(\frac{-30}{10}\right)^2}\sqrt{\frac{2077}{10} - \left(\frac{-7}{10}\right)^2}}$$

$$r = \frac{1862 - 10\ (-3)\ (-0.7)}{10\sqrt{186 - 9}\ \sqrt{207.7 - 0.49}}$$

$$= \frac{1862 - 10\ (2.1)}{10\sqrt{177}\ \sqrt{207.21}}$$

$$= \frac{1862 - 21}{10 \times 13.3 \times 14.39}$$

$$= \frac{1841}{1914.507}$$

$= 0.962$ (approx.)

***Partial Correlation***

Controlling the effect of a third variable on the bi-variate relationship by cross-tabulation or partial table method is quite common in the empirical research. However, the method has a serious drawback that limits its use when the number of cases relatively small. The partial cross-tabulation involves subdivision of the sample into gradually smaller subgroups. This reduces the size of cell frequency, thus its reliability and validity is questionable.

An alternative to method of control is the partial correlation. This is a mathematical process of adjustment of the bi-variate correlation, demand to nullify the effect of third variable (control variable) on the independent and dependent variables. The formula for calculation of the partial correlation co-efficient is as given below:

$$\Upsilon_{12.3} = \frac{\Upsilon_{12} - (\Upsilon_{1.3})\,(\Upsilon_{.23})}{\sqrt{1 - \Upsilon_{13}^{2}}\;\sqrt{1 - \Upsilon_{2.3}^{2}}}$$

Where X1 = independent variable
X2 = dependent variable
X3 = control variable

Let us suppose that we have found that there is strong correlation between 'awareness' and 'wage differential' (¡c.70). The researcher introduces third variable experience (control) as he has found that this variable is also correlated with wage differential (¡c.50) and 'awareness' (¡=.40). As such he wants to know the correlation' with the effect of 'experience' removed.

Thus we have:
X1 = Awareness (independent variable)
X2 = Wage differential (independent variable)
X3 = Experience (control variable)

We also have
ϒ1.2 (Correlation coefficient between X1 and X2)= .70
ϒ1.3 (Correlation coefficient between X1 and X3)= .40
ϒ2.3 (Correlation coefficient between X2 and X3)= .50

The symbol on the right hand side of the decimal point indicates the variable to be controlled. Thus ¡12.3 would mean correlation coefficient between variable 1 and variable 2 after controlling the effects of variable. In the present example it would mean the correlation between 'awareness' and 'wage differential' after, nullifying the effect of 'experience'. A partial correlation with one control is referred as a first order partial correlation to distinguish it from a bi-variate correlation often known as a zero-order correlation.

The partial correlation for wage differential and awareness can now be calculated as follows:

$$\Upsilon_{12.3} = \frac{.70 - (.40)\,(.50)}{\sqrt{1-(.40)^2}\;\sqrt{1-(.50)^2}}$$

$$= \frac{.70 - .20}{\sqrt{1-.16}\;\sqrt{1-.25}}$$

$$= \frac{.50}{\sqrt{.84}\;\sqrt{.75}}$$

$$= \frac{.50}{.92 \quad X \quad .87} = \frac{.50}{.80} = .625$$

Thus, we can see that the original relationship (¡=. 70) has been reduced to .625 showing the effect of the third variable. Though there is decrease in strength of relationship but still enough. The square of the coefficient of partial correlation reflects the proportion of variation left unexplained by the control variable. Thus, about 39 per cent [$¡^2$= $(.625)^2$ =. 39] is explained by 'awareness' after removing the effect of 'experience'.

**Multivariate Analysis**

So far, we have discussed the relation between two variables where one independent variable is to determine the dependent variable question. In rarity particularly in social sciences however, there is hardly any situation where one independent variable determines the dependent variable. Often we have situations where a set of independent variable is associated with dependent variable. In other words, more often several independent variables contribute to the prediction of the dependent variable. Multiple Regression is commonly used to estimate the effect of multiple independent variables. (Readers are advised to refer books listed under FOR FURTHER READING for procedure to calculate measures like Multiple Regression Analysis).

**Calculation of the Coefficient of Correlation by Rank Differences (Spearman's Rho 'r' )**

Where the direct qualitative measurement of the phenomenon under study is not possible, for example efficiency, intelligence etc., rank-difference method correlation is applied for finding out the degree of correlation. The formula for computing rank correlation is:

$$R = 1 - \frac{6 \Sigma D^2}{N(N^2 - 1)}$$

Where R denotes coefficient of rank correlation between paired ranks, D denotes the differences between the paired ranks and N stands for the number of pairs. The following example would illustrate the above formula:

**TABLE 14.4**
**RANKING OF SOCIAL WORKERS ACCORDING TO THEIR EFFICIENCY BY TWO DIFFERENT JUDGES**

| *Social Worker* | *Ranking by Judge A* | *Ranking by Judge B* |
|---|---|---|
| A | 3 | 4 |
| B | 9 | 7 |
| C | 6 | 6 |

*(Contd.)*

*(Contd.)*

| *Social Worker* | *Ranking by Judge A* | *Ranking by Judge B* |
|---|---|---|
| D | 5 | 8 |
| E | 1 | 1 |
| F | 2 | 3 |
| G | 4 | 2 |
| H | 7 | 5 |
| I | 8 | 10 |
| J | 10 | 9 |

**TABLE 14.5**

| *Social worker* | *Ranking by Judge A* | *Ranking by Judge B* | $D = (R^1 - R^2)$ | $D^2$ |
|---|---|---|---|---|
| A | 3 | 4 | -1 | 1 |
| B | 9 | 7 | +2 | 4 |
| C | 6 | 6 | 0 | 0 |
| D | 5 | 8 | -3 | 9 |
| E | 1 | 1 | 0 | 0 |
| F | 2 | 3 | -1 | 1 |
| G | 4 | 2 | +2 | 4 |
| H | 7 | 5 | +2 | 4 |
| I | 8 | 10 | -2 | 4 |
| J | 10 | 9 | +1 | 1 |

$N = 10$ $\Sigma D^2 = 28$

$$R = 1 - \frac{6 \Sigma D^2}{N(N^2 - 1)}$$

$$= 1 - \frac{6 \times 28}{10 \times (10^2 - 1)}$$

$$= 1 - \frac{168}{10 \times (100 - 1)}$$

$$= 1 - \frac{168}{10 \times (99)}$$

$$= 1 - \frac{168}{990}$$

$$= 1 - 0.1696969$$

$$= 0.83 \text{ (approximately)}$$

**Chi-square Test**

The $\chi^2$ (Greek letter $\chi^2$ and pronounced as Ki-square) test provides us with a method to evaluate whether or not frequencies which have been empirically observed differ significantly from those which would be expected under a certain set of theoretical assumption. For example, suppose specialization and place of residence have been cross classified and the data summarized in the following 2 x 3 contingency table:

**TABLE 14.7**

**RELATIONSHIP BETWEEN SPECIALISATION PREFERENCE AND PLACE OF RESIDENCE**

| *Place of Residence* | *Specialization Preference* | | | *Total* |
|---|---|---|---|---|
| | *MPSW* | *URCD* | *FCW* | |
| Urban | 38 | 20 | 12 | 70 |
| Rural | 10 | 26 | 6 | 42 |
| Total | 48 | 46 | 18 | 112 |

The proportions of urban people are 38/48 = 0.79, 20/46 – 0.34, and 12/18 = 0.67 (rounded to two decimals) for three specialization. We would then want to know whether or not these differences were statistically significant.

To this end, we can assume null hypothesis: that there are no differences between urban and rural in the choice of specialisation. This means that the proportions of urban and rural people should be the same in each of the three specialisations. On the basis of the assumption that the null hypothesis is correct we can compute a set of frequencies that would be expected given these marginal totals. In other words, we can compute the number of students of MPSW and would be expected to be urbanites and compare this figure with that actually obtained.

If the null hypothesis is true, we can compute a common proportion as:

$$\frac{38+20+12}{48+46+18} = \frac{70}{112} = 0.625$$

With this estimate we would expect 48 x (0.625)=30 students opting for MPSW, 46 x (0.625) = 28.75 students opting for URCD and 18 x (0.625) = 11.25 students opting for FCW from 70 urbanites. Subtracting these figures from the respective sizes of the three samples, we find that 48 – 30 = 18opting for MPSW, 46 – 28.75 = 17.25 opting for URCD and 18 – 11.25 = 6.25 opting for FCW from 42 persons from rural areas.

These results are shown in the following table, where expected frequencies are shown in parentheses.

**TABLE 14.8**

| *Place of Residence* | *Specialization Preference* | | | *Total* |
|---|---|---|---|---|
| | *MPSW* | *URCD* | *FCW* | |
| Urban | 38(30) | 20(28.75) | 12(11.25) | 70 |
| Rural | 10(18) | 26(17.25) | 6(6.75) | 42 |
| Total | 48 | 46 | 18 | 112 |

To test the null hypothesis we compare the expected and observed frequencies. The comparison is based on the following **c**$^2$ statistics.

$$\chi^2 = \sum \frac{(O-E)^2}{E}$$

Where O stands for observed frequencies and E stands for expected frequencies.

**TABLE 14.9**
**COMPUTATION OF $\chi^2$**

| $O$ | $E$ | $O - E$ | $(O - E)^2$ | $\frac{(O - E)^2}{E}$ |
|---|---|---|---|---|
| 38 | 30.00 | 8.00 | 64.0000 | 2.1333 |
| 10 | 18.00 | 8.00 | 64.0000 | 3.5555 |
| 20 | 28.75 | 8.75 | 76.5625 | 2.6630 |
| 26 | 17.25 | 8.75 | 76.5625 | 4.4384 |
| 12 | 11.25 | 0.75 | 0.5625 | 0.0500 |
| 6 | 6.75 | 0.75 | 0.5625 | 0.0833 |
| 112 | 112.00 | | | $\chi^2 = 12.9237$ |

## Calculation of Degree of Freedom

$$df = (c - 1)(r - 1)$$

Where *df* stands for the degrees of freedom, *c* for the number of columns and *r* for the number of rows.

Thus in 2 x 3 table (Table 14.8)

$$df = (3 - 1)(2 - 1) = 2 \times 1 = 2$$

## The Paired t – test

**TABLE 17.1**
**SELF ESTEEM SCORES OF 10 CHILDREN**

| *Students* | *Pre-test scores (X)* | *Post-test Scores(Y)* | *D=(Y-X)* | *$D^2$* |
|---|---|---|---|---|
| 1 | 9 | 12 | 3 | 9 |
| 2 | 8 | 10 | 2 | 4 |
| 3 | 15 | 15 | 0 | 0 |
| 4 | 12 | 14 | 2 | 4 |
| 5 | 8 | 14 | 6 | 36 |
| 6 | 4 | 11 | 7 | 49 |
| 7 | 6 | 10 | 4 | 16 |
| 8 | 3 | 8 | 5 | 25 |

*(Contd.)*

*(Contd.)*

| *Students* | *Pre-test scores (X)* | *Post-test Scores(Y)* | *D=(Y-X)* | *$D^2$* |
|---|---|---|---|---|
| 9 | 3 | 8 | 5 | 25 |
| 10 | 2 | 8 | 6 | 36 |
| n = 10 | | | $\Sigma D = 40$ | $\Sigma D^2 = 204$ |

$$SS = \Sigma D^2 - \frac{(\Sigma D)^2}{N}$$

$$= 204 - \frac{(40)^2}{10}$$

$$= 204 - 160 = 44$$

$$S^2 = \frac{SS}{\text{'df}} = \frac{44}{9} = 4.89$$

$$t = \frac{\bar{X}}{\sqrt{S^2/n}} = \frac{4}{\sqrt{4.89/10}}$$

$$= \frac{4}{0.489} = \frac{4}{0.699} = 5.7225$$

**The t – test for Independent Samples**

The t – test for two independent samples examines the difference between their means to see how close or apart they are. Let us consider the data given in the Table 17.2

The data compares scores obtained by two groups of students say for example a group of Master Degree students and a group of Bachelor's Degree students on a scale designed to measure attitude towards AIDS patients. A social work teacher is interested in studying whether there is significant difference among the two groups of students with regard to their attitude towards AIDS patients. The social work teacher selects the two groups of students randomly and administers the test. The scores at the interval level of measurement are presented in the Table.

| Step | Procedure | Application to Table 17.2 |
|---|---|---|
| 1. | Square the scores of X and Y column to get $X^2$ and $Y^2$ values. | $= (8)^2 = 64, (11)^2 = 121, (9)^2 = 81, ....$<br>$= (12)^2 = 144, (9)^2 = 81, (6)^2 = 36, .....$ |
| 2. | Find the sums of columns X, Y, $X^2$ and $Y^2$ | $\Sigma x = 100 \quad \Sigma y = 90$<br>$\Sigma x^2 = 1132 \quad \Sigma y^2 = 864$ |
| 3. | Compute Mean Scores for column X and Y | $\bar{X} = \frac{100}{10} = 10 \quad \bar{Y} = \frac{90}{10} = 9$ |
| 4. | Compute Variance sum of squares for X and Y column | $SSx = \Sigma x^2 - \frac{(\Sigma x)^2}{n}$<br>$= 1132 - \frac{(100)^2}{10} = 1132 - 1000$<br>$= 132$<br>$SS_y = \Sigma y^2 - \frac{(\Sigma y)^2}{N}$<br>$= 864 - \frac{(90)^2}{10} = 864 - 810$<br>$= 54$ |
| 5. | Find out the sum of squares | $SS_c = SS_x + SS_y$<br>$= 132 + 54 = 186$ |
| 6. | Find out the combined $SS_c$ degrees of freedom for two sets of data ($df_c$) | '$df_x = n - 1 = 10 - 1 = 9$<br>***$df_y = n - 1 = 10 - 1 = 9$***<br>***$df_c = df_x + df_y = 9 + 9 = 18$*** |
| 7. | Compute combined variances $S^2_c$ | $S^2_c = SS_c/df_c = 186/18 = 10.33$ |
| 8. | Compute 't' by using the formula<br>$t = \frac{X - Y}{\sqrt{S^2_c\left(\frac{1}{n_x} + \frac{1}{n_y}\right)}}$ | $= \frac{10 - 9}{\sqrt{10.33\left(\frac{1}{10} + \frac{1}{10}\right)}}$<br>$= \frac{1}{\sqrt{10.33 \times .2}}$<br>$= \frac{1}{\sqrt{2.066}}$ |

$$= \frac{1}{1.43}$$

$$= .699$$

Let us call the scores obtained by Master degree students as X scores and the Bachelor's degree students as Y scores. The first step in calculating t – test for two independent samples is to square the scores of X and Y columns to get $X^2$ and $Y^2$ values.

The next step is to sum up the columns to find out åX, åY, å$X^2$ and å$Y^3$. This is followed by calculation of means of X and Y columns, that is X and Y.

## The t – test for Independent Samples

**Table 17.2**

| *S.No.* | *Scores obtained by Master Degree students (X)* | *$X^2$* | *Scores obtained by Bachelor's Degree (Y)* | *$Y^2$* |
|---|---|---|---|---|
| 1 | 8 | 64 | 12 | 144 |
| 2 | 11 | 121 | 9 | 81 |
| 3 | 9 | 81 | 6 | 36 |
| 4 | 12 | 144 | 5 | 25 |
| 5 | 16 | 256 | 8 | 64 |
| 6 | 10 | 100 | 12 | 144 |
| 7 | 7 | 49 | 11 | 121 |
| 8 | 16 | 256 | 10 | 100 |
| 9 | 6 | 36 | 10 | 100 |
| 10 | 5 | 25 | 7 | 49 |
| n = 10 | $\Sigma X = 100$ | $\Sigma X^2 = 1132$ | $\Sigma Y = 90$ | $\Sigma Y^2 = 864$ |

The procedure for calculating 't' is given below;

$$SSx = \Sigma x^2 - \frac{(\Sigma x)^2}{n}$$

$$= 1132 - \frac{(100)^2}{10} = 1132 - 1000$$

$= 132$

$$SS_y = \Sigma y^2 - \frac{(\Sigma y)^2}{N}$$

$$= 864 - \frac{(90)^2}{10} = 864 - 810$$

$= 54$

$SS_c = SS_x + SS_y$
$= 132 + 54 = 186$

'$df_x = n - 1 = 10 - 1 = 9$

$df_y = n - 1 = 10 - 1 = 9$
$df_c = df_x + df_y = 9 + 9 = 18$
$S^2_c = SS_c/df_c = 186/18 = 10.33$
$S^2_c = SS_c/df_c = 186/18 = 10.33$

$$= \frac{10 - 9}{\sqrt{10.33 \quad \frac{1}{10} + \frac{1}{10}}}$$

$$= \frac{1}{\sqrt{10\ .33 \text{ X } .2}}$$

$$= \frac{1}{\sqrt{2.066}}$$

$$= \frac{1}{1.43}$$

$= .699$

**The One-Way Analysis of Variance**

**ALCOHOL INVOLVEMENT INDEX SCORES**

| *Group A* | $A^2$ | *Group B* | $B^2$ | *Group C* | $C^2$ |
|---|---|---|---|---|---|
| 14 | 196 | 38 | 1444 | 34 | 1156 |
| 20 | 400 | 42 | 1764 | 40 | 1600 |
| 22 | 484 | 24 | 576 | 30 | 900 |
| 18 | 324 | 12 | 144 | 48 | 2304 |
| 30 | 900 | 40 | 1600 | 58 | 3364 |
| $\Sigma A = 104$ | $\Sigma A^2 =$ | $\Sigma B = 156$ | $\Sigma B^2 =$ | $\Sigma C = 210$ | $\Sigma C^2 =$ |
| | 2304 | | 5528 | | 9324 |

$n_1 = 5$

$n_2 = 5$

$n_3 = 5$

$$n = n_1 + n_2 + n_3$$

$$= 5 + 5 + 5$$

$$= 15$$

$$\Sigma T = \Sigma A + \Sigma B + \Sigma C$$

$$= 104 + 156 + 210$$

$$= 470$$

The social worker establishes a null hypothesis that there are no differences between the groups who have been given different treatments.

The procedure of calculating 'f' test is as under;

| *Step* | *Procedure* | *Application to Table 17.3* |
|---|---|---|
| 1. | Find out the squares of scores in each of the three column | $= (14)^2 = 196, (20)^2 = 400, ....$<br>$= (38)^2 = 1444, (42)^2$<br>$= 1764,..... = (34)^2 = 1156, (40)^2$<br>$= 1600,.....$ |
| 72. | Find the sums of values in each of the three column | $\Sigma A = 104 \quad \Sigma A^2 = 2304$<br>$\Sigma B = 156 \quad \Sigma B^2 = 5528$<br>$\Sigma C = 210 \quad \Sigma C^2 = 44100$ |
| 3. | Add the sums of the values of each of the tree columns ($\Sigma T$) | $\Sigma T = \Sigma A + \Sigma B + \Sigma C$<br>$= 104 + 156 + 210 = 470$ |
| 4. | Compute $\Sigma^2$ | $\Sigma T^2 = \Sigma A^2 + \Sigma B^2 + \Sigma C^2$<br>$= 2340 + 5528 + 44100$<br>$= 51968$ |
| 5. | Compute sum of square of total scores (SST) | $SST = \Sigma T^2 \frac{(\Sigma T)^2}{n}$<br>$= 51968 - \frac{(470)^2}{15}$<br>$= 51968 - 14726.667$<br>$= 37241.333$ |
| 6. | Compute sum of squares between the scores (SSB) | $SS_B = \frac{(\Sigma A)^2}{n_1} + \frac{(\Sigma B)^2}{n_2} + \frac{(\Sigma C)^2}{n_3} - \frac{(\Sigma T)}{n_t}$<br>$= \frac{(104)^2}{5} + \frac{(156)^2}{5} + \frac{(210)^2}{5} - \frac{(470)^2}{15}$<br>$= 2163.2 + 4867.2 + 8820 - 14726.667$<br>$= 15850.4 - 14726.667$<br>$= 1123.733$ |
| 7. | Compute Error $SS_W = SST - SSB$ | $= 37241.33 - 1123.733$<br>$= 36117.597$ |
| 8. | Prepare a summary table | Table 17.4 |

**TABLE 17.4**
**SUMMARY TABLE**

| *Source of Variation* | *df* | *SS* | *Mean Squares* |
|---|---|---|---|
| Between measurement | K-1=3-1=2 | 1123.733 | 561.8665 |
| Within measurement | N-K=15-3=12 | 36117.597 | 3009.8 |
| Total | N-1=15-1=14 | 37241.33 | |

K=Number of Groups
N=Total Number of Observations

$$\text{F Ratio} = \frac{SS_B}{SS_W}$$

$$F2,12 = \frac{1123.733}{36117.597} = 0.031$$

# Appendix B
# Random numbers

| | | | | |
|---|---|---|---|---|
| 10 09 73 25 33 | 76 52 01 35 86 | 34 67 35 48 76 | 80 95 90 91 17 | 39 29 27 49 45 |
| 37 54 20 48 05 | 64 89 47 42 96 | 24 80 52 40 37 | 20 63 61 04 02 | 00 82 29 16 65 |
| 08 42 26 89 53 | 19 64 50 93 03 | 23 20 90 25 60 | 15 95 33 47 64 | 35 08 03 36 06 |
| 99 01 90 25 29 | 09 37 67 07 15 | 38 31 13 11 65 | 88 67 67 43 97 | 04 43 62 76 59 |
| 12 80 79 99 70 | 80 15 73 61 47 | 64 03 23 66 53 | 98 95 11 68 77 | 12 17 17 68 33 |
| | | | | |
| 66 06 57 47 17 | 34 07 27 68 50 | 36 69 73 61 70 | 65 81 33 98 85 | 11 19 92 91 70 |
| 31 06 01 08 05 | 45 57 18 24 06 | 35 30 34 26 14 | 86 79 90 74 39 | 23 40 30 97 32 |
| 85 26 97 76 02 | 02 05 16 56 92 | 68 66 57 48 18 | 73 05 38 52 47 | 18 62 38 85 79 |
| 63 57 33 21 35 | 05 32 54 70 48 | 90 55 35 75 48 | 28 46 82 87 09 | 83 49 1Z 56 24 |
| 73 79 64 57 53 | 03 52 96 47 78 | 35 80 83 42 82 | 60 93 52 03 44 | 35 27 38 84 35 |
| | | | | |
| 98 52 01 77 67 | 14 90 56 86 07 | 22 10 94 05 58 | 60 97 09 34 33 | 50 50 07 39 98 |
| 11 80 50 54 31 | 39 80 82 77 32 | 50 72 56 82 48 | 29 40 52 42 01 | 52 77 56 78 57 |
| 83 45 29 96 34 | 06 28 89 80 83 | 13 74 67 00 78 | 18 47 54 06 10 | 68 71 17 78 17 |
| 88 68 54 02 00 | 86 50 75 84 01 | 36 76 66 79 51 | 90 36 47 64 93 | 29 60 91 10 62 |
| 99 59 46 73 48 | 87 51 76 49 69 | 91 82 60 89 28 | 93 78 56 13 68 | 23 47 83 41 13 |
| | | | | |
| 65 48 11 76 74 | 17 46 85 09 50 | 58 04 77 69 74 | 73 03 95 71 86 | 40 21 81 65 44 |
| 80 12 43 56 35 | 17 72 70 80 15 | 45 31 82 23 74 | 21 11 57 82 53 | 14 38 55 37 63 |
| 74 35 09 98 17 | 77 40 27 72 14 | 43 23 60 02 10 | 45 52 16 42 37 | 96 28 60 26 55 |
| 69 91 62 68 03 | 66 25 22 91 48 | 36 93 68 72 03 | 76 62 11 39 90 | 94 40 05 64 18 |
| 09 89 32 05 05 | 14 22 56 85 14 | 46 42 75 67 88 | 96 29 77 88 22 | 54 38 21 45 98 |

*(Contd.)*

*(Contd. Appendix-B)*

| | | | | |
|---|---|---|---|---|
| 91 49 91 45 23 | 68 47 92 76 86 | 46 16 28 35 54 | 94 75 08 99 23 | 37 08 92 00 48 |
| 80 33 69 45 98 | 26 94 03 68 58 | 70 29 73 41 35 | 53 14 03 33 40 | 42 05 08 23 41 |
| 44 10 48 19 49 | 85 15 74 79 54 | 32 97 92 65 75 | 57 60 04 08 81 | 22 22 20 64 13 |
| 12 55 07 37 42 | 11 10 00 20 40 | 12 86 07 46 97 | 96 64 48 94 39 | 28 70 72 58 15 |
| 63 60 64 93 29 | 16 50 53 44 84 | 40 21 95 25 63 | 43 65 17 70 82 | 07 20 73 17 90 |
| | | | | |
| 61 19 69 04 46 | 26 45 74 77 74 | 51 92 43 37 29 | 65 39 45 95 93 | 42 58 26 05 27 |
| 15 47 44 52 66 | 95 27 07 99 53 | 59 36 78 38 48 | 82 39 61 01 18 | 33 21 15 94 66 |
| 94 55 72 85 73 | 67 89 75 43 87 | 54 62 24 44 31 | 91 19 04 25 92 | 92 92 74 59 73 |
| 42 48 11 62 13 | 97 34 40 87 21 | 16 86 84 87 67 | 03 07 11 20 59 | 25 70 14 66 70 |
| 23 52 37 83 17 | 73 20 88 98 37 | 68 93 59 14 16 | 26 25 22 96 63 | 05 52 28 25 62 |
| | | | | |
| 04 49 35 24 94 | 75 24 63 38 24 | 45 86 25 10 25 | 61 96 27 93 35 | 65 33 71 24 72 |
| 00 54 99 76 54 | 64 05 18 81 59 | 96 11 96 38 96 | 54 69 28 23 91 | 23 28 72 95 29 |
| 35 96 31 53 07 | 26 89 80 93 54 | 33 35 13 54 62 | 77 97 45 00 24 | 90 10 33 93 33 |
| 59 80 80 83 91 | 45 42 72 68 42 | 83 60 94 97 00 | 13 02 12 48 92 | 78 56 52 01 06 |
| 46 05 88 52 36 | 01 39 09 22 86 | 77 28 14 40 77 | 93 91 08 36 47 | 70 61 74 29 41 |
| | | | | |
| 32 17 90 05 97 | 87 37 92 52 41 | 05 56 70 70 07 | 86 74 31 71 57 | 85 39 41 18 38 |
| 69 23 46 14 06 | 20 11 74 52 04 | 15 95 66 00 00 | 18 74 39 24 23 | 97 11 89 63 38 |
| 19 56 54 14 30 | 01 75 87 53 79 | 40 41 92 15 85 | 66 67 43 68 06 | 84 96 28 52 07 |
| 45 15 51 49 38 | 19 47 60 72 46 | 43 66 79 45 43 | 59 04 79 00 33 | 20 82 66 95 41 |
| 94 86 43 19 94 | 36 16 81 08 51 | 34 88 88 15 53 | 01 54 03 54 56 | 05 01 45 11 76 |

*Source*: The RAND Corporation, *A Million Random Digits,* Free Press, Glencoe, Ill., 1955, pp. 1-3, with the kind permission of the publisher.

**Appendix B Random numbers** *(Continued)*

*(Contd. Appendix-B)*

| | | | | |
|---|---|---|---|---|
| 20 85 77 31 56 | 70 28 42 43 26 | 79 37 59 52 20 | 01 15 96 32 67 | 10 62 24 83 91 |
| 15 63 38 49 24 | 90 41 59 36 14 | 33 52 12 66 65 | 55 82 34 76 41 | 86 22 53 17 04 |
| 92 69 44 82 97 | 39 90 40 21 15 | 59 58 94 90 67 | 66 82 14 15 75 | 49 76 70 40 37 |
| 77 61 31 90 19 | 88 15 20 00 80 | 20 55 49 14 09 | 96 27 74 82 57 | 50 81 69 76 16 |
| 38 68 83 24 86 | 45 13 46 35 45 | 59 40 47 20 59 | 43 94 75 16 80 | 43 85 25 96 93 |
| | | | | |
| 25 16 30 18 89 | 70 01 41 50 21 | 41 29 06 73 12 | 71 85 71 59 57 | 68 97 11 14 03 |
| 65 25 10 76 29 | 37 23 93 32 95 | 05 87 00 11 19 | 92 78 42 63 40 | 18 47 76 56 22 |
| 36 81 54 36 25 | 18 63 73 75 09 | 82 44 49 90 05 | 04 92 17 37 01 | 14 70 79 39 97 |
| 64 39 71 16 92 | 05 32 78 21 62 | 20 24 78 17 59 | 45 19 72 53 32 | 83 74 52 25 67 |
| 04 51 52 56 24 | 95 09 66 79 46 | 48 46 08 55 58 | 15 19 11 87 82 | 16 93 03 33 61 |
| | | | | |
| 83 76 16 O8 73 | 43 25 38 41 45 | 60 83 32 59 83 | 0l 29 14 13 49 | 20 36 80 71 26 |
| 14 38 70 63 45 | 80 85 40 92 79 | 43 52 90 63 18 | 38 38 47 47 61 | 41 19 63 74 80 |
| 51 32 19 22 46 | 80 08 87 70 74 | 88 72 25 67 36 | 66 16 44 94 31 | 66 91 93 16 78 |
| 72 47 20 00 08 | 80 89 01 80 02 | 94 81 33 19 00 | 54 15 58 34 36 | 35 35 25 41 31 |
| 05 46 65 53 06 | 93 12 81 84 64 | 74 45 79 05 61 | 72 84 81 18 34 | 79 98 26 84 16 |
| | | | | |
| 39 52 87 24 84 | 82 47 42 55 93 | 48 54 53 52 47 | 18 61 91 36 74 | 18 61 11 92 41 |
| 81 61 61 87 11 | 53 34 24 42 76 | 75 12 21 17 24 | 74 62 77 37 07 | 58 31 91 59 97 |
| 07 58 61 61 20 | 82 64 12 28 20 | 92 90 41 31 41 | 32 39 21 97 63 | 61 19 96 79 40 |
| 90 76 70 42 35 | 13 57 41 72 00 | 69 90 26 37 42 | 78 46 42 25 01 | 18 62 79 08 72 |
| 40 18 82 81 93 | 29 59 38 86 27 | 94 97 21 15 98 | 62 09 53 67 87 | 00 44 15 89 97 |
| | | | | |
| 34 41 48 21 57 | 86 88 75 50 87 | 19 15 20 00 23 | 12 30 28 07 83 | 32 62 46 86 91 |
| 63 43 97 53 63 | 44 98 91 68 22 | 36 02 40 09 67 | 76 37 84 16 05 | 65 96 17 34 88 |
| 67 04 90 90 70 | 93 39 94 55 47 | 94 45 87 42 84 | 05 04 14 98 07 | 20 28 83 40 60 |
| 79 49 50 41 46 | 52 16 29 02 86 | 54 15 83 42 43 | 46 97 83 54 82 | 59 36 29 59 38 |
| 91 70 43 05 52 | 04 73 72 10 31 | 75 05 19 30 29 | 47 66 56 43 82 | 99 78 29 34 78 |

# Appendix C
# Distribution of t

| df | Level of significance for one-tailed test | | | | | |
|---|---|---|---|---|---|---|
| | *.10* | *.05* | *.025* | *.01* | *.005* | *.0005* |
| | *Level of significance for two-tailed test* | | | | | |
| | *.20* | *.10* | *.025* | *.02* | *.01* | *.001* |
| 1 | 3.078 | 6.314 | 12.706 | 31.821 | 63.657 | 636.619 |
| 2 | 1.886 | 2.920 | 4.303 | 6.965 | 9.925 | 31.598 |
| 3 | 1.638 | 2.353 | 3.182 | 4.541 | 5.841 | 12.941 |
| 4 | 1.533 | 2.132 | 2.776 | 3.747 | 4.604 | 8.610 |
| 5 | 1.476 | 2.015 | 2.571 | 3.365 | 4.032 | 6.859 |
| 6 | 1.440 | 1.943 | 2.447 | 3.143 | 3.707 | 5.959 |
| 7 | 1.415 | 1.895 | 2.365 | 2.998 | 3.499 | 5.405 |
| 8 | 1.397 | 1.860 | 2.306 | 2.896 | 3.355 | 5.041 |
| 9 | 1.383 | 1.833 | 2.262 | 2.821 | 3.250 | 4.781 |
| 10 | 1.372 | 1.812 | 2.228 | 2.764 | 3.169 | 4.587 |
| 11 | 1.363 | 1.796 | 2.201 | 2.718 | 3.106 | 4.437 |
| 12 | 1.356 | 1.782 | 2.179 | 2.681 | 3.055 | 4.318 |
| 13 | 1.350 | 1.771 | 2.160 | 2.650 | 3.012 | 4.221 |
| 14 | 1.345 | 1.761 | 2.145 | 2.624 | 2.977 | 4.140 |
| 15 | 1.341 | 1.753 | 2.131 | 2.602 | 2.947 | 4.073 |
| 16 | 1.337 | 1.746 | 2.120 | 2.583 | 2.921 | 4.015 |
| 17 | 1.333 | 1.740 | 2.110 | 2.567 | 2.898 | 3.965 |
| 18 | 1.330 | 1.734 | 2.101 | 2.552 | 2.878 | 3.922 |
| 19 | 1.328 | 1.729 | 2.093 | 2.539 | 2.861 | 3.883 |
| 20 | 1.325 | 1.725 | 2.086 | 2.528 | 2.845 | 3.850 |
| 21 | 1.323 | 1.721 | 2.080 | 2.518 | 2.831 | 3.819 |
| 22 | 1.321 | 1.717 | 2.074 | 2.508 | 2.819 | 3.792 |
| 23 | 1.319 | 1.714 | 2.069 | 2.500 | 2.807 | 3.767 |
| 24 | 1.318 | 1.711 | 2.064 | 2.492 | 2.797 | 3.745 |
| 25 | 1.316 | 1.708 | 2.060 | 2.485 | 2.787 | 3.725 |

*(Contd.)*

*(Contd. Appendix-C)*

| *df* | *Level of significance for one-tailed test* | | | | | |
|---|---|---|---|---|---|---|
| | *.10* | *.05* | *.025* | *.01* | *.005* | *.0005* |
| | *Level of significance for two-tailed test* | | | | | |
| | *.20* | *.10* | *.025* | *.02* | *.01* | *.001* |
| 26 | 1.315 | 1.706 | 2.056 | 2.479 | 2.779 | 3.707 |
| 27 | 1.314 | 1.703 | 2.052 | 2.473 | 2.771 | 3.690 |
| 28 | 1.313 | 1.701 | 2.048 | 2.467 | 2.763 | 3.674 |
| 29 | 1.311 | 1.699 | 2.045 | 2.462 | 2.756 | 3.659 |
| 30 | 1.310 | 1.697 | 2.042 | 2.457 | 2.750 | 3.646 |
| 40 | 1.303 | 1.684 | 2.021 | 2.423 | 2.704 | 3.551 |
| 60 | 1.296 | 1.671 | 2.000 | 2.390 | 2.660 | 3.460 |
| 120 | 1.289 | 1.658 | 1.980 | 2.358 | 2.617 | 3.373 |
| ? | 1.282 | 1.645 | 1.960 | 2.326 | 2.576 | 3.291 |

# Appendix D

**Table of critical values of *U* in the Mean-Whitney test**
(*Continued*) Critical values of U at a = 0.05 with direction predicted or at a = .10 with direction not predicted

| $n_1$ \ $n_2$ | 9 | 10 | 11 | 12 | 13 | 14 | 15 | 16 | 17 | 18 | 19 | 20 |
|---|---|---|---|---|---|---|---|---|---|---|---|---|
| 1 | | | | | | | | | | | 0 | 0 |
| 2 | 1 | 1 | 1 | 2 | 2 | 2 | 3 | 3 | 3 | 4 | 4 | 4 |
| 3 | 3 | 4 | 5 | 5 | 6 | 7 | 7 | 8 | 9 | 9 | 10 | 11 |
| 4 | 6 | 7 | 8 | 9 | 10 | 11 | 12 | 14 | 15 | 16 | 17 | 18 |
| 5 | 9 | 11 | 12 | 13 | 15 | 16 | 18 | 19 | 20 | 22 | 23 | 25 |
| 6 | 12 | 14 | 16 | 17 | 19 | 21 | 23 | 25 | 26 | 28 | 30 | 32 |
| 7 | 15 | 17 | 19 | 21 | 24 | 26 | 28 | 30 | 33 | 35 | 37 | 39 |
| 8 | 18 | 20 | 23 | 26 | 28 | 31 | 33 | 36 | 39 | 41 | 44 | 47 |
| 9 | 21 | 24 | 27 | 30 | 33 | 36 | 39 | 42 | 45 | 48 | 51 | 54 |
| 10 | 24 | 27 | 31 | 34 | 37 | 41 | 44 | 48 | 51 | 55 | 58 | 62 |
| 11 | 27 | 31 | 34 | 38 | 42 | 46 | 50 | 54 | 57 | 61 | 65 | 69 |
| 12 | 30 | 34 | 38 | 42 | 47 | 51 | 55 | 60 | 64 | 68 | 72 | 77 |
| 13 | 33 | 37 | 42 | 47 | 51 | 56 | 61 | 65 | 70 | 75 | 80 | 84 |
| 14 | 36 | 41 | 46 | 51 | 56 | 61 | 66 | 71 | 77 | 82 | 87 | 92 |
| 15 | 39 | 44 | 50 | 55 | 61 | 66 | 72 | 77 | 83 | 88 | 94 | 100 |
| 16 | 42 | 48 | 54 | 60 | 65 | 71 | 77 | 83 | 89 | 95 | 101 | 107 |
| 17 | 45 | 51 | 57 | 64 | 70 | 77 | 83 | 89 | 96 | 102 | 109 | 115 |
| 18 | 48 | 55 | 61 | 68 | 75 | 82 | 88 | 95 | 102 | 109 | 116 | 123 |
| 19 | 51 | 58 | 65 | 72 | 80 | 87 | 94 | 101 | 109 | 116 | 123 | 130 |
| 20 | 54 | 62 | 69 | 77 | 84 | 92 | 100 | 107 | 115 | 123 | 130 | 138 |

# Appendix E

## Table of critical values of T in the Wilcoxon matched-pairs signed-ranks test

| N | *Level of significance, direction predicted* | | |
|---|---|---|---|
| | *.025* | *.01* | *.005* |
| | *Level of significance, direction not predicted* | | |
| | *.05* | *.02* | *.01* |
| 6 | 0 | - | - |
| 7 | 2 | 0 | - |
| 8 | 4 | 2 | 0 |
| 9 | 6 | 3 | 2 |
| 10 | 8 | 5 | 3 |
| 11 | 11 | 7 | 5 |
| 12 | 14 | 10 | 7 |
| 13 | 17 | 13 | 10 |
| 14 | 21 | 16 | 13 |
| 15 | 25 | 20 | 16 |
| 16 | 30 | 24 | 20 |
| 17 | 35 | 28 | 23 |
| 18 | 40 | 33 | 28 |
| 19 | 46 | 38 | 32 |
| 20 | 52 | 43 | 38 |
| 21 | 59 | 49 | 43 |
| 22 | 66 | 56 | 49 |
| 23 | 73 | 62 | 55 |
| 24 | 81 | 69 | 61 |
| 25 | 89 | 77 | 68 |

*Source*: F. Wilcoxon, *Some Rapid Approximate Statistical Procedures,* American Cyanamid Company, New York, 1949, table I, p. 13, with the kind permission of the author and publisher; as adapted in S. Siegel, *Nonparametric Statistics,* McGraw-Hill Book Company, New York, 1956, table G.

# Appendix F

## Distribution of $x^2$

Probability

| df | .99 | .98 | .95 | .90 | .80 | .70 | .50 | .30 | .20 | .10 | .05 | .02 | .01 | .001 |
|---|---|---|---|---|---|---|---|---|---|---|---|---|---|---|
| 1 | $.0^3157$ | $.0^3628$ | .00393 | .0158 | .0642 | 198 | .455 | 1.079 | 1.642 | 2.706 | 3.841 | 5.412 | 6.635 | 10.827 |
| 2 | .0201 | .0404 | .103 | .211 | .446 | .713 | 1.386 | 2.408 | 3.219 | 4.605 | 5.991 | 7.824 | 9.210 | 13.815 |
| 3 | .115 | .185 | .352 | .584 | 1.005 | 1.424 | 2.366 | 3.655 | 4.642 | 6.251 | 7.815 | 9.837 | 11.341 | 16.268 |
| 4 | .297 | .429 | .711 | 1.064 | 1.649 | 2.195 | 3.357 | 4.878 | 5.989 | 7.779 | 0.488 | 11.668 | 13.277 | 18.465 |
| 5 | .554 | .752 | 1.145 | 1.610 | 2.343 | 3.000 | 4.351 | 6.064 | 7.280 | 9.236 | 11.070 | 13.388 | 15.086 | 20.617 |
| 6 | .872 | 1.134 | 1.635 | 2.204 | 3.070 | 3.828 | 5.398 | 7.231 | 8.558 | 10.695 | 12.592 | 15.033 | 16.812 | 22.457 |
| 7 | 1.239 | 1.564 | 2.167 | 2.833 | 3.822 | 9.671 | 6.396 | 8.383 | 9.803 | 12.017 | 14.067 | 16.622 | 18.475 | 24.322 |
| 8 | 1.646 | 2.032 | 2.733 | 3.990 | 9.594 | 5.527 | 7.394 | 9.529 | 11.030 | 13.362 | 15.507 | 18.168 | 20.090 | 26.125 |
| 9 | 2.088 | 2.532 | 3.325 | 4.168 | 5.380 | 6.393 | 8.393 | 10.656 | 12.242 | 14.684 | 16.919 | 19.679 | 21.666 | 27.877 |
| 10 | 2.558 | 3.059 | 3.940 | 4.865 | 6.179 | 7.267 | 9.342 | 11.781 | 13.442 | 15.097 | 18.307 | 21.161 | 23.209 | 29.588 |

*(Contd.)*

*(Contd. Appendix-F)*

| df | .99 | .98 | .95 | .90 | .80 | .70 | .50 | .30 | .20 | .10 | .05 | .02 | .01 | .001 |
|---|---|---|---|---|---|---|---|---|---|---|---|---|---|---|
| 11 | 3.053 | 3.609 | 4.575 | 5.578 | 6.989 | 8.148 | 10.341 | 12.899 | 14.631 | 17.275 | 19.675 | 22.618 | 24.725 | 31.264 |
| 12 | 3.571 | 4.178 | 5.226 | 6.304 | 7.807 | 9.034 | 11.340 | 14.011 | 15.812 | 18.549 | 21.026 | 24.054 | 26.217 | 32.909 |
| 13 | 4.107 | 4.765 | 5.892 | 7.042 | 8.634 | 9.926 | 12.340 | 15.119 | 16.985 | 19.812 | 22.362 | 25.472 | 27.688 | 34.528 |
| 14 | 4.660 | 5.368 | 6.571 | 7.790 | 9.467 | 10.821 | 13.339 | 16.222 | 18.151 | 21.064 | 23.685 | 26.873 | 29.141 | 36.123 |
| 15 | 5.229 | 5.985 | 7.261 | 8.547 | 10.307 | 11.721 | 14.339 | 17.322 | 19.311 | 22.307 | 24.996 | 28.259 | 30.578 | 37.697 |
| 16 | 5.812 | 6.614 | 7.962 | 9.312 | 11.152 | 12.624 | 15.338 | 18.418 | 20.465 | 23.542 | 26.296 | 29.633 | 32.000 | 39.252 |
| 17 | 6.408 | 7.255 | 8.672 | 10.085 | 12.002 | 13.531 | 16.338 | 19.511 | 21.615 | 24.769 | 27.587 | 30.995 | 33.409 | 40.790 |
| 18 | 7.015 | 7.906 | 9.390 | 10.865 | 12.857 | 19.440 | 17.338 | 20.601 | 22.760 | 25.989 | 28.869 | 32.346 | 39.805 | 42.312 |
| 19 | 7.633 | 8.567 | 10.117 | 11.651 | 13.716 | 15.352 | 18.338 | 21.689 | 23.900 | 27.204 | 30.144 | 33.687 | 36.191 | 43.820 |
| 20 | 8.260 | 0.237 | 10.851 | 12.443 | 14.578 | 16.266 | 19.337 | 22.775 | 25.038 | 28.412 | 31.410 | 35.020 | 37.566 | 45.315 |
| 21 | 8.897 | 9.915 | 11.591 | 13.290 | 15.445 | 17.182 | 20.337 | 23.858 | 26.171 | 29.615 | 32.671 | 36.343 | 38.932 | 46.797 |
| 22 | 9.542 | 10.600 | 12.338 | 14.041 | 16.314 | 18.101 | 21.337 | 24.939 | 27.301 | 30.813 | 33.924 | 37.659 | 40.289 | 48.268 |
| 23 | 10.196 | 11.293 | 13.091 | 14.848 | 17.187 | 19.021 | 22.337 | 26.018 | 28.429 | 32.007 | 35.172 | 38.968 | 41.638 | 49.728 |
| 24 | 10.856 | 11.992 | 13.848 | 15.659 | 18.062 | 19.943 | 23.337 | 27.096 | 29.553 | 33.196 | 36.415 | 40.270 | 92.980 | 51.179 |
| 25 | 11.524 | 12.697 | 14.611 | 16.473 | 18.940 | 20.867 | 24.337 | 28.172 | 30.675 | 34.382 | 37.652 | 41.566 | 44.314 | 42.620 |

*(Contd.)*

*(Contd. Appendix-F)*

| df | .99 | .98 | .95 | .90 | .80 | .70 | .50 | .30 | .20 | .10 | .05 | .02 | .01 | .001 |
|---|---|---|---|---|---|---|---|---|---|---|---|---|---|---|
| 26 | 12.198 | 13.409 | 15.379 | 17.292 | 19.820 | 21.792 | 25.336 | 29.246 | 31.795 | 35.563 | 38.885 | 42.856 | 45.642 | 54.052 |
| 27 | 12.879 | 14.125 | 16.151 | 18.114 | 20.703 | 22.719 | 26.336 | 30.319 | 32.912 | 36.741 | 90.113 | 41.140 | 46.963 | 55.476 |
| 28 | 13.565 | 14.847 | 16.928 | 18.939 | 21.588 | 23.647 | 27.336 | 31.391 | 34.027 | 37.916 | 41.337 | 45.410 | 48.278 | 56.893 |
| 29 | 14.256 | 15.574 | 17.708 | 19.768 | 22.475 | 24.577 | 28.336 | 32.461 | 35.139 | 39.087 | 42.557 | 46.693 | 49.588 | 58.302 |
| 30 | 14.953 | 16.306 | 18.493 | 20.599 | 23.364 | 25.508 | 29.336 | 33.530 | 36.250 | 40.256 | 43.773 | 47.962 | 50.892, | 59.703 |

For larger values of df, the expression $2x^2$- 2df - 1 may be used as a normal deviate with unit variance, remem-bering that the probability for $x^2$ corresponds with that of a single tail of the normal curve. A slightly more complex trans-formation, which gives far better approximations for relatively small values of *v*, is

7 ° I ~X' - 1w ( 1 - 2I9v) *ll1w ~2J9v*

(See A. C. Acock and G. R. Stavig: "Normal Deviate Approximations of $x^2$" *Perceptual and Motor Skills,* Vol. 42, p. 220, 1976)

SOURCE: Table I is reprinted from Table IV of R. A. Fisher and F. Yates, *Stotistical Tables for Biological, Agricultural and Medical Research* (1948 ed.), published by Oliver & Boyd Ltd., Edinburgh and London, by permission of the authors and publishers.

# Appendix G
## Distribution of *F* (*Continued*)

$p = .05$

| $n_2$ \ $n_1$ | 1 | 2 | 3 | 4 | 5 | 6 | 8 | 12 | 24 | ? |
|---|---|---|---|---|---|---|---|---|---|---|
| 1 | 161.4 | 199.5 | 215.7 | 224.6 | 230.2 | 234.0 | 238.9 | 243.9 | 249.0 | 254.3 |
| 2 | 18.51 | 19.00 | 19.16 | 19.25 | 19.30 | 19.33 | 19.3T | 19.41 | 19.45 | 19.50 |
| 3 | 10.13 | 9.55 | 9.28 | 9.12 | 9.01 | 8.94 | 8.84 | 8.74 | 8.64 | 8.53 |
| 4 | 7.71 | 6.94 | 6.59 | 6.39 | 6.26 | 6.16 | 6.04 | 5.91 | 5.77 | 5.63 |
| 5 | 6.61 | 5.79 | 5.41 | 5.19 | 5.05 | 4.95 | 4.82 | 4.68 | 4.53 | 4.36 |
| 6 | 5.99 | 5.14 | 4.76 | 4.53 | 4.39 | 4.28 | 4.15 | 4.00 | 3.84 | 3.67 |
| 7 | 5.59 | 4.74 | 4.35 | 4.12 | 3.97 | 3.87 | 3.73 | 3.57 | 3.41 | 3.23 |
| 8 | 5.32 | 4.46 | 4.07 | 3.84 | 3.69 | 3.58 | 3.44 | 3.28 | 3.12 | 2.93 |
| 9 | 5.12 | 4.26 | 3.86 | 3.63 | 3.48 | 3.37 | 3.23 | 3.07 | 2.90 | 2.71 |
| 10 | 4.96 | 4.10 | 3.71 | 3.48 | 3.33 | 3.22 | 3.07 | 2.91 | 2.74 | 2.54 |
| 11 | 4.84 | 3.98 | 3.59 | 3.36 | 3.20 | 3.09 | 2.95 | 2.79 | 2.61 | 2.40 |
| 12 | 4.75 | 3.88 | 3.49 | 3.26 | 3.11 | 3.00 | 2.85 | 2.69 | 2.50 | 2.30 |
| 13 | 4.67 | 3.80 | 3.41 | 3.18 | 3.02 | 2.92 | 2.77 | 2.60 | 2.42 | 2.21 |
| 14 | 4.60 | 3.74 | 3.34 | 3.11 | 2.96 | 2.85 | 2.70 | 2.53 | 2.35 | 2.13 |
| 15 | 4.54 | 3.68 | 3.29 | 3.06 | 2.90 | 2.79 | 2.64 | 2.48 | 2.29 | 2.07 |

*(Contd.)*

*(Contd. Appendix-G)*

$p = .05$

| $n_2$ \ $n_1$ | 1 | 2 | 3 | 4 | 5 | 6 | 8 | 12 | 24 | ? |
|---|---|---|---|---|---|---|---|---|---|---|
| 16 | 4.49 | 3.63 | 3.24 | 3.01 | 2.85 | 2.74 | 2.59 | 2.42 | 2.24 | 2.01 |
| 17 | 4.45 | 3.59 | 3.20 | 2.96 | 2.81 | 2.70 | 2.55 | 2.38 | 2.19 | 1.96 |
| 18 | 4.41 | 3.55 | 3.16 | 2.93 | 2.77 | 2.66 | 2.51 | 2.34 | 2.15 | 1.92 |
| 19 | 4.38 | 3.52 | 3.13 | 2.90 | 2.74 | 2.63 | 2.48 | 2.31 | 2.11 | 1.88 |
| 20 | 4.35 | 3.49 | 3.10 | 2.87 | 2.71 | 2.60 | 2.45 | 2.28 | 2.08 | 1.84 |
| 21 | 4.32 | 3.47 | 3.07 | 2.84 | 2.68 | 2.57 | 2.42 | 2.25 | 2.05 | 1.81 |
| 22 | 4.30 | 3.44 | 3.05 | 2.82 | 2.66 | 2.55 | 2.40 | 2.23 | 2.03 | 1.78 |
| 23 | 4.28 | 3.42 | 3.03 | 2.80 | 2.64 | 2.53 | 2.38 | 2.20 | 2.00 | 1.76 |
| 24 | 4.26 | 3.40 | 3.01 | 2.78 | 2.62 | 2.51 | 2.36 | 2.18 | 1.98 | 1.73 |
| 25 | 4.24 | 3.38 | 2.99 | 2.76 | 2.60 | 2.49 | 2.34 | 2.16 | 1.96 | 1.71 |
| 26 | 4.22 | 3.37 | 2.98 | 2.74 | 2.59 | 2.47 | 2.32 | 2.15 | 1.95 | 1.69 |
| 27 | 4.21 | 3.35 | 2.96 | 2.73 | 2.57 | 2.46 | 2.30 | 2.13 | 1.93 | 1.67 |
| 28 | 4.20 | 3.34 | 2.95 | 2.71 | 2.56 | 2.44 | 2.29 | 2.12 | 1.91 | 1.65 |
| 29 | 4.18 | 3.33 | 2.93 | 2,70 | 2.54 | 2.43 | 2.28 | 2.10 | 1.90 | 1.64 |
| 30 | 4.17 | 3.32 | 2.92 | 2.69 | 2.53 | 2.42 | 2.27 | 2.09 | 1.89 | 1.62 |
| 40 | 4.08 | 3.23 | 2.84 | 2.61 | 2.45 | 2.34 | 2.18 | 2.00 | 1.79 | 1.51 |
| 60 | 4.00 | 3.15 | 2.76 | 2.52 | 2.37 | 2.25 | 2.10 | 1.92 | 1.70 | 1.39 |
| 120 | 3.92 | 3.07 | 2.68 | 2.45 | 2.29 | 2.17 | 2.02 | 1.83 | 1.61 | 1.25 |
| ? | 3.84 | 2.99 | 2.60 | 2.37 | 2.21 | 2.09 | 1.94 | 1.75 | 1.52 | 1.00 |

Value of n1 and n2 represents the degrees of freedom associated with the larger and smaller estimates of variance respectively

## Appendix G
## Distribution of *F* (*Continued*)

$p = .01$

| $n_2$ \ $n_1$ | 1 | 2 | 3 | 4 | 5 | 6 | 8 | 12 | 24 | ? |
|---|---|---|---|---|---|---|---|---|---|---|
| 1 | 4052 | 4999 | 5403 | 5625 | 5764 | 5859 | 5981 | 6106 | 6234 | 6366 |
| 2 | 98.49 | 99.01 | 99.17 | 99.25 | 99.30 | 99.33 | 99.36 | 99.42 | 99.46 | 99.50 |
| 3 | 34.12 | 30.81 | 29.46 | 28.71 | 28.24 | 27.91 | 27.49 | 27.05 | 26.60 | 26.12 |
| 4 | 21.20 | 18.00 | 16.69 | 15.98 | 15.52 | 15.21 | 14.80 | 14.37 | 13.93 | 13.46 |
| 5 | 16.26 | 13.27 | 12.06 | 11.39 | 10.97 | 10.67 | 10.27 | 9.89 | 9.47 | 9.02 |
| 6 | 13.74 | 10.92 | 9.78 | 9.15 | 8.75 | 8.47 | 8.10 | 7.72 | 7.31 | 6.88 |
| 7 | 12.25 | 9.55 | 8.45 | 7.85 | 7.46 | 7.19 | 6.84 | 6.47 | 6.07 | 5.65 |
| 8 | 11.26 | 8.65 | 7.59 | 7.01 | 6.63 | 6.37 | 6.03 | 5.67 | 5.28 | 4.86 |
| 9 | 10.56 | 8.02 | 6.99 | 6.42 | 6.06 | 5.80 | 5.47 | 5.11 | 4.73 | 4.31 |
| 10 | 10.04 | 7.56 | 6.55 | 5.99 | 5.64 | 5.39 | 5.06 | 4.71 | 4.33 | 3.91 |
| 11 | 9.65 | 7.20 | 6.22 | 5.67 | 5.32 | 5.07 | 4.74 | 4.40 | 4.02 | 3.60 |
| 12 | 9.33 | 6.93 | 5.95 | 5.41 | 5.06 | 4.82 | 4.50 | 4.16 | 3.78 | 3.36 |
| 13 | 9.07 | 6.70 | 5.74 | 5.20 | 4.86 | 4.62 | 4.30 | 3.96 | 3.59 | 3.16 |
| 14 | 8.86 | 6.51 | 5.56 | 5.03 | 4.69 | 4.46 | 4.14 | 3.80 | 3.43 | 3.00 |
| 15 | 8.68 | 6.36 | 5.42 | 4.89 | 4.56 | 4.32 | 4.00 | 3.67 | 3.29 | 2.87 |
| 16 | 8.53 | 6.23 | 5.29 | 4.77 | 4.44 | 4.20 | 3.89 | 3.55 | 3.18 | 2.75 |
| 17 | 8.40 | 6.11 | 5.18 | 4.67 | 4.34 | 4.10 | 3.79 | 3.45 | 3.08 | 2.65 |
| 18 | 8.28 | 6.01 | 5.09 | 4.58 | 4.25 | 4.01 | 3.71 | 3.37 | 3.00 | 2.57 |
| 19 | 8.18 | 5.93 | 5.01 | 4.50 | 4.17 | 3.94 | 3.63 | 3.30 | 2.92 | 2.49 |
| 20 | 8.10 | 5.85 | 4.94 | 4.43 | 4.10 | 3.87 | 3.56 | 3.23 | 2.86 | 2.42 |

(*Contd.*)

*(Contd. Appendix-G)*

$p = .01$

| $n_2$ \ $n_1$ | 1 | 2 | 3 | 4 | 5 | 6 | 8 | 12 | 24 | ? |
|---|---|---|---|---|---|---|---|---|---|---|
| 21 | 8.02 | 5.78 | 4.87 | 4.37 | 4.04 | 3.81 | 3.51 | 3.17 | 2.80 | 2.36 |
| 22 | 7.94 | 5.72 | 4.82 | 4.31 | 3.99 | 3.76 | 3.45 | 3.12 | 2.75 | 2.31 |
| 23 | 7.88 | 5.66 | 4.76 | 4.26 | 3.94 | 3.71 | 3.41 | 3.07 | 2.70 | 2.26 |
| 24 | 7.82 | 5.61 | 4.72 | 4.22 | 3.90 | 3.67 | 3.36 | 3.03 | 2.66 | 2.21 |
| 25 | 7.77 | 5.57 | 4.68 | 4.18 | 3.86 | 3.63 | 3.32 | 2.99 | 2.62 | 2.17 |
| 26 | 7.72 | 5.53 | 4.64 | 4.14 | 3.82 | 3.59 | 3.29 | 2.96 | 2.58 | 2.13 |
| 27 | 7.68 | 5.49 | 4.60 | 4.11 | 3.78 | 3.56 | 3.26 | 2.93 | 2.55 | 2.10 |
| 28 | 7.64 | 5.45 | 4.57 | 4.07 | 3.75 | 3.53 | 3.23 | 2.90 | 2.52 | 2.06 |
| 29 | 7.60 | 5.42 | 4.54 | 4.04 | 3.73 | 3.50 | 3.20 | 2.87 | 2.49 | 2.03 |
| 30 | 7.56 | 5.39 | 4.51 | 4.02 | 3.70 | 3.47 | 3.17 | 2.84 | 2.47 | 2.01 |
| 40 | 7.31 | 5.18 | 4.31 | 3.83 | 3.51 | 3.29 | 2.99 | 2.66 | 2.29 | 1.80 |
| 60 | 7.08 | 4.98 | 4.13 | 3.65 | 3.34 | 3.12 | 2.82 | 2.50 | 2.12 | 1.60 |
| 120 | 6.85 | 4.79 | 3.95 | 3.48 | 3.17 | 2.96 | 2.66 | 2.34 | 1.95 | 1.38 |
| ? | 6.64 | 4.60 | 3.78 | 3.32 | 3.02 | 2.80 | 2.51 | 2.18 | 1.79 | 1.00 |

Value of y and n2 represent the degrees of freedom associated with the larger and smaller estimates of varience respectively.

Source : Table J is abridged from Table V of ft. A. Fisher and F. Yates, *Statistical Tables for Biological, Agricultural and Medical. Research* (1948 ed.), published by Oliver & Boyd, Ltd., Edinburgh and London, by permission of the authors and publishers.

**Appendix G Distribution of** *F* *(Continued)*

$p = .001$

| $n_2$ \ $n_1$ | 1 | 2 | 3 | 4 | 5 | 6 | 8 | 12 | 24 | ? |
|---|---|---|---|---|---|---|---|---|---|---|
| 1 | 405284 | 500000 | 540379 | 562500 | 576405 | 585937 | 598144 | 610667 | 623497 | 636619 |
| 2 | 998.5 | 999.0 | 999.2 | 999.2 | 999.3 | 999.3 | 999.4 | 999.4 | 999.5 | 999.5 |
| 3 | 167.5 | 148.5 | 141.1 | 137.1 | 134.6 | 132.8 | 130.6 | 128.3 | 125.9 | 123.5 |
| 4 | 74.14 | 61.25 | 56.18 | 53.44 | 51.71 | 50.53 | 49.00 | 47.41 | 45.77 | 44.05 |
| 5 | 47.04 | 36.61 | 33.20 | 31.09 | 29.75 | 28.84 | 27.64 | 26.42 | 25.14 | 23.78 |
| 6 | 35.51 | 27.00 | 23.70 | 21.90 | 20.81 | 20.03 | 19.03 | 17.99 | 16.89 | 15.75 |
| 7 | 29.22 | 21.69 | 18.77 | 17.19 | 16.21 | 15.52 | 14.63 | 13.71 | 12.73 | 11.69 |
| 8 | 25.42 | 18.49 | 15.83 | 14.39 | 13.49 | 12.86 | 12.04 | 11.19 | 10.30 | 9.34 |
| 9 | 22.86 | 16.39 | 13.90 | 12.56 | 11.71 | 11.13 | 10.37 | 9.57 | 8.72 | 7.81 |
| 10 | 21.04 | 14.91 | 12.55 | 11.28 | 10.48 | 9.92 | 9.20 | 8.45 | 7.64 | 6.76 |
| 11 | 19.69 | 13.81 | 11.56 | 10.35 | 9.58 | 9.05 | 8.35 | 7.63 | 6.85 | 6.00 |
| 12 | 18.64 | 12.97 | 10.80 | 9.63 | 8.89 | 8.38 | 7.71 | 7.00 | 6.25 | 5.42 |
| 13 | 17.81 | 12.31 | 10.21 | 9.07 | 8.35 | 7.86 | 7.21 | 6.52 | 5.78 | 4.97 |
| 14 | 17.14 | 11.78 | 9.73 | 8.62 | 7.92 | 7.43 | 6.80 | 6.13I | 5.41 | 4.60 |
| 15 | 16.59 | 11.34 | 9.34 | 8.25 | 7.57 | 7.09 | 6.47 | 5.81 | 5.10 | 4.31 |
| 16 | 16.12 | 10.97 | 9.00 | 7.94 | 7.27 | 6.81 | 6.19 | 5.55I | 4.8.5 | 4.06 |
| 17 | 15.72 | 10.66 | 8.73 | 7.68 | 7.02 | 6.56 | 5.96 | 5.32 | 4.63 | 3.85 |
| 18 | 15.38 | 10.39 | 8.49 | 7.46 | 6.81 | 6.35 | 5.76 | 5.13 | 4.45 | 3.67 |
| 19 | 15.08 | 10.16 | 8.28 | 7.26 | 6.61 | 6.18 | 5.59 | 4.97 | 4.29 | 3.52 |
| 20 | 14.82 | 9.95 | 8.10 | 7.10 | 6.46 | 6.02 | 5.44 | 4.821 | 4.151 | 3.38 |

*(Contd.)*

(Contd. Appendix-G)

**Appendix G Distribution of** $F$ *(Continued)*

$p = .001$

| $n_2$ \ $n_1$ | 1 | 2 | 3 | 4 | 5 | 6 | 8 | 12 | 24 | ? |
|---|---|---|---|---|---|---|---|---|---|---|
| 21 | 14.59 | 9.77 | 7.94 | 6.95 | 6.32 | 5.88 | 5.31 | 4.70 | 4.03 | 3.26 |
| 22 | 14.38 | 9.61 | 7.80 | 6.81 | 6.19 | 5.76 | 5.19 | 4.58 | 3.92 | 3.15 |
| 23 | 14.19 | 9.47 | 7.67 | 6.69 | 6.08 | 5.65 | 5.09 | 4.48 | 3.82 | 3.05 |
| 24 | 14.03 | 9.34 | 7.55 | 6.59 | 5.98 | 5.55 | 4.99 | 4.39 | 3.74 | 2.97 |
| 25 | 13.88 | 9.22 | 7.45 | 6.49 | 5.88 | 5.46 | 4.91 | 4.31 | 3.66 | 2.89 |
| 26 | 13.74 | 9.12 | 7.36 | 6.41 | 5.80 | 5.38 | 4.83 | 4.24 | 3.59 | 2.82 |
| 27 | 13.61 | 9.02 | 7.27 | 6.33 | 5.73 | 5.31 | 4.76 | 4.17 | 3.52 | 2.75 |
| 28 | 13.50 | 8.93 | 7.19 | 6.25 | 5.66 | 5.24 | 4.69 | 4.11 | 3.46 | 2.70 |
| 29 | 13.39 | 8.85 | 7.12 | 6.19 | 5.59 | 5.18 | 4.64 | 4.05 | 3.41 | 2.64 |
| 30 | 13.29 | 8.77 | 7.05 | 6.12 | 5.53 | 5.12 | 4.58 | 4.00 | 3.36 | 2.59 |
| 40 | 12.61 | 8.25 | 6.60 | 5.70 | 5.13 | 4.73 | 4.21 | 3.64 | 3.01 | 2.23 |
| 60 | 11.97 | 7.76 | 6.17 | 5.31 | 4.76 | 4.37 | 3.87 | 3.31 | 2.69 | 1.90 |
| 120 | 11.38 | 7.31 | 5.79 | 4.95 | 4.42 | 4.04 | 3.55 | 3.02 | 2.40 | 1.56 |
| ? | 10.83 | 6.91 | 5.42 | 4.62 | 4.10 | 3.74 | 3.27 | 2.74 | 2.13 | 1.00 |

# Appendix H
# Values of z for given values of r

| $r$ | .000 | .001 | .002 | .003 | .004 | .005 | .006 | .007 | .008 | .009 |
|---|---|---|---|---|---|---|---|---|---|---|
| .000 | .0000 | .0010 | .0020 | .0030 | .0040 | .0050 | .0060 | .0070 | .0080 | .0090 |
| .010 | .0100 | .0110 | .0120 | .0130 | .0140 | .0150 | .0160 | .0170 | .0180 | .0190 |
| .020 | .0200 | .0210 | .0220 | .0230 | .0240 | .0250 | .0260 | .0270 | .0280 | .0290 |
| .030 | .0300 | .0310 | .0320 | .0330 | .0340 | .0350 | .0360 | .0370 | .0380 | .0390 |
| .040 | .0400 | .0410 | .0420 | .0430 | .0440 | .0450 | .0460 | .0470 | .0480 | .0490 |
| .050 | .0501 | .0511 | .0521 | .0531 | .0541 | .0551 | .0561 | .0571 | .0581 | .0591 |
| .060 | .0601 | .0611 | .0621 | .0631 | .0641 | .0651 | .0661 | .0671 | .0681 | .0691 |
| .070 | .0701 | .0711 | .0721 | .0731 | .0741 | .0751 | .0761 | .0771 | .0782 | .0792 |
| .080 | .0802 | .0812 | .0822 | .0833 | .0842 | .0852 | .0862 | .0872 | .0882 | .0892 |
| .090 | .0902 | .0912 | .0922 | .0933 | .0943 | .0953 | .0963 | .0973 | .0983 | .0993 |
| .100 | .1003 | .1013 | .7024 | .1034 | .1044 | .1054 | .1064 | .1074 | .1081 | .1094 |
| .110 | .1105 | .1115 | .1125 | .1135 | .1145 | .1155 | .1160 | .1175 | .1185 | .1195 |
| .120 | .1206 | .121d | .1226 | .1236 | .1246 | .1257 | .1267 | .1277 | .1287 | .1297 |
| .130 | .1308 | .1318 | .1328 | .1338 | .1348 | .1358 | .1368 | .1379 | .1389 | .1399 |
| .140 | .1409 | .1419 | .1430 | .1440 | .1450 | .1460 | .1470 | .1481 | .1491 | .1501 |

*(Contd.)*

(Contd. Appendix-H)

| r | .000 | .001 | .002 | .003 | .004 | .005 | .006 | .007 | .008 | .009 |
|---|---|---|---|---|---|---|---|---|---|---|
| .150 | .1511 | .1522 | .1532 | .1542 | .1552 | .1563 | .1573 | .1583 | .1593 | .1604 |
| .160 | .1614 | .1624 | .1634 | .1644 | .1655 | .1665 | .1676 | .1686 | .1696 | .1706 |
| .170 | .1717 | .1727 | .1737 | .1748 | .1758 | .1768 | .1779 | .1789 | .1799 | .1810 |
| .180 | .1820 | .1830 | .1841 | .1851 | .1861 | .1872 | .1882 | .1892 | .1903 | .1913 |
| .190 | .1923 | .1934 | .1944 | .1954 | .1965 | .1975 | .1986 | .1996 | .2007 | .2017 |
| .200 | .2027 | .2038 | .2048 | .2059 | .2069 | .2079 | .2090 | .2100 | .2111 | .2121 |
| .210 | .2132 | .2142 | .2153 | .2163 | .2174 | .2184 | .2194 | .2205 | .2215 | .2226 |
| .220 | .2237 | .2247 | .2258 | .2268 | .2279 | .2289 | .2300 | .2310 | .2321 | .2331 |
| .230 | .2342 | .2353 | .2363 | .2374 | .2384 | .2395 | .2405 | .2416 | .2127 | .2437 |
| .240 | .2448 | .2458 | .2469 | .2480 | .2490 | .2501 | .2511 | .2522 | .2533 | .2543 |
| .250 | .2554 | .2565 | .2575 | .2586 | .2597 | .2608 | .2618 | .2629 | .2640 | .2650 |
| .260 | .2661 | .2672 | .2682 | .2693 | .2704 | .2715 | .2726 | .2736 | .2747 | .2758 |
| .270 | .2769 | .2779 | .2790 | .2801 | .2812 | .2823 | .2833 | .2844 | .2855 | .2866 |
| .280 | .2877 | .2888 | .2898 | .2909 | .2920 | .2931 | .2942 | .2953 | .2964 | .2975 |
| .290 | .2986 | .2997 | .3008 | .3019 | .3029 | .3040 | .3051 | .3062 | .3073 | .3084 |
| .300 | .3095 | .3106 | .3117 | .3128 | .3139 | .3150 | .3161 | .3172 | .3183 | .3195 |
| .310 | .3206 | .3217 | .3228 | .3239 | .3250 | .3261 | .3272 | .3283 | .3294 | .3305 |
| .320 | .3317 | .3328 | .3339 | .3350 | .3361 | .3372 | .3384 | .3395 | .3406 | .3417 |
| .330 | .3428 | .3439 | .3451 | .3462 | .3473 | .3484 | .3496 | .3507 | .3518 | .3530 |
| .340 | .3541 | .3552 | .3564 | .3575 | .3586 | .3597 | .3609 | .3620 | .3632 | .3643 |

(Contd.)

*(Contd. Appendix-H)*

| *r* | .000 | .001 | .002 | .003 | .004 | .005 | .006 | .007 | .008 | .009 |
|---|---|---|---|---|---|---|---|---|---|---|
| .350 | .3654 | .3666 | .3677 | .3689 | .3700 | .3712 | .3723 | .3734 | .3746 | .3757 |
| .360 | .3769 | .3780 | .3792 | .3803 | .3815 | .3826 | .3838 | .3850 | .3861 | .3873 |
| .370 | .3884 | .3896 | .3907 | .3919 | .3931 | .3942 | .3954 | .3966 | .3977 | .3989 |
| .380 | .4001 | .4012 | .4021 | .4036 | .4047 | .4059 | .4071 | .4083 | .4094 | .4106 |
| .390 | .4118 | .4130 | .4142 | .4153 | .4165 | .4177 | .4189 | .4201 | .4213 | .4225 |
| .400 | .4236 | .4248 | .4260 | .4272 | .4284 | .4296 | .4308 | .4320 | .4332 | .4344 |
| .410 | .4356 | .4368 | .4380 | .4392 | .4404 | .4416 | .4429 | .4441 | .4453 | .4465 |
| .420 | .4477 | .4489 | .4501 | .4513 | .4526 | .4538 | .4550 | .4562 | .4574 | .4587 |
| .430 | .4599 | .4611 | .4623 | .4636 | .4648 | .4660 | .4673 | .4685 | .4697 | .4710 |
| .440 | .4722 | .4735 | .4747 | .4760 | .4772 | .4784 | .4797 | .4809 | .4822 | .4835 |
| .450 | .4847 | .4860 | .4872 | .4885 | .4897 | .4910 | .4923 | .4935 | .4948 | .4961 |
| .460 | .4973 | .4986 | .4999 | .5011 | .5024 | .5037 | .5049 | .5062 | .5075 | .5088 |
| .470 | .5101 | .5114 | .5126 | .5139 | .5152 | .5165 | .5178 | .5191 | .5204 | .5217 |
| .480 | .5230 | .5243 | .5256 | .5279 | .5282 | .5295 | .5308 | .5321 | .5334 | .5347 |
| .490 | .5361 | .5374 | .5387 | .5400 | .5413 | .5427 | .5440 | .5453 | .5466 | .5480 |

Source : Albert E. Waugh, Statistical Tables and Problems, McGraw-Hill Book Company, New York, 1952, table A11, pp. 40-41, with the kind permission of the author and publisher

# Bibliography


Anderson, J. et. al. (1970). *Thesis and Assignment Writing.* New Delhi : Wiley Eastern Limited.

Ackoff, R.L. ( 1953) *The Design of Social Research,* Chicago: University of Chicago Press.

Bailey, Kenneth D. (1978). *Methods of Social Research*, London: The Free Press.

Baker, L. Therese. (1988) *Doing Social Research,* New York: McGraw Hill.

Black, James A. and Champion, Dean J.(1976). *Methods and Issues in Social Research,* New York: John Wiley.

Blalock, H.M.(1988). *Social Statistics*, Auckland. Mc Graw Hill.

Brace, Nicola. et. al.(2003). *SPSS for Psychologists*, New York : Palgrave McMillan.

Buckinggham, A, and Saunders, P. (2004). *The Survey Methods Workbook*, Cambridge : Polity Press.

Craft, John. (1990). *Statistics and Data Analysis for Social Workers*, Illinois : Peacock Publishers.

Doby. J.T. et al. (1953). *An Introduction to Social Research,* London: Harrisburg : Stackpole Co.

Festinger. L. and Katz. D. (eds.). (1953). *Research Methods in the Behavioral Sciences,* New York: The Dryden Press.

Goode. W.J. and Hatt. P.K. (1952). *Methods of Social Research*, New York, McGraw Hill.

Guilford, J. P. (1950). *Fundamental Statistics in Psychology and Education*. 2nd ed. New York : McGraw Hill.

Kerlinger, Fred R.( 1964). *Foundations of Behavioural Research* Delhi, Surjeet Publications.

Kidder, Louise H. (1981) *Research Methods in Social Relations,* New York: Holt.

Krishef, Curtis H. (1987). *Fundamentals of Statistics for Human Services and Social Work*, Boston: Duxbury Press.

Lal Das, D.K., (2000) *Practice of Social Research : Social Work Perspective*, Jaipur : Rawat Publications.

Lal Das, D.K., (2005)*Designs of Social Research : Social Work Perspective*, Jaipur : Rawat Publications.

Lundberg, G. A.( 1946). *Social Research*, New York : Longman.

Miller. D.C. (1964). *Handbook of Research Design and Social Measurement* New York : David Mckey Co.

Mohsin, S.M. (1984). *Research Methods in Behavioural Sciences,* Calcutta : Orient and Longman Lmited.

Monette, Duane R. et. al. (1986). *Applied Social Research: Tool For the Human Services*, Chicago: Holt.

Moser, C.A. and Kalton, (1975). *Survey Methods in Social Investigation* London : Heinemann Educational Books.

Nachmias D and Nachmias C.(1981). *Research Methods in the Social Sciences*, NewYork : St. Martins press.

O'Leary, Zina.(2004). *The Essential Guide to Doing Research,* New Delhi : Vistar Publications.

Oppenheim, N.A.(1966).*Questionnaire Design and Attitude Measurement*, New York: Basic Books.

Philip, A.E. et. al.( 1975). *Social Work Research*, and The Analysis of Social Data, Oxford: Peragon Press.

Ramachandran. P. (2000).*User Friendly Research and Statistics for Social Work.*

Secunderabad : Andhra Pradesh Social Service Society.

Rubin, Allen and Babbie E.(1989). *Research Methodology for Social Work*, Belmohf, California, Wadsworth.

Sellitz. G. et. al. (1973). *Research Methods in Social Relations* New York: Holt. Rinehart and Winston (3rd edition.

Stouffer. S.A. *Social Research to Test ideas* New York: Free Press of Glencoe, 1962.

Suchman, E.A. (1953). *The Principles of Research Design.* In John T Dobyet. al., An Introduction to Social Research, New York: TheStackpole.

Wilkinson, T.S. and Bhandarkar, P.L. (1977). *Methodology and Techniques of Social Research*: Bombay: Himalayan.

Young. P.V. (1953) *Scientific Social Surveys and Research* Englewood Cliff. N.J. Prentice Hall .

# Index